The
Brilliance
of
Yorktown

A March of History,
1781 Command and Control, Allied Style

by Herman O. Benninghoff, II

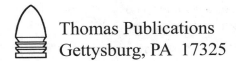
Thomas Publications
Gettysburg, PA 17325

Copyright © 2006 Herman O. Benninghoff, II

Printed and bound in the United States of America

Published by THOMAS PUBLICATIONS
P.O. Box 3031
Gettysburg, Pa. 17325

ISBN-1-57747-123-7

Cover illustrations, *Washington and Rochambeau at Yorktown* and *Cornwallis at Yorktown, 1781* by Don Troiani, www.historicalartprints.com.

THOMAS PUBLICATIONS publishes books about the American Colonial era, the Revolutionary War, the Civil War, and other important topics. For a complete list of titles, please visit our website at:

www.thomaspublications.com

Dedicated to those who came before
so that we may move ahead.

Contents

Foreword

In the Fall of 2006, the United States will celebrate the 225th anniversary of the victory at Yorktown. The surrender of Lord Cornwallis on October 19, 1781, to a combined Franco-American force under the supreme command of General George Washington and the *comte* de Rochambeau as well as to a French naval squadron under Admiral de Grasse riding at anchor in the York River, constituted a crucial step on the road to independence for these United States. Anniversaries have always provided an impetus for studying historic events, and the Yorktown Campaign has been the subject of many a monograph as well. For the Centennial of the siege in 1881, Henry P. Johnston published his *The Yorktown Campaign and the Surrender of Cornwallis, 1781*. On the occasion of the sesquicentennial, 50 years later in 1931, Colonel H.L. Landers published *The Virginia Campaign and the Blockade and Siege of Yorktown, 1781*. Then in 1963 came Thomas Fleming's *Beat the Last Drum* followed by Burke Davis' *Campaign that won America* in 1970, and a flurry of publications for the Bicentennial celebrations of the American Revolutionary War. But the surprising fact that all but Colonel Landers' government-sponsored study are still in print vividly shows the need for a fresh look not just at the 21 days of the siege as Jerome Greene recently offered in his *The Guns of Independence: The Siege of Yorktown, 1781* (2005) but at the campaign as a whole. Yet meritorious as an updated narrative might be, even if it were expanded chronologically over the whole year of 1781, and spread geographically over all of the thirteen rebellious colonies as Richard M. Ketchum has recently attempted to do in his *Victory At Yorktown: The Campaign That Won The Revolution* (2005), there would still remain a gap.

This gap, which called for a study analyzing the Yorktown Campaign from the view point of Command and Control of this first example of allied (America and France) as well as joint (land and sea) warfare in American history, has been addressed, and closed through the *The Brilliance of Yorktown* by well-known Revolutionary War historian Herman O. Benninghoff. Following on the heels of his acclaimed *Valley Forge: A Genesis for Command and Control, Continental Army Style* (2001), Benninghoff has applied his considerable skill to a Command and Control-based analysis of the campaign that in retrospect ended the war. The ultimate military purpose of warfare, as defined in U.S. Army Field Manual 100-5, *Operations,* is "the destruction of the enemy's armed forces and will to fight." The nine Principles of War, which if properly implemented will achieve this goal are outlined in the 1994 edition of Field Manual 100-5:

Mass: the need to concentrate combat power at the decisive place and time.

Objective: direct every military operation towards a single, clearly defined, decisive, and attainable objective.

Offensive: Seize, retain, and exploit the initiative.

Surprise: Strike the enemy at a time, at a place, or in a manner for which he is unprepared.

Economy of force: Allocate minimum essential combat power to secondary efforts.

Maneuver: Place the enemy in a position of disadvantage through the flexible application of combat power.

Unity of Command: For every objective, unity of effort under one responsible commander must be ensured.

Security: Never permit the enemy to acquire an unexpected advantage.

Simplicity: Prepare clear, uncomplicated plans and clear, concise orders to ensure thorough understanding.

By applying these principles, which are the glue that hold *The Brilliance of Yorktown* together, to the 1781 campaign, or more precisely to the series of events that culminated in the siege of Yorktown, Benninghoff's study begins where others end. He is not interested in the siege itself but rather in the efforts which brought the armies to Yorktown. In doing so, Benninghoff casts his net wide chronologically, beginning his narrative with the *marquis* de Lafayette's departure for France in January, 1779. The geographic reach of his work is equally inclusive: it extends from France across the Atlantic Ocean to Newport, Rhode Island, and south to Yorktown, Virginia. Neither is the study confined to an analysis of the decision-making process in Washington's head-quarters in Newburgh or White Plains or to Baron Steuben's, Lafayette's and Nathanael Greene's ever-changing center of operations in Virginia and the Carolinas. Benninghoff is as much at home in General Rochambeau's war-office in the Vernon House in Newport and in the Odell House in Philipsburg as he is in Sir Henry Clinton's quarters in New York City and Cornwallis' tent as His Lordship meanders across Virginia to his final destination at Yorktown. This approach allows Benninghoff to "Compare and Contrast" the almost diametrically opposed approaches to the war reigning in the opposing camps.

If Rochambeau's and Admiral de Grasse's unquestioning, if at times reluctant, sub-ordination to Washington's leadership established *Unity of Command* on the side of the allies, that same aspect was painfully lacking on the British side where Sir Henry, Lord Cornwallis and Admiral Arbuthnot viewed each other with distrust and at times worked toward opposing goals. If Washington stayed focused on his *Objective*, a military victory over British forces be they in New York City or Virginia, Clinton and Cornwallis did not share a common objective. By deciding not to pursue Cornwallis into Virginia, and conversely by first deciding to mass his forces outside New York City and then, in mid-August 1781, by marching the largest feasible number of troops to Virginia, Greene and Washington applied the principles of *Mass* and *Economy of Force* at exactly the time when Clinton and Cornwallis divided their forces.

The clandestine disengagement from New York City, the stealing of a few days' marches from Clinton on the way to Trenton and Philadelphia, was as brilliant in its *Simplicity* as it was an example of near perfect timing, of *Maneuver* and *Surprise* that kept Sir Henry in New York City guessing as to Washington's intentions, all under the unified *Command* of Washington. That command not only included the movements of Lafayette in Virginia but also the coordination of the movement of Washington's and Rochambeau's land forces with the vessels of Admiral de Grasse while retaining the focus on Cornwallis, the *Objective* of the campaign. Benninghoff is at his best when he shows how Washington, by detaching Lafayette with a small number of Continentals to Virginia in early 1781, gained *Security* from that quarter while addressing the need for *Economy of Force*. Once the campaign of 1781 had started, the allies remained on the *Offensive*, at New York as well as on the march to Virginia.

The ultimate success of the campaign, and Benninghoff makes that very clear, was made possible only by the contributions and sacrifices, the hard work of thousands of ordinary Americans along the routes to Yorktown and in Virginia and the suffering of the soldiers of the Continental Army. Their efforts were coordinated by a small group of dedicated Americans such as Superintendent of Finance Robert Morris, Quartermaster-General Timothy Pickering, Baron Steuben and Virginia Governor Thomas Nelson. But there are not only heroes in this study: Thomas Jefferson emerges as anything but an effective war-time governor, and Baron Steuben, though sincere in his efforts, was clearly out of his element in Virginia. After a terrifying beginning, viz. the mutinies of the New Jersey and Pennsylvania Lines, 1781 turned into the year when everything that could go right for America went right, and everything that could go wrong for Britain went wrong. The success of the campaign is all the more surprising in view of the formidable hurdles of history, even Washington had earned his spurs fighting against the French, language, religion and culture, which separated these unlikely allies. French financial, political, military and naval support were crucial for victory in 1781: there was no American navy that could have prevented Graves from evacuating

Cornwallis in September, 1781. If coordination of the campaign on the tactical and strategic level was difficult enough, it was no easier on the political level in view of the divergent national agendas pursued in Philadelphia and Versailles. Call it good fortune, providence or fate — no matter how careful the planning and how resourceful the troops and then quarter-master, no matter how much "Command and Control" Washington, Rochambeau and de Grasse exerted over their forces, there were aspects they could not control: the winds and the seas, the interception or delivery of letters or decisions made in Versailles and Whitehall. What ultimately decided the outcome of the campaign was the simple fact that in 1781, unlike in previous campaigns, fortune shone on America's arms and Benninghoff is honest enough to admit as much.

If the goal of *The Brilliance of Yorktown* is to show the Yorktown campaign as a model of the expert and successful application of the *Principles of War,* Benninghoff has achieved his goal, and his book will constitute a welcome and valuable addition to an already large library on the Yorktown Campaign.

Robert A. Selig, Ph.D.
Holland, MI
June 2006

Acknowledgements

Any writer knows that the creation and publication of a manuscript requires a team effort-the collective effort of many people who often work tirelessly and selfishly to provide encouragement, information, clarity, and constructive suggestions. For this book, their assistance was vital to improve my many awkward drafts. While the writer is credited in the byline, contributions from so many others deserve credit for any positive considerations of the work.

It is impossible to thank or mention all who made significant contributions with encouragement and action. Without their assistance this book would have never been completed.

I would also like to offer a posthumous thanks to all the individuals who performed and recorded the actions reported in this work. They were amazing people during a critical time of American history. They provided a rich legacy and reservoir of correspondence, documents, and other information that made it easy for me to snoop into their business. I am humbled to have the privilege of reporting some of their life's experiences, albeit with a twenty-first century anachronistic influence. They were the real heroes in American history.

Preparation of any manuscript is filled with emotional highs and lows, but in my case I always had someone at the low lows to give a boost of encouragement and, at the high highs, to channel my exuberance into reality. I was blessed with just such a person, my wife Joan, and a historian in her own right. She performed above and beyond the call of duty spending many hours to review and edit numerous drafts. Often finding humorous and ridiculous mistakes — then there was the unenviable task of making corrections without bruising my ego.

I am indebted to the folks at Thomas Publications for their constructive massage of the text and the special effort of Sally and Jim Thomas for their patient effort to improve the story; their wit and wisdom was most appreciated.

Robert A. Selig, Ph.D. was most helpful in fine-tuning the manuscript as well as supplying the forward. His knowledge of the subject matter is unsurpassed. Bob's participation as historical consultant to Washington-Rochambeau Revolutionary Route was a crucial assistance in the final stages of review and preparation.

A special gratitude is due the staff of the American Revolution Center (ARC), Tom Daly, President and CEO, and ZeeAnn Mason, Senior Vice President, for their encouragement, also Arc's Board of Directors, especially Gerry Lenfest. In addition, ARC's Board of Scholars which include fellow members David McCullough, Chairman, Tom Fleming, Don Higginbotham, and Rick Beeman were an inspiration.

Some of the people who directly or indirectly influenced the creation of this book are deserving of more appreciation than they can imagine: Joe Rubinfine, Robert N. Hill, DeWitt Bailey, Ph. D., Varena Barr Hill, Gordon Wood Ph.D., Don Troiani, Stanley W. Frambes, William (Pete) Musser, Robert K. Wright PhD, Dona McDermott, Stacey Swigert, George C Neumann, and Robert L. McNeil, Jr.

Institutions that were most helpful include: the Valley Forge National Historical Park Library and manuscript collection, Valley Forge PA; The David Library of the American Revolution, Washington Crossing, PA; Clements Library, University of Michigan; National Archives, Washington, DC and Philadelphia.

All of the above were responsible for the accuracies in the book and the mistakes are mine.

Introduction

During the 1781 Yorktown campaign, George Washington was the driving force, but Rochambeau and Lafayette were the fuel.

How two armies, one American, the other French, allied in a common cause, moved over seven hundred miles over land and water to Virginia, on the longest trek of American military history, against impossible odds, is an amazing story. Even more amazing is that both armies were further subdivided to ease logistical and supply difficulties where the defeat or capture of any unit placed the entire mission at risk.

The brilliance of the Yorktown victory that assured United States independence was the result of people who moved these armies in an incredible time of forty-two days and prepared Virginia as a base of support, exercising unprecedented command and control, Allied style.

Several excellent books detail the Yorktown siege, which formally began on October 6, 1781, and ended with a British surrender on October 20. But few accounts pay more than superficial attention to the mass movement of allied forces to Yorktown. The trek is an exciting people story filled with full a range of human emotions and behavior – personal intrigues, contention, antagonism, jealousy, despair, incompetence, valor, mutiny and an incredible amount of good luck.

The story begins in Boston Harbor on a cold January morning in 1779. A ship headed for France carried a passenger with the United States future as a mission. The passenger was Major General the Marquis de Lafayette on his way to the Royal Court at Versailles, France. His Versailles experiences involved people with little in common, yet they developed unimaginable relationships to describe a process, which eventually determined United States' independence. Paris decisions brought new life to military events in North America where the Continental Army was near collapse. Only the dedication and determination of a few, combined with extraordinary luck, preserved Washington's main army. Meanwhile, in the South, two Continental armies were destroyed within a year. The enemy planned to separate southern states, economically and politically, from their northern brothers. If successful, any hope of independence ended. Extraordinary luck intervened on behalf of the American cause.

In early 1781, Washington's main Continental Army was deployed around New York City and the French ally in Newport, Rhode Island. At the time, Virginia's political situation was a quagmire of chaos and incompetence, hardly a platform to support a major offensive, especially from Allied forces located so far away. But the enemy changed strategy and concentrated its southern forces in Virginia. On the surface, the enemy moves were a tactical success, but later became a strategic disaster.

How the Allies arrived at Yorktown, Virginia, and gained the victory is a warm personal tale of people and an army constantly on the edge of destruction and failure as it moved toward Virginia. Supported by a French ally, the Continental Army survived to overcome impossible odds.

Preparation of Virginia to host an onslaught of invading armies, friend and foe, is a story with immense historical consequences. From the plan's inception, success of the Virginia trek was questionable, at best foolhardy and more likely an aberration. For forty-two precarious days the Allies moved toward Virginia. Every day of the journey suffered obstacles, but people united to move forces exceeding six thousand nearly seven hundred miles – still the longest trek in American military history. Critical to success was a rendezvous with the French navy, weeks out of contact, and offering no guaranteed arrival.

Almost miraculously, Allied armies reached Yorktown and eventual victory, but only through efforts forged by personal relationships of icons in United States history: George Washington, Nathanael Greene, Lafayette, King Louis XVI, General Rochambeau, Admiral De Grasse, Baron von Steuben and Governors Thomas Jefferson and Thomas Nelson of Virginia along with thousands of "common soldiers." Even British admirals and generals contributed. Throughout the 1781 Virginia campaign, George Washington was an engine driving American independence, but Lafayette and Rochambeau provided fuel.

This story is a result of examining other people's business, especially personal letters and documents that reveal unheralded efforts by individuals who impacted the campaign to Yorktown. At times, it is a raw story of fear, inflated egos, anger, stubbornness, jealousy, contentiousness, selfishness, and distrust woven into historical context.

Seeds of the campaign germinated in Paris in 1780, influenced by Marquis de Lafayette and instituted by Louis XVI, King of France. Good fortune joined the American cause with General Rochambeau's appointment as commander of French Auxiliaries to serve in the United States.

When French forces arrived at Newport, Rhode Island, in 1780, there was an agonizing period as personal relationships matured. Almost a year passed while Washington and Rochambeau *measured* each other.

But before the campaign succeeded, radical changes transformed Virginia's political and military situation. Continental Army Major Generals von Steuben and Lafayette were embroiled in the intrigues of state politics. With determined effort, they forced changes while confronting a brilliant tactical enemy.

Complicating a tenuous Virginia military situation was the arrival of a large naval force commanded by French Admiral De Grasse, with limited time for duty in North America. His arrival was crucial to Allied operations, but did not guarantee success. Victory required an Allied unity of effort on a scale without precedent. This effort provided a critical ingredient in the command and control process for the Yorktown victory. The enemy's inability to achieve a similar unity of effort sealed their defeat.

❖ 1 ❖

Lafayette – A Fugitive from Justice?

*I am very grateful to God when I reflect on my
good fortune in being his wife*

A cold wind swirled through Boston Harbor on the sunny morning of January 11, 1779. The Continental Navy Frigate *Alliance* bumped against the dock as the crew grabbed lines to cast free. The *Alliance* carried fifty-six guns on two decks and was recently commissioned. Built in Portsmouth, Rhode Island, outfitted in Boston, she was the pride of the Continental Navy.[1] Captain Pierre Landais was trained as a French naval officer and now served in the Continental Navy.[2] Landais was "ingenious," a well behaved man, "an able and experienced officer."[3] He stood upright on the quarterdeck, observing all activities which brought the ship to life. He was especially interested in actions taking place off the bow in front of the *Alliance*.

Ten men shouted in cadence from an open boat and pulled on long wooden oars; the sea danced and splashed as the oars relentlessly penetrated the water's surface. A mist rose in blue green agony from agitated waters and occasionally froze into ice slivers, then shattered from the incessant bitter wind.

The men pulled harder on the oars against a taunt line attached to the big ship's bow. The large ship held back, resisting, but then moved. Slowly gathering speed, the *Alliance* appeared helpless as she moved from inner harbor to open sea. Sailors scurried around the deck and tugged on long lines and sheets to hoist and steady sails. Officers shouted commands, but no one seemed to listen; after years of experience the sailors knew what to do. An explosion followed as the wind, in a sudden, deafening, angry burst filled the sails. The towline was released quickly from the small boat and pulled quickly into the *Alliance*. The oarsmen shouted a cheer and some waved hats but few in the crew reacted, for they were too busy. The ship vibrated, came alive, and lurched ahead in determined motion to the open sea. Captain Landais was pleased. The ship headed for Brest, France.

A lone figure watched the commotion with quiet interest. He held tight with both hands to the port rail. Once at sea the ship creaked, groaned and strained as it pitched and rolled and picked up speed. When the ship moved, the figure reinforced his footing on a deck slippery from sea spray that splashed across the entire ship. The activities performed to bring the ship to life seemed nothing less than mass confusion to the figure who was the only passenger on deck. Every one else was crew.

Several layers of protective clothing left little exposed to distinguish his features, other than a shortness in stature. Occasionally, when a face showed under the round hat tightly pulled against the ears, a hawkish countenance appeared with a prominent nose.

In France, he was addressed as Marie Joseph de Motier, Marquis de Lafayette, and in the United States, as Major General Marquis de Lafayette. In 1777, at nineteen, he was commissioned the youngest major general in the Continental Army. Now, nearly twenty-one, he possessed a military leave for a trip home to France. Although young and a bit egotistical, he had a pleasing personality. His short height, approximately five feet, five inches, was capped with facial features rather long in proportion and a head that tilted up to address taller colleagues. In discussions, his eyes twinkled and suggested a thought or two hidden and not shared, but at times they reflected sadness. He was not shy; he loved to talk and once engaged in conversation, his speech was delightful. His French accent on English words with a flowery vocabulary, sometimes mispronounced, was often expressed with a bit of humor.

Lafayette was born in 1757 and lost both his father and mother "before he" reached age thirteen. In some quarters he was described as a "wealthy orphan." At sixteen he married fourteen-year-old Marie Adrienne Francoise de Noailles from "one of the most powerful" families in France. Lafayette read widely about political and military events throughout Europe and North America. Captivated "by romantic ideas of the American" cause, in 1775, he decided to join them.

The Marquis had another, not so romantic, reason to join the Americans: retribution. Lafayette's father had been killed in action against British forces during the Seven Years War. Seeing an opportunity for revenge, he arrived in America in the summer of 1777. At the time his English vocabulary was limited, but now, two years later, the vocabulary had expanded, adding depth to his conversations and written communications.

Lafayette demonstrated perceptive and persuasive powers soon after his arrival in America. Washington, usually cautious and even suspicious of foreign pretenders for Continental Army commissions, took an immediate liking to the young Frenchman. They first met at a tavern in Philadelphia and began a lifelong friendship, which benefitted Washington, the Continental Army, and the American cause.

Two years later, after hard military service for the American cause, Lafayette headed home. Fiercely loyal to Washington, he had fought bravely in a number of battles. At the Battle of Brandywine, his first military engagement, he was wounded after displaying meritorious action.

But now, standing there on deck, Lafayette suffered a twinge of anguish. The trip home was filled with both danger and destiny. The danger was his and the destiny involved success or failure of American independence. Many times during his two years' service in North America, he had experienced loneliness and wished to be back in France with all the comforts afforded by a young wife and influential family. America was a strange land with even stranger customs, few European comforts, and a foreign language. In America, he had faced hardships unimaginable at home and without compensation, for he had volunteered and paid all his expenses.

The *Alliance* was fully alive when she reached the open sea. Wind filled all sails with such a force the ship drove forward splashing great pillars of foam and spray over the bow, cascading as far as the stern. Lafayette watched with a nostalgic stare at the shores of America and wondered if he would see them again. Soon they disappeared over the western horizon.

He was convinced that "the beauty, strength, and perfection of the *Alliance* is a sure omen of my safe voyage."[4] Yet he understood the reality of his situation. Recognition from his American friends, especially Washington, about the importance of this trip, massaged the ego, but he wondered if this ambition for recognition had over-ruled good judgment. He faced a host of indeterminate challenges. An immediate danger was capture by a British Man of War, always lurking off Boston harbor to prey on American ships.

Earlier, when the trip was first planned, Captain Landais had orders to get the ship "in readiness as soon as possible" and "prepare suitable accommodations" for Major General Lafayette and a small staff, but above all keep this secret "lest the enemy should get intelligence and watch for the ship."[5] Captain Landais was informed that Lafayette "is a nobleman of France highly esteemed by Congress as a zealous and able friend to the American cause.[6]

Fortunately the "ingenious" captain and his speedy vessel avoided enemy interception, but not excitement. When the ship reached the "Banks of Newfoundland" a violent storm struck in the middle of the night. Most harrowing was the awful noise; the sea thundering against the wooden hull sounded like cannon fire. The hull responded with creaks and groans in a torturous agony that promised certain disintegration. The topmast snapped, but with all the noise, no one noticed until later. A "great deal of water" poured over the decks and threatened the crew. Some unfortunate sailors washed from side to side, but miraculously grabbed something to hold and avoided going overboard.

Lafayette was terrified, and convinced they would sink in spite of assurances from Captain Landais to the contrary.[7] If he got out alive, he promised never to travel across the ocean again. But eventually the storm subsided. The ship was lucky and escaped with only a loss of the topmast, which was quickly repaired.

By nature Lafayette was a ponderer, someone who considered various strategies. He needed to develop a plan of action for his arrival. Most worrisome was what to expect from authorities and family. During his tumultuous service in North America, Lafayette was too busy to worry about the consequences of his previous situation in France. Now, in the confines of the cabin, with its gimbaled grate and small fire to protect against the winter air, there was time.

No matter how he tried to ignore the subject, Lafayette was a fugitive from French justice. In 1777, during his first trip, the king had ordered him not to go to America; instead he was ordered to Marseilles.[8] A royal order was issued for his arrest. The English government protested furiously at the prospect of one from such a prominent French family going to assist rebellious colonies. It was an act of war, some English politicians claimed, but France and England were not at war – an embarrassing situation for the French government. Lafayette ignored the royal orders; in fact, he defied them and hastened south toward the Spanish border. By then, the Lafayette affair was a full-blown international incident covered in both French and English newspapers. "If he did not want to cut himself off forever from his country," he was ordered to Paris immediately. Instead, he crossed the border into Spain to avoid arrest. During the wait in Spain, he received a deluge of correspondence with threats, warnings, and encouragements. The angriest came from his father-in-law. The letters from his family "were terrible," he wrote, except from his wife.

At the time the Lafayettes had one child, a daughter born in 1775, and another on the way. The infant daughter died in 1777 during his service in North America. Some members of the family viewed his passion for America as a youthful, irresponsible act. But Adrienne, his wife, "whom he had left without a word of farewell," nor explanation, never offered "a word of reproach." She only prayed, "to bring [her husband] back safely from the war in America."[9]

Suddenly, early one afternoon, as Lafayette sat in the cabin addressing letters, cannon fire erupted – two shots together – then, seconds later, a third. After hastily wrapping himself in a large woolen cloak and mantle, he rushed up on deck. There, off in the distance, were two ships, motionless. The *Alliance's* cannon fire had signaled them to halt and *turn to*. The Americans lowered long boats with armed boarding parties and rowed toward the ships.

Lafayette watched as cannon crews held a direct aim, ready to fire immediately if the ships, well within range, made any challenging moves. They were Swedish vessels with British cargoes of value and offered no resistance to the speedier well-armed American ship. Their British cargoes entitled the Americans to consider them lucrative prizes of war.

Later, when the *Alliance*, followed by the two prize ships under the command of boarding crews, arrived a short distance from the French coast, whispers of mutiny drifted through the ship. Before departure, the crew was hastily assembled and pressed from prisoners of war. With the mutinous intentions uncovered, suspected perpetrators were overpowered and trouble avoided.[10] After the extraordinary short time of twenty-six days, the French coast was reached on February 6, 1779.[11] Lafayette gambled that his return would meet with less rancor, because now France was officially allied with the United States. He thought only "of rejoining my family and friends," from "whom I had heard nothing for eight months," but he decided to go directly to court and resolve his personal situation before the family was involved in possible recriminations. By the time he arrived at the imposing ministry buildings at Versailles, he suffered from a terrible state of anxiety. But fortune smiled on him. "M. de Poix," his wife's cousin, met him.[12] Word had somehow reached the ministry that Lafayette was on the way. De Poix introduced him "to all the ministers." He "was questioned, complimented, and exiled." But to his great relief, the exile was to his father-in-law's Paris residence.[13]

Immediately a message went to Lafayette's father-in-law with a request to inform his wife Adrienne of her husband's presence in France. The family had no information about the trip, other than vague references sent over time that he might return soon. There were many reasons to avoid committing travel details to writing. The British were well aware of Lafayette's importance to the American cause. With information in their hands from intercepted correspondence, a major attempt would be made for his capture.

In the late months of 1778, before his return to France, Lafayette carried out extensive discussions with Washington and Congressional delegates about the American cause and the shaky financial condition. Lafayette volunteered to return to France and enlist family influence for American support. But his situation as a fugitive in France was either unknown or ignored by Americans. Lafayette decided to risk the penalties of fugitive status and return home to appeal on behalf of the American cause. World affairs changed dramatically after he left France, a change he hoped would modify his status. France and Britain had officially declared war and France was allied with the United States.

When his father in law, Jean de Noailles, duc d'Ayen, received Lafayette's message he staggered in disbelief. The duc d'Ayen was a *marchal de camp* in the French army with influence at the royal court and well known throughout French military and financial circles. He made two very quick moves: a servant went upstairs to inform Adrienne of her husband's arrival and a carriage was ordered to fetch his son-in-law. Lafayette was in no mental state to wait for transportation; his heart pounded with uncertainty about what reception he might receive from family members.

He arrived almost before his message. The duc d'Ayen heard a commotion outside the drawing room. The door opened and his tearful son-in-law rushed forward. There was a short hesitation then a warm embrace, but few words. Seconds passed, and Lafayette turned and faced the doorway. There she was, the most beautiful sight he had seen in two years. Tears poured down cheeks and she raced with open arms to embrace her husband. It was a long passionate embrace oblivious to the gathering family members who, by now, erupted in joy.

Happily, Adrienne wrote to relatives:

Paris, February 16, 1779

There is no need for me to tell you of my happiness, my dear aunts, because we have asked the Abbe Fayon to inform you of it with the greatest possible care, but I do need to share that happiness with you. It is easy to believe and hard to express! The price this happiness has cost me may be compared only with this joy. Monsieur de Lafayette has returned, as modest and as charming as when you last saw him, his sensibility undiminished. In the midst of our joy, we are distressed at not being able to go to embrace you at once and to share with you a grief that we feel very deeply. We even fear that the joy of his return will renew that sorrow in you.

Monsieur de Lafayette is now in the king's disfavor and is forbidden to appear in any public place. We hope this will not last long, but he cannot risk being away, nor will he be able to leave for some time after the restriction ends since he must take advantage of the king's good will when it is offered him. Besides, his conversation with the ministers gave them an idea but not a complete understanding of who he is, and they all spoke of it appreciatively....[14]

Aware that her husband's family was concerned about his state of mind and his safety, and wanted badly to see him, Adrienne continued her letter:

His modesty has even increased, and he finds endless means of praising others without speaking of himself. He seems completely unbiased about everyone, even the persons he loves most. In short, my dear aunts, in the midst of the greatest dangers God has preserved for us the most distinguished and lovable person in the world. Let us bless him, let us pray for him. I am very grateful to God when I reflect on my good fortune in being his wife. I am distressed at being so much less gracious than he is, and I hope that my affection makes up for what I lack in charm.

I speak confidently to you of the state of my heart, my dear aunts, but I am very much concerned with what you must be suffering. Everything that rends your hearts saddens mine, and I am sorry that you cannot see our delightful hero. If you should try to come to see him, I would take care of finding you lodgings – in a convent or elsewhere – with enthusiasm inspired by the desire of seeing you and the joy your visit will bring him.... I speak to you of this matter quite seriously because I greatly fear that Monsieur de Lafayette will not be able to go to see you for a long time, and this grieves him.

He has gone out just now to take care of some essential business. He should return in time to write you, but I am always afraid that his business will take him longer than he expects. Do consider his feelings, share our happiness, pity us for not being able to share it with you ourselves, my dear aunts, and accept this testimony of the sincere, tender, and respectful attachment that I have sworn to you for life.

Noailles de Lafayette[15]

Lafayette's gamble, that the French alliance would change his fugitive status, worked. Word drifted back from royal sources that with proper contrition the situation might improve more. On February 19, Lafayette appealed to the king and offered contrition for past misdeeds. "The misfortune of having displeased Your Majesty produces such sorrow" and I will "not try" to offer excuses for my actions, only "the real motives." The love "of my country, the desire to witness the humiliation of her enemies, a political instinct" that the past was unjust: "these, Sire, are the reasons that governed the part I took in the American cause." A royal reply arrived immediately. Lafayette was released from all restrictions, but with a warning, which he described:

...when my freedom was restored I was advised to avoid those places where the public might consecrate my disobedience. On my arrival I had enjoyed the honor of being consulted by all the ministers and, what was far better, being kissed by all the ladies. The kissing stopped the following day, but I retained the confidence of the ministry much longer and enjoyed both favor at Versailles and popularity in Paris. They spoke well of me in all circles.... The times have changed somewhat, but I have retained what I would have chosen: popular favor and the affection of the people I love.[16]

He even received an official French commission as captain of "king's Dragoons."[17]

The Marquis employed charm, enthusiasm, and sincerity to enter the royal realm of influence. He observed political activities at court and interpersonal relationships to find people with influence who might help the Americans. He kept a stream of continual communications with prominent Americans. "I must" visit the King "before seeing any Body of the Royal family," he wrote to Benjamin Franklin. "I understand" it will "be at 11 o'clock" today. Then

"I will See the Ministers, and to morrow morning I'll have the pleasure" to visit you and discuss "what is the Matter at Versailles."

Lafayette was disappointed by the visit with ministers. All they expressed was unofficial interest and curiosity. They wanted to know more about his experiences, stories, and opinions. Court officials listened, asked questions, whispered to each other. There was no rejection of his proposals, but neither was any encouragement offered. After weeks of frustration at the lack of official responses, Lafayette decided on another initiative. He presented a detailed written proposal for France's participation in the military affairs of North America. To Lafayette's relief, the initiative worked. On July 18, 1779, he made an official presentation that included details for a proposed "expeditionary force" for America.[18] The plan's completeness was impressive and indicated months of preparation. Although not rejected, there was still no official reaction. But this time Lafayette sensed a desire by royal officials to help. For the first time, he felt encouraged and accepted as an authority on American military affairs.

The wait dragged on. Was there something he could do better to persuade the ministers that military assistance for the Americans was an opportunity to regain international prominence after the terrible defeat of the Seven Years War? He felt helpless. After the initial rush of interest to hear Lafayette's presentation, there was no official reaction. He waited and time drifted by without official comments. The delayed response brought another concern. Lafayette had heard nothing about the current situation in America. For all he knew the American resistance had collapsed and the Continental Army disbanded. Any day news could arrive that the war was over and the Americans had failed. Finally a few letters arrived from Washington and others, which confirmed the Continental Army's continued existence.

In Paris, nothing happened. Lafayette decided on a new move. He continued to "lay siege to ministers" and influential friends, but revised the plan after consultations with court officials and military advisors, assuring their input was included. The refined plan was submitted to the Comte de Vergennes, French Minister of Foreign Affairs. Within days, to his joy, Lafayette was summoned to the ministry for immediate in-depth discussions. After months of lobbying, there was a positive reaction from both government and King. He spent the rest of January and all of February preparing detailed operational plans. Manpower, materiel, and financial needs were analyzed. Lafayette was ecstatic and found it difficult to focus on the tedious preparation. He had to satisfy French political, financial and military concerns.

Government ministers expressed skepticism and asked many questions. Of major concern was the Continental Army's viability and Washington's competence; if the Americans collapsed with French forces in North America, how could they avoid capture or annihilation? What type of association would French forces have with the Continental Army? How would a command structure work? There were suspicions about American trustworthiness. Would Americans abandon the alliance in return for independence and join Britain against France? Lafayette answered with clarity and candor based on his Continental Army experience and personal acquaintance with Washington. He emphasized that the Americans would never join against the French. His sincere answers satisfied officials; they agreed to move forward on a broad scale of additional American support. The new French initiative, based on Lafayette's proposal, was original, creative, and progressive. Strategic moves included deployment of land forces to America under the command of General Rochambeau, although initially Lafayette had suggested himself for the command.

In unprecedented action, the proposal recommended appointment of General Washington as supreme commander of all French forces, land and sea, in North America. The proposal's acceptance was a shock. Lafayette, a previous fugitive from French justice, had performed life saving transfusions for American independence and gained popularity with the King. One reason for the bond was similarity in age; the King was twenty-six and Lafayette, a twenty-three year old Major General in the Continental Army.

Lafayette rose to near hero status with the French public who saw him as Washington's friend and confidant.[19] High praise for his dedication and bravery was sent to the king in official correspondence from Washington and Congress. The accounts emphasized Lafayette's loyalty to King and country while he served with distinction as a Major General in the Continental Army.

Lafayette was convinced the French initiative guaranteed continuation of American resistance and an eventual Allied victory. He experienced pride at the turn of events and frustration over how to communicate such glorious news to Washington and Congress. Under the best of conditions, communications required weeks, sometimes months. Even then, a plan like this with subtle complexities would generate a multitude of questions that required detailed explanations and answers. In the meantime, he could only hope that unforeseen events in North America did not occur to dash opportunities provided by new strategic plans.

Additional joyful news arrived on December 24, 1779. Adrienne was in Passy, near Paris, visiting relatives and awaiting the birth of their child. She presented her husband with a Christmas gift, "a long-hoped for son and heir." He was christened "George Washington, marquis de Lafayette"[20]

With everything going so well, Lafayette faced a dilemma: whether to remain in France as a national hero, enjoying the personal comforts of wife, family, and friends, or return to America. No one in America would blame him if he remained in France. The family, especially his young wife, had suffered enough, losing a daughter during the previous absence, and now he had an infant son. Lafayette considered sending a messenger with news accounts of his accomplishments. If he remained in France, he could justify the decision as necessary to follow up on the new initiatives. But after several days of deep deliberation, he was uncomfortable – a letter simply would not do. No messenger had the full and intimate details necessary to answer questions and give explanations. Lafayette was the only one who knew the people involved on both sides of the Atlantic and there was no one with Lafayette's ability to convey in-depth information or address "touchy" issues when they arose.

After anguishing over many personal considerations, Lafayette decided to rejoin Washington, the Continental Army, and deliver the news in person. Once the decision was made, a big burden disappeared. He was excited at the opportunity to participate in military operations for the glory of France, the United States, and of course, himself.

Next, he notified the king and government ministers of plans to return to North America, then informed friends, relatives, and close family associates. He used the public acclaim to attract private financial support for supplies. The cargo was carefully selected to include much-needed military provisions and materiel: clothing, arms and shoes. Every day Lafayette grew more impatient and anxious to leave, but deliveries took forever. At last a departure date was scheduled and the official ministry notification published, "M. le Marquis de Lafayette is returning to America to resume his service as major general with our allies."[21]

Then without warning he was summoned to Paris. When he reached the city on March 5, 1780, he went to Versailles, always impressive but very threatening when uncertainty was in the air. Almost immediately he was ushered to a meeting room with several royal representatives who sat behind a small oblong table. Conversation was cordial, supportive and general. No specific issues were addressed; the king's representatives were polite and respectful. Lafayette wondered why he was there. He waited patiently. It was a French custom to go in many trivial directions before coming to the point. At last the meeting's purpose was revealed – a secret letter was handed to Lafayette for personal delivery to Washington. The letter described arrangements for increased French aid and support. There was specific information that described French financial, material and manpower support, an enormous accomplishment for young Lafayette.[22]

The new French initiative was "due entirely to the persuasion" and "persistence" of Lafayette.[23] After the meeting, Lafayette, exuberant and excited, returned home and completed the preparations for America.

On March 1, five days before Lafayette received the letter for Washington, Louis XVI, King of France, issued instructions to Jean Baptiste Donatien de Vimeur, Comte de Rochambeau who, at fifty-five, was twenty-nine years his king's senior.[24] They were radical, special instructions and described the first organization for an Allied unity of command with an American commander-in-chief.

Rochambeau was born on July 1, 1725, "in the church of Sainte-Madeline de Vendome" in France.[25] His military career began during "the War of the Austrian Succession" when Rochambeau "performed with great distinction." Later, in the Seven Years War, he was promoted to "lieutenant general."[26] Associates described Rochambeau as "clear-sighted, deliberate" and "a strict disciplinarian," but not "a military genius."[27] After France was embarrassed by defeat in the Seven Years War, Rochambeau joined a small group of young officers who attempted French Army reorganization, in spite of "inertia" from an entrenched military bureaucracy supported by "indifference of the Versailles court."[28]

At last, on Saturday, March 11, 1780, Lafayette was aboard the frigate *L'Hermione,* a French warship docked in the harbor of La Rochelle. The captain was ordered by the king to hold the ship in readiness and "to take orders" from the marquis and carry him to America.[29] Lafayette traveled with a respectable entourage; one that befitted a king's emissary on his way to a foreign land to conduct official royal business of a secret nature. The king's prestige was at stake and a proper image was necessary to project the mission's importance. Eight servants, a secretary, and a number of military aides accompanied Lafayette.[30]

Weather conditions delayed departure; wind and tide must be just right. Lafayette used the time preparing correspondence. "I have an excellent frigate commanded by a charming captain; my lodging is the best possible," he informed a friend. But "it pains me cruelly to leave my friends and this separation afflicts my heart deeply."[31] The first departure on March 13, failed. Contrary weather forced the ship back to port. "Bad weather as well as the loss of a main yard obliged us to return to" port, Lafayette wrote to his wife. "Once the equinox has passed, we shall have superb winds, and I prefer to be in port rather than to thrash about uselessly on the sea."[32] Finally, on March 20, "We are going to sail," he wrote with joy.

After a voyage of thirty-seven days, Lafayette arrived in Boston harbor on April 26. During the voyage the Marquis reflected on many aspects of life since his last sea voyage in 1779. There were spectacular accomplishments in Paris for the American cause, but now came demands of equal effort from America. Lafayette had avoided reporting the "whole truth to Versailles." A report of the desperation would have guaranteed no additional forces for America. Lafayette had "avoided either telling or suppressing the truth."

The "news that Marquis de Lafayette had returned" brought excitement to all of Boston. His previous service in America made him "universally popular."[33] His first order of business was notifying Washington of his return. Before the ship docked, he sat pen in hand at a small table. He was in "the Mist of joy," he wrote. He found himself "again one of Your loving Soldiers...I have affairs of the utmost importance" to "Communicate to You alone." A "great public good" will derive from the information.[34] Minutes after the ship was secured in its berth, the letter was on the way.

At headquarters, "with tears in his eyes," Washington read "the lines [from] his young [Major General]."[35] Immediately he replied, "you do not tell me the route you are taking." He would send an escort, "you will be passing estates owned by Tories." He looked forward to embracing "you with all the warmth of an affectionate friend." When he reached headquarters there would be "a bed prepared for you."[36]

The next task, before heading for headquarters, was off-loading a boatload of cargo procured in France at Lafayette's expense. For the most part, these were military supplies desperately needed by the Continental Army: trousers, shoes, accoutrements and a variety of arms – all in short supply. Agents were located to deliver on an expedited basis. Fortunately, Lafayette was well known in Boston with trusted friends anxious to help in all the details. Awed by the reception, he wrote to a friend in France, "Well I am here again" and, "I assure you that the pleasure of seeing my friends again was a great joy for me. Nothing could have increased it more than the reception with which I was honored."[37] Before he left Boston to meet Washington, he spoke before the Massachusetts General Assembly and thanked them for the "flattering reception." He was pleased to be "on the American shore" and "again with my American fellow-soldiers."[38] Lafayette's return generated a wave of enthusiasm in the citizens of Boston. "Respects were paid by the Government as well as the People at Large to this prudent and gallant young Nobleman," an American wrote."[39]

Finally with welcoming events concluded, Lafayette rushed to meet Washington at Morristown, New Jersey, three hundred miles from Boston. All along the route, there were a deluge of questions about France; what can be expected; will they send more help? Lafayette was delighted with public attention and interest, but he carefully avoided disclosure of confidential information intended for Washington. "I have already written you twice, my dear heart," he wrote to his wife. The "expressions of goodwill with which they have overwhelmed me cannot be repeated without a pompous air, for which you know I have not much taste."

On May 10, an elated Lafayette reached Morristown and a reunion. He met a swarm of staff and senior officers who hooted, hollered, and shouted questions. Every face beamed with a smile, and every eye had a tear. At last with a big smile, glassy eyes, and a snappy salute he faced Washington who with great difficulty held his emotions, but then a smile broke through a usually well-controlled countenance. Immediately Lafayette was ushered into headquarters and a private room of the big mansion.[40]

Hours were spent with selected staff members, exchanging explanations, questions, and answers about the French initiative. All agreed the news injected a needed morale boost to the American cause. In "the flickering light of a candle," Lafayette read instructions "from Louis XVI" that placed "French auxiliary forces, military and naval, under the supreme command" of Washington.[41] It was a spectacular achievement, something the commander-in-chief never expected. Tears of joy swelled Washington's eyes and for a moment words escaped him. Lafayette conveyed the circumstances in eloquence and a manner intended to give appropriate recognition for his accomplishments in Paris. He succeeded brilliantly; Washington knew well the American cause owed Lafayette an eternal debt of gratitude.

Next came the difficult part, explaining to Washington that he had not emphasized the deplorable conditions existing in North America, especially lack of reliable support from the population and government. With a French expedition about to arrive, a realistic picture of the North American situation would soon become obvious. Lafayette expected ridicule for his underestimation of the terrible conditions. Washington understood it was a nasty situation for the Marquis, especially for his prestige and reputation in France.

The commander-in-chief started intense action and demanded immediate support from the states and Congress to assure the French that there was a genuine effort by Americans to support their own cause. Lafayette wrote letters to Congress, the states, and the public in general, pleading for invigorated procurement efforts of sufficient means to conduct the war. He appealed to public pride, urging that American soldiers should not be disgraced and ridiculed for their deplorable situation in the eyes of a generous French ally.

Lafayette had good reason to make the appeal. He had absorbed a large personal debt to clothe, feed, and pay his own regiments. In a personal appeal to the ladies of Philadelphia and other towns, he encouraged a formation of local societies to raise funds and provide comforts for the soldiers. Lafayette was gratified; the appeal worked and the idea traveled throughout the states. It became fashionable at the "highest circles of society" to compete with other groups to provide clothing and comforts for the troops.[42]

❧ 2 ❧

A French Experience

❧ *Do not count on these Americans, or upon their* ❧
means; they are without money or credit

General Rochambeau departed from Brest, France, on April 15, 1780, with 5,028 officers and men embarked on thirty-six transports.[1] His son, the Vicomte de Rochambeau, accompanied him. "We have had the most excellent start and are sailing before the best northeast winds," Rochambeau wrote.[2] After eighty-seven days at sea and some violent storms, French forces anchored outside of Narragansett Bay a short distance from the town of Newport, Rhode Island, on July 10, 1780. They had been confined in damp stench-ridden holes of the transport ships for over three months. Food and water was either depleted or sour with most rations contaminated. Scurvy and other diseases were rampant with almost a third of the forces hospitalized.[3]

American pilots came on board late that day. The next day, Rochambeau and some staff officers landed at Newport; the entire fleet, directed by the pilots, then moved to Newport and anchored by early evening. Some 3000 British soldiers had occupied the city between December 1776 and October 1779. When they departed, little of any military value was left behind. The region was stripped of provisions, wood, clothing, and even personal items of value. Everything was carried as contraband on British military transports to New York.

Newport harbor was well known to the French who considered it a superb and spacious safe anchorage for deep draft warships. The topography was well suited for defenses with the entrance guarded by Fort Brenton, now manned by a few Americans. A small island in front of the main channel provided a base for building fortifications against a sea assault.[4]

Newport was fairly plain by European standards and offered little of the old-fashioned charm of European towns. Most houses were built of wood, an unusual building material to the French. The new arrivals strained to view the first Americans and their dwellings, but there were few signs of life. As

18th century view of the port of Brest, France.
This port was a major military embarkation point for soldiers and supplies
sent to North America during the American War for Independence.

Rochambeau reached Newport, "he was astonished to find...the shops were closed," and local people did not seem well "disposed in our favor," one French officer reported. They seemed more afraid of us than the enemy.[5]

An immediate threat was a British attack from the sea. Rochambeau's army was vulnerable, almost defenseless, during disembarkation. A campsite was needed with fortifications built and provisions secured. Accommodations for officers had to be arranged. Every hour counted and the French anxiously watched the harbor entrance for a British armada that could arrive at any time. While the harbor and bay area offered excellent defensive terrain, existing fortifications were inadequate and needed extensive expansion.

Washington anticipated that French forces at Newport required assistance on a massive scale beyond the town's ability. In early May he sent Brigadier General Heath to Newport to arrange cooperation. The Rhode Island deputy-governor met Heath and together they worked on arrangements to meet an influx of hungry allies. In advance of the main landing, a French commissary–general arrived to assist Heath in the general preparations. One of

Heath's major concerns was to "be careful that the allies [were treated fairly] in prices." Medical concerns were another consideration and Washington sent his personal physician and chief medical officer Doctor Craik to arrange for hospitals to receive any sick after the long voyage.[6]

Even with all the preparations they were woefully inadequate. The deluge of demands that arrived overnight far exceeded expectations and the number of sick and infirm was beyond the capacity of hospital accommodations. The financial situation was chaotic; how to pay for all the needs without hard currency? Heath was confronted with a depreciating Continental currency that held little attraction for the locals, adding immense difficulties to procurement. Another serious problem was insufficient manpower to assist the French. Most Continental Army units from the area had gone south to Washington or Greene. Only untrained militia remained in the region.

When the French arrived on July 10, Heath was in Providence, Rhode Island, arranging for supplies. A speedy courier brought the news and Heath headed to Newport, arriving at midnight on July 12. The next morning he joined Rochambeau for breakfast and offered all the services he could command. When he learned of the cool reception by the natives, Heath met with local officials and initiated a process of engagement between the community and the French allies, which resulted in immediate success. The "inhabitants of Newport" sent a proclamation: they were "sincerely desirous of affording their utmost aid and assistance to the fleet and army of His Most Christian Majesty." Prompting the initial cool reception was a feeling of defenselessness caused during the British occupation. The population had been "deprived of their firearms and accoutrements," and their homes "stripped of every resource."[7]

Rochambeau's first business was to quarter his troops; a difficult task "in a country where language is an obstacle." Providing even minimal food and water in the first few weeks challenged the region. General Heath had surveyed the area and found a secure camp location. He led Rochambeau accompanied by staff officers to the site, pointing out advantages. They agreed that the site was "a high and healthful location southeast of the town." Soon citizens of Newport made overtures and approached their allies with "great respect." Quickly, after Heath placed advertisements for "small meats and vegetables," to be paid for in "hard money," the markets opened. "The markets are very good [and] everything appears agreeable and satisfactory," Heath wrote.[8]

The troops did not fully disembark and locate in camp until July 19. After only two days' rest the French started "digging trenches and fortifying." They placed artillery where the enemy might attack. As anticipated, while the French worked frantically to complete fortifications, "about 20 sail were sighted heading for the island." The British men of war were a great incentive to the soldiers. Every hour counted in construction of defenses. "We were convinced they would attack" at any moment, wrote one soldier. Several days passed and expectations for an attack grew to a fever pitch; the wait was agonizing, but every hour's delay helped to improve defenses. Then, as suddenly as they appeared, the enemy retired and disappeared over the horizon. Was it a feint? Or would they return? It made little difference; the fortifications continued at a rapid pace.[9]

After initial coolness to the French (Americans called it shyness), relations between French soldiers and Newport residents advanced with surprising warmth and respect. But for many French officers and men this was the first time they had witnessed such strange customs and behavior, unlike anything in Europe. The interaction of American civilians with the French allies was a source of great concern for both Rochambeau and Washington. Bitterness remained from the French and Indian War, less than twenty years before. Isolating the French to minimize fraternization was considered. Washington realized that social relations developed with the French at Newport could influence public perception in the rest of the country. Interaction of French and Americans in Newport was followed closely in both Patriot and Loyalist press. Friction or antagonism discouraged hope for effective military cooperation.

Rochambeau was very sensitive to American perceptions. He held officers personally accountable for the actions of soldiers under their command. At Newport, Washington and Rochambeau faced their biggest public relations challenge of the war. While public relations success did not guarantee future operations, failure would surely cloud the future. As it turned out, the positive public relations developed at Newport became a model for the balance of the war. Remarkable accomplishments at Newport were the friendship and respect developed between French soldiers and residents, but it needed time to mature. Many soldiers sent letters home with observations of a culture very different from Europe.

Americans had strange building practices; at times they built houses outside of town and, after completion, put them on rollers for relocation in town, reported one soldier. Most houses seemed small and designed in simple architecture. The "houses are charming...wonderfully clean," an officer wrote. "The Americans do not possess much furniture [but it is] so clean you can see your face in it."[10]

Correspondence revealed a growing appreciation and fondness between the contrasting cultures. "In general [Americans] eat a great deal of meat [but] little bread...with vegetables." Their favorite dinner drinks are "grog, cider, or beer," and after dinner, Madeira wine. "When you go visiting, the master of the house never fails to offer you a drink [after he] takes one first...to your health." Most "Americans are tall and well built [but] do not live long." Some are "sixty or seventy," although "it is exceedingly uncommon" for them to reach the age of eighty.

Fraternization between American women and French soldiers at Newport was a major topic of conversation during the visit, and for years afterward. Discussions were carried out in whispers, smiles, and with the wink of an eye. While no dalliances are described, there is a certain amount of imagination and implication.

The "women have very little color, but nothing can compare with the whiteness and texture of their skin," wrote a French officer. They possess "charming figures [and] are all pretty, even beautiful," especially "in what one can imagine to be a woman's loveliest attribute." They are great dancers; "one is really struck with admiration." Unfortunately "they fall short" in one respect. After they leave the dance floor; they assume a "frigid manner [and] lose much of their charm," showing "little vivacity and gaiety." American women can become very boring, unless you "assume the burden of conversation...[a difficult task] when you do not know English [and can only animate it] with your French gaiety." The effort is worth the reward, for "when these beauties get to know us...we find them absolutely ravishing."

When the English occupied Newport, they portrayed the French as "odious." They were mean "and most abominable," the English claimed. As they became better acquainted, "Little by little the houses and shops were opened to us, [but with] outrageous prices," one soldier wrote. Eventually, "friendship and courtesy replaced the bad impressions we had formed of each other." Once invited into homes, the French were "received as brothers rather than foreigners." Americans offered "quarters in the town [and they] lodged us very well." Together they spent many evenings in candlelight learning each other's language and customs. There was time for in-depth discussions about the war, British tyranny, and the French king's benevolence. All in all the time advanced mutual understanding, trust, and respect.[11]

This interaction was a welcome relief to both Rochambeau and Washington but there were still military operations to plan. Rochambeau assessed the situation and was stunned by his conclusions: Washington's army was effectively bankrupt, almost totally without discretionary funds. Rochambeau offered an immediate infusion of financial support in the amount of approximately $600,000 (Spanish Pieces of Eight), followed quickly by another equal amount.[12] The cash was needed to procure arms, ammunition, clothing, and powder. In a confidential letter to Vergennes, the French Minister of Foreign Affairs in Paris, Rochambeau described a shocking state of affairs. "Send us troops, ships, money," he wrote. Do "not count on these

[Americans], or upon their means; they are without [money] or credit." Unreliable Continental Army troop returns were another of Rochambeau's concerns. Information was so inconsistent that any future plans using American numbers were questionable. "Washington commands sometimes 15,000, sometimes 3,000 men," Rochambeau reported.[13] Another annoying situation: "On my arrival [I found a number of letters] from the Marquis de Lafayette awaiting me; they are too voluminous for copies to be sent, and they contain a mass of excited and rather incoherent proposals."[14]

Soon after arrival, Rochambeau had sent a courier to Continental Army Headquarters and placed himself under Washington's command.[15] Surprisingly, Washington delayed meeting with the French general. He never fully explained this initial reaction toward Rochambeau, but justified his action by citing "dangers" to the army.[16] In behavior uncharacteristic of Washington, Rochambeau was not invited to headquarters, although both commanders knew a communication exchange process was essential.

Washington initiated immediate steps to create a secure, dependable exchange process. Letters alone were superficial, unable to completely explain military complexities between two officers who had never met and did not speak each other's language. The best way to explain the full nuances of language was through personal contact that allowed discussions and explanations. Exchanges between Washington and Rochambeau, would, at times, contain highly classified information, of great value to the enemy. Contacts through a third party, someone trusted and of sufficient stature to represent the commander-in-chief, was a possibility. Washington dispatched Major General Marquis de Lafayette as his personal representative to French Headquarters in Newport, a move Washington felt would impress Rochambeau, but the appointment had unexpected results; it created a firestorm of contention.

Back in July when French forces arrived in Newport, they faced potential disaster. Rochambeau recognized the task's enormity and engaged American agents with previous Continental Army Commissary experience.[17] French efforts to acquire domestic provisions strained available supplies, and procurement attempts were forced to go further afield.

Rochambeau quickly recognized that the American cause was in a state of crisis. The first letters sent home by French officers disclosed "the true situation" and were written with vivid descriptions "of disappointment and malice." By this time Rochambeau knew that Lafayette had inadequately disclosed the true situation in North America.

Rochambeau was puzzled by the political and military protocol of his American allies. The Continental Army's command structure had no European parallel. The relationships between Washington, the Continental Congress, and the thirteen state governments confused him. Rochambeau was schooled in the autocratic military forces of a monarchy with no ambiguity in the chain of command. Louis XVI had appointed Washington commander-in-chief of French Armies and Navies in North America. Allegiance of French military personnel was to Washington, not to the Continental Congress or individual states.

During the remainder of July, Washington and Rochambeau exchanged a series of "spirited" views.[18] Even from a distance, each man used the exchanges to gain a measure of the other. On July 21, 1780, Lafayette arrived at French headquarters as Washington's emissary.[19] Almost as soon as he arrived, British forces from New York attempted a land and sea assault against French positions at Newport. But "Considerable bickering" between British commanders, General Clinton and Admiral Arbuthnot eventually caused an abandonment of the assault.[20] The British commanders argued over command details; egos clashed and neither would share authority with the other.

At American headquarters, Washington studied Rochambeau's inclinations through communication exchanges.[21] He desperately wanted the French to share his passion for an attack on New York City. Rochambeau's arrival, with the French fleet under Admiral De Ternay's command, only enhanced Washington's passion for an attack.[22] For the first time there were sufficient allied military forces available to make a determined effort against New York and end the war. To Washington's dismay neither Rochambeau nor DeTernay exhibited enthusiasm for an attack against the city. The two French commanders wanted any decision deferred until additional forces arrived.[23] Frustrated by French attitudes and confident an assault would interrupt British supplies and strangle the city, Washington proposed an alternative: start a siege without a blockade.[24] Again the French reacted with passive resistance.

Lafayette was to facilitate communication and help spur the French into immediate joint action. His knowledge of languages, Rochambeau's and Washington's personalities, was expected to solidify a positive relationship between the two men. "The alliance ought to be cemented in affection, and you will be justly dear to both countries for the share you have in binding [the ties]," Washington wrote to Lafayette.[25]

Contrary views on a New York assault increased the friction between Rochambeau and Lafayette. Sharp verbal exchanges were followed by sneers; the two projected an intense clash of personalities. The situation demanded continuous meetings where Lafayette, Rochambeau, and Admiral De Ternay discussed tactical and strategic matters.[26] In spite of a British fleet's arrival at Newport, Lafayette pushed for action against New

York City.[27] Rochambeau resented the young Continental Army officer whom he viewed as pushy, self-aggrandizing, and impertinent. He still harbored anger over Lafayette's misleading assessment of military conditions in North America. The immediate contention was over chain of command; under no circumstances did Rochambeau intend to take orders from anyone but Washington. While Lafayette was a personal emissary, as far as Rochambeau was concerned, he was not Washington.

Lafayette's ego was bruised. He felt his rank as a Continental Army major general and status as Washington's representative elevated him to a privileged position, especially after his year in Paris meeting with French officials and the king. After all, he was responsible for Rochambeau's appointment. Lafayette fumed that Rochambeau recognized him as little more than a glorified messenger. He felt French resistance to an assault against New York was a political blunder. Unwillingness to fight projected a lack of sincerity to both Patriot and Loyalist sympathizers. Disappointed and angry, Lafayette returned to Washington's headquarters. He prepared a detailed report and presented his views on the matters discussed at Newport.[28] The report ignited a controversy between Rochambeau and Lafayette; Rochambeau was infuriated by the implications. One suggested a French responsibility to assure success of the American cause. Lafayette insisted the French presence in Rhode Island had no military advantage and they should immediately prepare for a junction with Washington and assault New York.[29]

Rochambeau, furious with Lafayette's report, emphasized again that he did not intend to accept orders unless they came directly from Washington.[30] Rochambeau considered Lafayette's approach an attempt to exercise direct command influence. Between August 12 and 27, the two exchanged heated words.[31] Almost by accident, Lafayette was informed of the contents in a private letter written by Rochambeau to a mutual friend. Now Lafayette was infuriated, for the letter seemed to demean Americans. An angry Lafayette wrote to the French Minister, Chevalier de la Luzerne, in Philadelphia and explained American behavior in a positive manner. Perhaps, he suggested, the Minister might offer "discreet advice" to Rochambeau.[32]

At first, Washington was unaware of the problem, but after reading copies of the exchanges, he encouraged Lafayette to make his peace with Rochambeau. "Through a little excess of plain speaking I have got into a slight controversy," Lafayette informed his wife. Humble and contrite, Lafayette prepared two letters dated August 18, 1780. "Allow me to acknowledge here that I explained myself very awkwardly," he wrote to both Rochambeau and the Chevalier de Ternay, in the first letter.[33] "If I have offended you, I ask your pardon for two reasons." First was his high esteem for Rochambeau; the second was his desire to do "that [which] may please you." His second letter, to Rochambeau only, was more personal:

In camp, August 18, 1780

Now that I have written to you a letter, Monsieur le Comte, in common with M. le Chevalier de Ternay, permit me to address myself to you with all the confidence of that tender friendship, that veneration I have felt for you and have tried to show you since my tenderest youth. Although the expressions in your letter show your usual kindness to me, I noticed some items there that, without being addressed to me personally, show me that my last epistle displeased you. After four months in which I have been busy day and night preparing people's minds to receive you, respect you, and love you; after all I have said to point out the advantages of your stay on Rhode Island and to use my influence in speaking to the people about this truth; finally, Monsieur le Comte, after everything my patriotism and my sentiments for you have imposed upon me, my heart cannot help but be affected at seeing you give my letter such an unfavorable interpretation and one that I never intended. If in the course of that letter I may have offended or displeased you or if, for example, you dislike the written account that General Washington asked of me and that I thought I should submit to you, I give you my word of honor that I thought I was doing something very simple, so simple indeed that I would have considerd the failure to do it as an injustice to you.

If like me, Monsieur le Comte, you had heard the second division talked about, if you knew how the English and the Tories try to persuade people that France wants only to stir up the fire and not to put it out, you would understand that the desire to silence this talk gives me perhaps too ardent a zeal. I confess to you in confidence, in the middle of a foreign land, that my vanity suffers when I see the French blockaded on Rhode Island, and the resentment I feel makes me tend to want action. As for what you tell me about Rhode Island, Monsieur le Comte, if I recounted for you what I have said, written, and placed in the papers; if you had seen me often amid a group of American peasants telling them about the conduct of the French in Newport; if you spend just three days here with me, you would see the injustice of that sort of reproach.

If I have offended you, I ask your pardon for two reasons; the first is that I love you; the second is that my intention is to do here all that may please you. Wherever I am just a private person, your orders will be law to me; and for the least of the French who are here I would make every sacrifice rather than not contribute to their glory, their satisfaction, and their union with the Americans. Such are, Monsieur le Comte, my sentiments, and although you imagined I had quite contrary ones in my heart, I am forgetting this injustice in order to think only of my devotion to you.

Lafayette[34]

In his own conciliatory way, Rochambeau responded:

Newport, August 27, 1780

Allow an old father, my dear Marquis, to reply to you as a cherished son whom he loves and esteems immensely. You know me well enough to believe that I do not need to be roused to action; at my age, when we have made a decision based on military and political considerations and to which we were forced by circumstances, no possible instigation could make me change without a direct order from my general. I am happy enough that, on the contrary, he tells me in his despatches that my ideas accord substantially with his own on all the bases that will enable us to turn this campaign into an offensive and that we differ only on certain details, on which the slightest explanation, and certainly his orders, will settle any difficulty. You are humiliated as a Frenchman, my dear friend, to see an English squadron here with a marked superiority of ships and frigates blockading the Chevalier de Ternay's squadron. But take comfort, my dear marquis.... If you had fought in the last two wars you would have heard of nothing but such blockades. I hope that M. de Guichen, on the one hand, and M. Gaston, on the other, will avenge us for all these momentary vexations.

It is always praiseworthy, my dear marquis, to believe the French are invincible, but I am going to confide in you a great secret based on forty years' experience. There are no troops easier to defeat [than] when they have lost confidence in their commander, and they lose that confidence immediately when they have been put in danger because of private or personal ambition. If I have been fortunate enough to keep their confidence thus far, I owe it to the most scrupulous examination of my conscience, in that, of the nearly 15,000 men who have been killed or wounded under my command in the varioius ranks and in the most murderous actions, I need not reproach myself that a single one was killed for my own advantage....

Be well assured, therefore, of my warmest friendship and that, if I have pointed out to you very gently the things in your last letter that displeased me, I concluded immediately that the warmth of your feelings and your heart had somewhat overheated the calmness and prudence of your judgment. Preserve this last quality in the council, and keep all of the first for the moment of action. This is still the old father Rochambeau speaking to his dear son Lafayette, whom he loves and will continue to love and esteem to his last breath.[35]

After declaring "everything I said was wrong" he asked to be pardoned, Lafayette wrote sheepishly to his wife, "which has had a wonderful effect." Now, "we are all on much better terms than ever before."[36]

Lafayette and Rochambeau needed two months to settle their differences. Rochambeau defined his position in the Allied chain of command. Compassionate but firm towards Lafayette, he accepted the Marquis as communications facilitator, but when orders were involved he expected to deal directly with Washington. Rochambeau, although angry at times, never projected an acrimonious temperament, rather a resolute image and a power of leadership charisma.[37]

Rochambeau had sent a letter placing his forces under Washington's command and requesting a meeting.[38] Washington resisted; his reluctance was influenced by experience. Two earlier attempts of military cooperation between French and American forces had ended in disaster. Washington faced both a military and political dilemma. Something had to be done to harness the military potential of allied forces or the alliance might collapse. But another failed attempt would have serious military consequences and horrendous political implications.

Several years earlier, on July 8, 1778, a unified Allied effort had been attempted at Newport with French naval forces under the command of Admiral D'Estaing. Before he reached Newport, D'Estaing was headed for New York. Washington, ecstatic at the prospect of French naval support against the city, prepared detailed plans for the attack. The French navy was to penetrate New York harbor and blockade any attempts by a British relief fleet. But a contingency, not considered, was the deep draft of French vessels. They could not cross the sandbar at the harbor entrance. Washington, inexperienced in tactical demands of naval warfare, missed a crucial consideration and the assault was abandoned.

Newport was the alternate target if New York was judged impractical. Approximately 5,000 British forces occupied Newport. A British defeat would have great propaganda value and signal the significance of American and French cooperation. American military forces assembled for the assault against Newport with high expectations. Soon it was glaringly apparent they lacked adequate training and supplies. Delays hampered American forces and exasperated Admiral D'Estang. The French had to wait while Americans assembled sufficient forces.

On August 10, 1779, a British relief fleet arrived near Newport. With a threat of entrapment in Newport harbor, D'Estaing left to engage the enemy fleet and informed his American allies he would return. Eventually, the Americans assembled sufficient forces, but found British defenses substantial and naval support needed to bombard the fortifications. D'Estaing was out of contact and now Americans fumed as they waited for the return of French naval support. Finally, on August 20, 1779, the fleet returned, but left at once for Boston and extensive repairs – an action Americans referred to as "shameful desertion."

The French departure sparked emotional diatribes, most from the American viewpoint. In public discussions and communications, references to earlier American delays were avoided. With the French navy's move to Boston, Americans were forced to give up attempts against Newport. A united Allied effort failed and the consequences were a political debacle. Some challenged

French dedication and willingness to support American efforts. Perceptions of the sordid affair spiraled out of control and developed into a propaganda mess. Washington tried to calm the emotions of officers and public officials who rushed to judgment. They blamed the French and questioned the value of an Alliance.[39]

On September 9, 1779, a second united allied assault was directed at the city of Savannah, Georgia. After a series of blunders, allies called off the siege and the French sailed away on October 24. When the assault began Admiral D'Estaing placed French troops on shore to join Americans in a spirited attack. Brilliant defense by British forces repulsed the allies and inflicted heavy casualties. Americans lost over two hundred men and the French more than six hundred, while British casualties were about 150.[40] But public explanations differed greatly between Newport and Savannah, where Patriot press reports avoided incriminations between Allies.[41]

The previous failures of these combined efforts made Washington cautious when he considered an Allied effort in 1780. Another failure had many political and military consequences and past experiences did not bode well for a good future. By this time Washington realized the need to demonstrate a successful unified Allied effort. Without success the whole idea of the Alliance came into question and the American cause was at risk.

A factor influencing Washington's caution was lack of personal experience with Rochambeau. Personal associations were part of Washington's mode of operation. This was essential on matters that involved life and death issues. The foundation for an effective unity of command was possible, especially after Rochambeau informed him upon arrival, "We are now sir under your command."[42]

Before Washington finished contemplating further allied opportunities, Americans suffered another military disaster. On September 6, 1780, Washington informed Maryland Governor Thomas Sim Lee of "disagreeable intelligence." Continental Army Major General Horatio Gates suffered a serious defeat at Camden, South Carolina.[43] Gates' defeat destroyed the southern Continental Army, leaving the entire south open to British conquest. "We have just received the most disagreeable advices from General Gates, of a defeat of the Army near Camden in South Carolina the 16th.of last month," Washington wrote to Rochambeau.[44] The Battle at Camden was the second defeat of the southern Continental Army within a year.[45] In May 1780, Major General Benjamin Lincoln lost a southern Continental Army when he surrendered at Charleston, South Carolina. "This event must have the worst effect upon the affairs of the Southern States," Washington acknowledged.[46]

Meanwhile, Rochambeau spent August and early September cementing relationships with the citizens of Newport and expanding the fortifications along the coast and around Narragansett Bay. In Newport, dances, receptions and other gatherings with French guests were marvelous social events. Great and glorious entertainment exposed both French and American customs to all. The affairs of Newport were reported in great detail and carried with interest in Patriot newspapers throughout the country, which now saw the French as comrades and friends.

In one unusual reception about twenty representatives visited Rochambeau from four Iroquois nations, including Oneidas and Tuscaroras. They came to offer their allegiance and services again to the American cause. (In 1778, at the Battle of Barren Hill in Pennsylvania, Oneida and Tuscarora warriors had helped to extract a Continental Army detachment under the command of Lafayette from a British encirclement, enabling them to return to Valley Forge.) The visit lasted four days. For the French soldiers the sight of these strange figures was unforgettable. Warriors demonstrated their prowess with dances, games, and an exhibition of scalping techniques.[47] The French were fascinated; it was great entertainment and relief from the drudgery of building entrenchments. "These barbarians go naked and paint their bodies different colors," wrote a French officer. "They pierce their nostrils…and likewise their ears." "[They are] fond of strong liquor and are always smoking." They "have many good qualities and are basically much less barbarous than they appear." They were sent home well satisfied and "loaded with gifts."[48]

At Washington's Headquarters the mood was anything but positive. The terrible news from Camden, South Carolina, jolted Washington, and he requested a meeting with Rochambeau as soon as possible. His caution gave way to desperation. Hartford, Connecticut, was the meeting place. "I hope we shall be able to combine some plan of future operation which events will enable us to execute," Washington wrote to Rochambeau. "Affairs of this Country absolutely require activity." Rochambeau was relieved; his irritation over Washington's previous delays for a personal meeting had been growing. Now at last they would meet.[49]

"Tomorrow I set out for Hartford, on an interview with the French General and Admiral," Washington informed Major General Nathanael Greene. "In my absence [your are in] command of the army [but I have] only one observation…it is not our business to seek an action or accept it, [unless with] advantageous terms."[50]

Washington left Tappan, New York, on September 17, accompanied by six aides including Lafayette, Henry Knox, and Alexander Hamilton. Rochambeau departed Newport with seven aides at about the same time. At this first face-to-face meeting of two soldiers who would influence United State's destiny, little of strategic importance was accomplished, but powerful interpersonal associations developed. Washington and Rochambeau observed and evaluated each other, although Rochambeau still considered Lafayette an "unwelcome intermediary," but necessary to translate exchanges for two men without fluency in the other's language.[51]

The conference ended abruptly with news that a British fleet of twenty-one ships had arrived at New York from the West Indies. The New York reinforcements postponed any immediate consideration for an assault on New York.[52] On September 28, Rochambeau returned to Newport and Washington to Tappan.

During his return trip to headquarters, Washington was informed of Benedict Arnold's traitorous actions. This was a blow to the commander-in-chief; Arnold was considered to be talented and loyal. "Who is there that we can trust?" he asked.[53] After returning to headquarters, he received news from Congress that Continental Army Major General Horatio Gates was to be suspended from command of the Southern Army. President Huntington requested Washington to choose Gates' successor.[54] On October 14, 1780, in a move with enormous consequences on the war's direction, Washington quickly appointed Major General Nathanael Greene to command another Southern Army.[55]

Rochambeau returned to headquarters pleased at the first meeting with his American commander-in-chief. Washington could be trusted. Although inexperienced when measured by European standards, he possessed stature, intelligence, and an innate understanding of military affairs. His power of leadership charisma was a quality Rochambeau both recognized and appreciated.

After consultations with his staff, Rochambeau planned a new course of action, which eventually defined the war's final phase. He decided to send his son and adjutant, Donatien Marie Joseph de Vimeur, Vicomte de Rochambeau, to France with instructions to encourage additional French support on a scale larger than previously considered.

Vicomte Rochambeau, age thirty, was ambitious. He readily accepted a personal mission to gain a presence away from his father's shadow. He and his father had left France with enormous support and encouragement from king and country. Thus, young Rochambeau anticipated a warm reception and broad support for the requests he carried. The opportunity for France to regain stature in world affairs was a compelling reason for sizable increased assistance for the Americans. He hoped his return would generate the same enthusiasm and hero status afforded Lafayette from his military adventure in North America. General Rochambeau was convinced of a British defeat if France committed increased support. Now, antagonism against Britain was spread throughout the world.

In October 1781, French troops at Newport had a frightening experience. "There was a terrible storm...the whole camp was blown apart," reported a

French officer. "The vessels anchored in the harbor dragged their anchors and, and several went aground." One "merchantman was dashed on the rocks and [destroyed]." Another vessel "went aground and broke her top mast." For many soldiers this was a first encounter with the ferocity of Mother Nature. "Nearly all the tents in the camp were blown down," wrote another officer. We "had a terrifying hurricane," yet another officer wrote.[56] Soldiers spent days repairing the camp, sewing the tents, and recovering lost items of clothing and equipment scattered all over the area.

Meanwhile, the Allies decided not to engage in any major military effort until France supplied "strong naval reinforcements" and additional financial support. As October closed, Rochambeau entered winter quarters at Newport. By this time, Newport had changed considerably. A town hall, "quite handsome," and built of brick was made into a "large hospital." The town has "a good public library" and the "meat market is built of brick and is rather pretty," described a French officer. Most of the "buildings consecrated to religious worship [are] used for our hospitals."

Fortifications were completed around the camp area. "The harbor, though rather difficult to enter, is one of the best in the world," they reported. "Easily a hundred vessels can winter there." A "small island at the entrance...is an excellent emplacement for a fort [with] a lighthouse [at] the harbor entrance." French soldiers were seen exploring all over the immediate area, delighted with its natural abundance. "The surrounding sea, and even the harbor, abounds in delicious fish – blackfish, lobster, eel, skate, mackerel, bluefish, succulent cod, and plenty of excellent oysters," one soldier wrote home. Newport was a paradise for those who considered themselves seafood connoisseurs. Not a day passed without the sight of off-duty Frenchmen fishing along the river and harbor banks.

On October 28, 1780, General Vicomte Rochambeau departed Newport, and reached France on November 15. In Paris he was shocked to find a dramatically changed situation. Visiting the court and ministries, he found that extensive reorganizations were instituted during General Rochambeau's absence. He was greeted with polite but uninterested reactions; some shunned and others ignored him. The Vicomte submitted a "memoir" detailing "the Necessity for an Increase in Sea and Land Forces in the United States."[57] To his astonishment, there was little enthusiasm; requests for increased support were rejected. He found individuals who "feared General Rochambeau's success," almost opposing him. Intrigues and jealousies abounded from ministers who possessed "erroneous ideas on the United States," and fostered a sullen resistance to increased assistance. Some even viewed a success by General Rochambeau in America a threat to their personal ambitions.

Dismayed, "very tired and quite dissatisfied," young Rochambeau departed France on March 24, 1781, for his return to North America. He agonized about the Paris disappointments and dreaded the prospect of revealing such news to his father.

Back in Newport on December 15, 1781, while the Vicomte engaged in the drama of Paris, General Rochambeau experienced a tragic event; his friend and associate Admiral De Ternay died suddenly. The citizens of Newport reacted with respect and sadness, and he was buried in the town's Baptist cemetery. Such gestures were further evidence of the increasing affection developing between the people of Newport and their French allies. He was succeeded by his second in command, Admiral Destouches.

❧ 3 ❧

1781 – A Horrible Beginning

*At what point this defection will stop, or how
extensive it may prove God only knows*

The year 1781 started with a series of disastrous events. If January troubles were an indication of the rest of the year, the Continental Army would collapse. In 1780 two Southern Continental armies were destroyed, the first at Charleston, South Carolina, in May 1780 and later in August at Camden, South Carolina. Now Washington faced another challenge, an insidious assault from within.

Before 1781, the army's major strength was a small, dedicated, and experienced officer corps.[1] Much of the patriotic zeal had faded in the civilian population. Time and circumstances had eroded hopes to preserve the American cause. An intangible power of leadership charisma and promises from a few Continental Army officers held the army together.

On January 1, the army trembled; mutiny infected its very existence. "Murmurs," complaints and threats always flourished just below the surface. While causes were obvious, immediate solutions were impossible. Washington faced threats on a scale he had never before encountered. They came in quick succession and demanded immediate action or the army would dissolve. The army watched; wrong responses could spread the scourge like a wildfire. Uncertain of the extent, Washington switched attention from a unified effort with the French ally to salvation of the Continental Army.

Small mutinous activities were nothing new. In June 1776, a member of Washington's Life Guard was charged with "passing counterfeit currency," convicted, and hanged.[2] Januaries were especially difficult. A hundred soldiers from the Massachusetts Continental line left West Point on January 1, 1780, for home, after their enlistments expired. They were pursued, captured, and returned, with some punished and a majority pardoned.[3] In June 1780, after a mutiny in the First New York Regiment, deserters were pursued and shot by Oneida Indians assigned to track them. This was the only time during the American War of Independence when Native Americans were used to track and kill white soldiers.[4]

On January 2, 1781, the first ominous reports arrived from General Anthony Wayne. Washington stared at the words, his head shook in disbelief, and an anguished expression crossed his face as the cold reality set in. "The most general and unhappy mutiny took place in" the Pennsylvania Line "about 9OClock Night," Wayne wrote. Every "exertion has been made by the Officers to [quell the] determination to Revolt." He reported success for the present, but added, "[how] long it will last God knows."[5]

Eleven regiments from Pennsylvania under Wayne's command stationed at Morristown, NJ, "mutinied and marched toward Philadelphia." The Continental Congress was their target and they intended a direct presentation of grievances.[6] Washington replied to Wayne in full support of his actions. He was satisfied "that everything possible was done" by Wayne and his officers "to check the mutiny."

Wayne's situation triggered another concern, the troops under Washington's command at headquarters. "I am advised by [my officers that the] temper of the troops" is uncertain.[7] Mutiny was contagious, and

Etching by unknown artist.

Brigadier General Anthony Wayne.

nobody knew how far the disease had spread. Would other units join the Pennsylvanians? Washington weighed the distinct possibility of a general uprising throughout the Continental Army. Too much attention encouraged mutineers to continue; too little allowed time to build a platform of support, inviting others to join. The situation was a powder keg with a small spark igniting dissolution of an entire army. Washington also sensed another problem. When the enemy realized the situation, they would make every effort to provide a spark.

The size of the mutiny was unparalleled – in excess of fifteen hundred men accompanied by their women and children.[8] On January 3, 1781, the mutineers marched into Princeton, New Jersey, "with Wayne...at a distance." As they marched, the situation grew increasingly ugly; "anger and alcohol made them" impossible to deal with.[9] They were a mob without organization, but with purpose. In spite of appearance, they retained some discipline. The "greatest order" was maintained, a British spy reported, "and if a man takes a fowl from an inhabitant he is severely punished."[10]

When Congress heard that mutineers were on the way, they panicked. Congressional delegates met with members of the Pennsylvania legislature. Congress blamed the Pennsylvania legislature and insisted they send representatives to hear the mutineers' complaints.[11] After several hours of tense discussions, they reached an agreement. President Joseph Reed of the Pennsylvania legislature and a small staff headed for New Jersey to meet the mutineers. Congress agreed to send representatives and join in discussions. Both members of Congress and the Pennsylvania Legislature were terrified at the possibility of a large group of mutinous soldiers loose in the city of Philadelphia; the political consequences were enormous. "We had to keep them away from here," one Philadelphian wrote.

Washington monitored the situation closely and kept in constant communication with Wayne. "Your influence has had a great share in preventing worse extremities," he informed Wayne. "I felt for your situation."[12]

Washington knew that the situation was precarious. At any moment, news could arrive of events triggering a collapse of the American cause. Rumors floated around camp about other units on the verge of joining the mutineers.

Meanwhile the Continental Army's entire chain of command was in a fragile state. The French Alliance was at stake. In a bold stroke of diplomacy, despite temptations to the contrary, Washington did not cover up the unfolding disaster. Instead he leveraged the situation to challenge both Congress and the states to increase assistance for the army. On January 5, in a "Circular" to the states and Congress, he wrote, "At what point this defection will stop, or how extensive it may prove God only knows." Presently "the Troops [directly under my command] remain quiet," and unaware of "this unhappy and alarming affair." How "long they will continue," is uncertain, because "they labor under [the same] pressing hardships," as "the Troops who have revolted."

Many and varied were the causes of this disastrous situation. One big deficiency was a lack "of pay for nearly twelve Months." The desperate need for "cloathing [and] provisions" was "beyond description." The potential consequences were chilling. "I give it decidedly as my opinion" that it will be impossible to keep "the army together much longer," Washington reported. "I have used every effort in my power to avert the evil that has come upon us, [and I will] continue to exert every means I am possessed of to prevent an extension of the Mischief."[13]

Most Congressional delegates had little understanding of the demands to keep an army together. Some delegates considered that the army exhorted frivolous financial needs on the country. In the past, Congress often dismissed complaints from the army as gross exaggerations, passing them on to individual state legislatures for corrective action.

Washington prepared Congress for the worst. He sent daily reports and kept Congress updated as the mutiny progressed. Occasionally, he had better news. The mutineers "shewed some signs of [an improved] disposition," he reported. They made no attempt to join the enemy. But Washington avoided dispatching Continental Army units to quell the mutineers, because there was no assurance "of the temper and affections of the Garrison," he reported. "Matters are now come to a Crisis."[14]

Mutiny destroyed discipline, but a wrong solution could be as destructive as the mutiny. Grievances had accumulated over time, involving "terms of enlistments." These were the main issues in the Pennsylvania Line on January 1, 1781. Who organized the mutiny was unclear, but a twelve man "Board of Sergeants" represented them. When the group reached Princeton, Wayne met and discussed complaints with the "Board of Sergeants." He was astonished, and concluded that their demands were "founded in principles of justice and honor."[15]

President Joseph Reed and General James Potter, a Pennsylvania militia officer, left Philadelphia on January 5, 1781. They arrived in Trenton, New Jersey, the next day. Congress sent a four-man committee to join Reed.[16]

Earlier, the mutineers had captured British emissaries sent to discuss support for their effort. British spies kept a close watch on the mutiny's development. Information flowed back and forth from headquarters in New York City. British intelligence officers made plans to stimulate any dissent. Fortunately, the mutineers avoided an association with the enemy and rejected their offers. When news reached Wayne and Reed of the rejection, a great mood of relief spread through Reed's group and Washington's headquarters. The rejection dispelled immediate concerns that the mutineers intended to accept British support.

In the meantime, Wayne offered a series of proposals to keep the mutineers from considering further encouragement from the enemy. The big concern was a British offer to pay mutineers back pay with incentives to join
forces against the "rebel" army.

During Wayne's discussions with the sergeants, he confirmed a whole
list of fraudulent enlistment practices. Men, often illiterate, were vulnerable to enlistment papers not reflecting conditions as explained and accepted; further discussions revealed a wide range of other abuses.[17] As
discussions proceeded, Wayne was more convinced of possible solution;
at no time, did the mutineers threaten to abandon the American cause for
enemy promises and pay. They demanded only fairness and justice.
Wayne decided on a course of action to end the mutiny quickly. He offered, "total amnesty" and Reed, after reviewing the details and notes,
honored the offer. The mutineers agreed and gave up their arms. The
mutiny was over, and a final episode was hanging the British emissaries
as spies on January 11, 1781.

On January 29, there was jubilant news. The "task was completed,"
Wayne informed Washington.[18] "Many of the mutineers who are discharged
are now pestering us to re-enlist them," an American officer wrote.[19] At headquarters there was great relief, but the situation continued to fester. Washington faced another issue as discontent spread. The solution to the one mutiny
spawned other problems. The "effects of temporary inlistments" are a source
of ruin, Washington wrote. The discontent "arising from this source" con-
taminates the entire Pennsylvania Line.[20]

During the Reed and Wayne discussions with the sergeants, Washington
remained in the background. Later he explained why; once "the civil authority
[had] undertaken to settle the dispute" it was improper for me to interfere "in
their conciliatory measures."

Washington breathed a sigh of relief, but he feared aftershocks. At least
temporarily catastrophe was avoided, but mutineers had gained negotiating
status in the Continental Army – a status no professional army in the world
tolerated. Under the circumstances, Washington believed Reed and Wayne
had extracted the best solution. But he knew the solution was both expedi-
ent and political, not military. Officers from the Pennsylvanian Line resented
their exclusion from negotiations, and strongly opposed the solution, which
gave mutineers an elevated importance.[21]

During the episode, Washington informed others of developments. The
Pennsylvania Line was "composed of foreigners," he wrote to Rochambeau,
and, "The rest of our army" struggles "under the same difficulties."[22]

The perils of a political settlement arrived quickly. On January 20,
1781, a smaller group from New Jersey's Continental Line mutinied. The

causes mirrored Pennsylvania's problem.[23] But this time the solution differed; it was military, not political.[24]

Washington acted immediately upon notification of the New Jersey mutiny. This situation "must be brought to a [conclusion] favorable to subordination, or the army is ruined," he wrote Colonel Israel Shreve, commander of New Jersey troops. The mutineers' only alternative is "to unconditional submission [and] the more decisively you are able to act the better."[25] Washington was "determined at all hazards to put a stop to such proceedings, [which otherwise would] prove the inevitable dissolution of the Army."[26]

The entire Continental Army, the French, and the enemy watched. The solution must involve an obvious, quick and deliberate extinction of mutinous spirit, before it spreads "through the remainder of the army."[27] But Shreve hesitated. The thought of action against people from his home state was unpalatable. He was uncommitted in his response to an angry Washington who considered Shreve more motivated by political concerns than a need to save the Army. Without hesitation, Washington ordered forces, under the command of Major General Robert Howe from North Carolina, against "the mutineers [to] compel [them into] unconditional submission." Washington was adamant. "If you succeed in compelling the revolted troops to surrender you will instantly execute a few [of the leaders]," he ordered.[28] Howe marched forces through snow at night and arrived "at the huts" of the mutineers. During the deployment, Howe heard rumors that his own soldiers might "not prove faithful" against the mutineers. He assembled the troops and "harangued" them about the "heinousness of the crime of mutiny." At the conclusion there was a consensus that the orders would be followed "with alacrity."[29]

Washington informed Rochambeau:

> It is with equal mortification and regret, I find myself obliged to add to that, the account of a second mutiny, which I had apprehended and which has lately taken place in the Jersey troops. When the advices came away it was only partial, that corps being divided into several detachments, but it was imagined the revolt the one part had been in consequence of a pre-concerted plan between the whole and that the remainder would follow the example. Immediately on receiving the intelligence I sent a detachment from these posts under the command of Major General Howe, with orders to compel the mutineers to unconditional submission, and I have requested the civil Authority not to interpose with any terms of conciliation. It appears to me essential that this spirit should be suppressed by force and by an examplary punishment of the principal instigators of the defection.[30]

Hard action was needed, he told Rochambeau, and he continued his letter:

> The complaints and demands of these mutineers resemble, those of the Pennsylvanians. It is hard to say with certainty how far the disposition which has now appeared may extend itself among troops who have so many causes of dissatisfaction; but I hope we shall be able to stop the progress of the evil here.[31]

Rochambeau was sympathetic, but shocked at the extent of turmoil in the Continental Army. The French general observed intently how Washington handled the situation. As a seasoned military officer, he developed a great respect for Washington's honesty and effort to keep him informed.

After the "Jersey mutiny" was quelled, Washington informed Congressional and state authorities that a few of "the principal incendiaries" were executed on the spot. The mutiny "is now completely subdued and superceded by a genuine penitence," he wrote. "But having punished the guilty and supported authority, it now becomes proper to do justice."[32] The punishments were dramatic, open and precedent-setting. Three of the most "atrocious offenders" were selected, tried "on the spot," convicted and sentenced "to be immediately shot." The firing squad was, "Twelve of the guiltiest mutineers" who "under threat of death" were selected. Sentences were "administered one by one; after two had been executed, the third being less criminal...received a pardon."[33]

On January 29, a relieved Washington informed General Rochambeau, "I have the pleasure to inform your Excellency that the detachment sent" to quell the mutineers "surrounded them and demanded immediate surrender." They complied "without the least attempt to resist. Two of the principal actors were executed on the spot [and I am convinced] the spirit of the mutiny is completely subdued and will not show itself."[34]

January 1781 was over, and insidious challenges resolved. The army was preserved and steeled by the discipline of a military solution to mutiny. Congress and the states did attempt to redress the army's grievances; "the Army fared" much "better after January 1781 than before."[35]

With the mutinies quelled, Washington turned attention to reconstruction of the army. Major General Horatio Gates' defeat in at Camden placed the entire south open for British conquest. There was no assurance that any realistic southern command existed.

4

Southern Reconstruction

I trust, the experience of error will enable us to act better in the future

With the January mutinies over, optimism at Washington's headquarters did not improve; a cloud of pessimism hung over the camp. By early 1781, British military power in the southern states reduced Continental Army activities to little more than harassment operations. British domination was growing and there was no indication of change.

In late 1780, Washington sent Major General Nathanael Greene to reconstruct a third southern command. At best only shattered Continental Army remnants remained following the destruction of two previous southern commands in 1780.

Greene was thirty-eight years old, from Rhode Island, and a big man for the times, about five feet ten or eleven inches tall with prominent facial features and robust in stature, around two hundred pounds, but he rode a horse well. Sandy hair was streaked with gray and his flashing blue eyes exuded a sense of melancholy under a high forehead. Anyone in Greene's company quickly recognized an air of quiet charisma. He possessed an obvious sense of humor and a straightforward manner; he enjoyed conversation, but was an exceptionally good listener. A good joke always received an animated response driven by a "vivacious and spirited temperament."[1] In military endeavors, his temperament was a mixed blessing; at times he was bold, audacious, and daring. He suffered defeat and disappointment with deep anxiety. On occasion, these traits contributed to Greene's difficulties, and drove him to "impetuous or headstrong" actions. Although generally healthy, he was asthmatic and had a decided limp caused by a stiff knee, probably from a boyhood accident.

Greene was not in the military through a natural progression. Raised in a strict Quaker family, his father, a Quaker preacher, owned a farm and an iron business where Nathanael worked long hours as a boy. His formal education was limited to reading, writing, and arithmetic, but he demonstrated a strong

aptitude in all three. As a youth his passion was reading, which "overshadowed all other forms of recreation;" reading about military affairs fascinated
him. Although not shy or a stranger with the opposite sex, his father made
every effort to curb "worldly mindedness."[2] The family iron business flourished, and after Nathanael's father died in November 1770, he formed a part-
nership with his brothers to continue the business, now one of the largest in
Rhode Island. On July 20, 1774, Nathanael married Catherine Littlefield after a short courtship. She was nineteen, thirteen years his junior, and described
as "pretty, vivacious, witty, and flirtatious."[3]

Etching by Alonzo Chapel.

Major General Nathanael Greene.

In the spring of 1773, Nathaniel attended one of his earliest military gatherings in Connecticut, called to protest a number of incidents involving British actions against the American colonists. Later, in December 1773, after the Boston Tea Party, Greene's involvement in militia activities grew in intensity, especially after the British Parliament invoked the odious Intolerable Acts.

Greene's advance in rank was less than spectacular, and helped along to some extent by political influence. Eventually he was recognized by the Rhode Island Assembly as a man with "military talent" and appointed on April 22, 1775, three days after the events at Lexington and Concord, to the rank of "brigadier general to command an Army of Observation."[4] On May 20, 1775, Greene ordered his army to Massachusetts and Boston to help "preserve the Liberties of America."

At headquarters on July 5, 1775, on the hills overlooking Boston, Nathanael Greene first met George Washington, the man who would exercise a dramatic influence over the rest of his life. Their meeting was an instant success; both men took "a great liking to each other."[5] During this early association, Washington recognized extraordinary qualities in Greene. He was marked as worthy of Washington's confidence, something "preserved" throughout the war.

Washington saw in Greene an officer with a capacity for strategic thinking. Although lacking battlefield experience, he possessed intellect and willingness to learn. Greene was bright and projected confidence with military bearing, but without arrogance. Above all, he was a team player, a quality Washington admired and desperately needed. As it turned out, Washington's early assessment of Greene was one of his most accurate. After serving his country and commander-in-chief with loyalty and dedication for more than five years, Major General Nathanael Greene was on the threshold of his most epic military experience and challenge.

Washington considered preservation of the South essential to survival of the United States and an integral part of any military strategy. He believed the best tactic to save the South was an assault against New York City; it would force the British to send reinforcements from the South for the city's defense. Rochambeau had a different view; he considered British forces in and around the city too large for a successful attack and regarded the harbor as a challenge to navigation. Meanwhile, southern coastal ports were closer to French operations in the West Indies, providing an opportunity for expeditious cooperation and delivery of planned reinforcements.

As Washington and Rochambeau wrestled with a strategy to harness the combined potential of their military forces, challenges to the Continental Army's survival changed from mutinies to logistics. Supply problems resulted from poor coordination between Congress, states, militias, and a foreign ally.

Lack of a central financial authority created logistical nightmares with no prospects for improvement. Lack of money and supplies threatened the Continental Army's existence.

"We must not despair; the game is yet in our hands; to play it well is all we have to do. And I trust, the experience of error will enable us to act better in the future," Washington wrote in early 1781. With controlled optimism, he continued, "A cloud may yet pass over us; individuals may be ruined, and the country at large, or particular States [may undergo] temporary distress; but certain I am, that [we can] bring the war to a happy conclusion."[6] Later in 1781, after the Yorktown victory, Washington acknowledged, "The interposing hand of Heaven, in the various instances of our extensive preparations for this operation, has been most conspicuous and remarkable."[7] There are, he continued, "abundant reasons to thank Providence, for its many favorable interpositions in our behalf. It has, at times, been my only dependence; for, all other resources seemed to have failed us."[8] But before these sentiments were expressed, a difficult, bloody and complex next phase of war began.

Washington's appointment of Nathanael Greene to command the southern theater was a crucial organizational decision, but the assignment of Major General Baron von Steuben and other competent officers to Greene as subordinates started a winning southern strategy. As events progressed, Washington's southern assignments dominated the war's outcome.

On October 14, 1780, Washington told Greene that Congress had directed, "me to order a Court of Inquiry to be held on the conduct of Major General Gates, as Commander of the Southern Army." They also directed "me to appoint an Officer [of] my choice" to that command. "[I appoint you] and from the pressing situation of affairs in that quarter, [you are to] arrive there, as soon as circumstances will possibly admit."[9]

After the past military disasters, the assignment to create a third southern Continental Army command seemed an impossible task. The South possessed no financial or supply base to support extended Continental Army activities. Washington knew that to leave the South under British domination removed hope for independence or a union of American states. But he understood the difficulties Greene faced:

> I am aware, that the command you are entering upon will be attended with peculiar embarrassments; but the confidence I have in your abilities, which determined me to choose you for it, assures me you will do everything the means in your power will permit to surmount them and stop the progress of the evils which have befallen and still menace the Southern states.
> You may depend on all the support I can give you.[10]

Aware of the slim chances for success, Washington agonized over the decision to send a favored subordinate on a mission destined for almost certain failure, but Greene was the best he had. At Valley Forge, during the horrible winter of 1777-78, with the army's logistical situation a disaster, only after a personal appeal from Washington did Greene reluctantly accept the thankless appointment of quartermaster general. Grimly, through dogged determination, he revamped the quartermaster department. Greene changed policies and organization to rescue the army's supply system from disintegration to an adequate but struggling organization. The selection of anyone other than Greene for the southern command only increased the already impossible odds against success. In a command decision with immeasurable consequences, Washington sent Greene.

For Greene, it was an independent field command, away from Washington's protective shadow and an opportunity to demonstrate his military talents. Field commands were the prized appointments by all Continental Army senior officers. Greene was well aware that he faced a daunting task. His boldness, daring, and propensity for audacity would serve him well in this appointment.

Greene's first challenge was to create an organization. Experienced officers were scarce, but Washington helped with another organizational move. If Greene agreed and Congress approved, Major General Baron von Steuben was to go "Southward with you," under Greene's command. In addition Washington moved to "put Major Lee's corps [Light Horse Harry's Cavalry] under marching orders, and as soon as he is ready, I will send him to join you."[11] Steuben was an officer with extensive experience in training, essential for reconstruction of an army. Major Light Horse Harry Lee, future father of Robert E. Lee, was one of the Continental Army's finest cavalry officers.

Washington's next action was to publicly announce Greene's appointment. Important politicians and military officers received notice of Greene's responsibilities and the need for their support. Assistance from Governors Thomas Sim Lee of Maryland and Thomas Jefferson of Virginia were vital. Washington pressed them to create a process "for the regular support and subsistence of the Army in provisions, Forage and transportation." Greene's success was impossible without state support, which required the governors' active cooperation. "I am well aware of the embarrassments under which the Southern States labor, and of the many difficulties, which are to be surmounted." He expressed confidence they would make "the most vigorous exertions" in the present circumstances to help General Greene, an officer with "fortitude and integrity" who had his "entire confidence."[12]

Then, on October 23, 1780, Washington wrote directly to the proud, sensitive, and sometimes irascible Baron von Stueben. As "to the Southward there is an army to be created, the mass of which is without any formation at all, I have recommended to Congress to send you with General Greene to the Southern Army." He continued with, "Assure yourself that wherever you are, my best wishes for your happiness and success attend you."[13] These sentiments were not idle expressions; Washington appreciated the Baron's abilities. Steuben had injected *esprit de corps*, drill and military discipline into the army at the Valley Forge encampment in 1778. His demonstrated ability and loyalty was necessary to reconstitute a new southern army. But Washington never imagined the political firestorm caused when Steuben arrived unshielded, in a culture of southern politics.

When Washington appointed Greene, he was unaware of the first good news after a series of southern disasters. On October 7, 1780, at Kings Mountain, South Carolina, a battle occurred. British Major Patrick Ferguson with Loyalist forces of approximately one thousand were, for all practical purposes, destroyed by a group of American "Over the Mountain Men." Although not inflicted by Continental Army forces, Ferguson's defeat buoyed very depressed southern patriot morale. The result had an immediate Patriot propaganda value. Loyalist support slowed and the British were forced to restrain tactical efforts.

Generals Greene and Steuben arrived in Virginia on November 8, 1780, and to their dismay encountered chaos and panic. After a short stay, Greene headed for the Carolinas, anxious to recover any vestiges of a Continental Army and southern command before the British destroyed all hope of a revival. Virginia's military situation was so deplorable that Greene left Steuben as "the temporary Continental Army commander."

Baron von Steuben's quasi-independent command required interaction with politicians and local military commanders. For him this was a new experience. Initially, he received cooperation and praise, but as he uncovered logistical, and organizational incompetence, his gruff, no-nonsense approach strained personal relationships and inflamed Virginian sensitivities. Never adept at political persuasion, he was alone and in command of untrained militias. Aggressively he criticized both individuals and organizations. While despised by some for his unabridged descriptions of Virginia's failed war effort, he uncovered systemic problems with potentially disastrous consequences. He had no patience for obstructionists. The Baron directed outbursts of temper and profanity at individuals considered deficient or incompetent, regardless of their political or social standing. The validity of his complaints and accusations were ignored by bruised Virginia sensitivities.

To the Baron, incompetence without correction was immoral. Local politicians, aided by poorly coordinated and trained militias, were responsible for Virginia's defense. Infuriated, he unleashed a scathing temper on politicians and militias when they failed to respond to orders and discharge their duties. With "great pain," the Baron informed Greene, "Affairs are very little advanced" since he had departed from Richmond. Generals who command state forces operate "at the head of their separate armies," he wrote. Steuben found chaos, confusion, and incompetence in all aspects of the Virginia military situation. Especially dangerous, he explained, was an ineffective chain of command caused by ineptness of the Governor and legislature.[14] Meanwhile, friction escalated between Virginia officials and Steuben.[15]

Suddenly British intervention slowed the growing animosity between Steuben and his political adversaries. In a letter of January 2, 1781, Governor Jefferson informed, "I have this moment received a confirmation of the arrival of a hostile Fleet consisting of 19 Ships, 2 Brigs, and 10 Sloops and Schooners." The enemy's "destination from the intelligence of deserters and some captured mariners, whom they put on shore, is some where up the river, supposed to be Petersburg." Desperate, Jefferson offered, "We shall be very glad of the aid of your counsel in determining on the force to be collected, and other circumstances necessary" to oppose this intrusion."[16]

American traitor Benedict Arnold commanded the new enemy forces, which arrived in Virginia. Arnold was dispatched from New York on December 20, 1780, and arrived in Virginia on December 29. His objective was the city of Richmond, which he entered unopposed on January 5.[17] The following day, after destroying various buildings, he left unchallenged for Westover, Virginia.[18] "Arnold has landed in Virginia, Burnt all the Public Buildings," wrote a shocked Virginia politician. Although he had only "1500 men not a shot was fired at him."[19]

Without success, the Baron tried to rally some militia and Continental recruits. "But the military resources of Virginia were devoid of effective organization," he wrote, "[and] the state was unable to arm and equip them."[20] Arnold's forces marauded with impunity, eventually occupying Portsmouth, Virginia. After repeated attempts, Steuben finally assembled "between 3,000 and 4,000 militia."[21] Although an inadequate number for a frontal attack, Steuben employed his forces skillfully and blunted Arnold's further intrusions into Virginia. In retrospect, Steuben was convinced, if exposed directly to British regulars, the militia would scatter.

On January 17, as tensions and turmoil unfolded in Virginia, a significant Continental Army victory occurred at Cowpens, South Carolina. To Washington, who was deeply embroiled with mutiny at the time, Cowpens was a gift from heaven, a clear victory against British regulars by Continental Army and militia units commanded by Brigadier General Morgan. Forces assembled in the newly formed southern command achieved the victory.

The victory was a propaganda coup reported expansively in Patriot broadsides and newspapers. It came at just the right time and demonstrated a successful resurgence of the southern command under two veteran Continental

Etching by J.F.E. Prud'homme.

Brigadier General Daniel Morgan.

Army officers, Morgan and Greene, assisted by "indigenous" forces (militia). British regulars suffered an embarrassing defeat. A major consequence of the victory on future British operations was significant depletion of General Cornwallis' intelligence gathering force of British cavalry.

Cowpens also was a decisive Continental Army victory with important political gains: Southern Loyalists were discouraged and reluctant to take up British arms. In addition, it deflected attention from the mutinous affairs of January and provided Washington with a needed public relations opportunity.

The perception of well-led Continental forces defeating the best units of the British Army was not lost on the French.

While military fortunes improved in the Carolinas, confusion and desperation still reigned between Governor Jefferson and Steuben. Contentious issues included Jefferson's perceived lack of urgency in solving Virginia's military deficiencies. Arnold's intrusions strained Jefferson's military administration. In a series of written exchanges between Jefferson and Steuben, the governor avoided any agreement to apply administrative pressures to defend Virginia. Build fortifications to "block the water route to the upcountry," Steuben pleaded, and keep Arnold hemmed in at Portsmouth.[22] Jefferson delayed, and when questioned by Steuben, he replied:

> The executive have not by the Laws of this State any power to call a freeman to labour even for the Public without his consent. From a review of these circumstances, I hope you will be persuaded that any delays which may have occurred have been produced by circumstances which it was not in our power to control, and not from either a want of attention, or inclination to the work.[23]

Bluntly, Jefferson replied the state's laws did not allow a response to British intrusions by invoking martial law. Steuben, in desperation, wrote to Washington on February 15 that, "The Executive Power is so confined that the Governor has it not in his power to procure me 40 negroes to work at Hoods."[24] A few Virginians were aware of deficiencies associated with the state's military affairs. James Madison, Virginia delegate to the Continental Congress, wrote:

> Having been long sensible that the security in the Country as high up as tide water reaches has been [due more] to ignorance & caution of the enemy than to [the area's] strength or inaccessibleness, I was much less astonished at the news. The rapid and unopposed advances of the Enemy appear unaccountable.[25]

Baron's von Steuben's effort in Virginia lacked political or public relations sophistication, but he uncovered deficiencies that needed correction before a sizeable allied army could move in and sustain offensive operations. As a preview of future events, the Baron's difficulties provided a blueprint with logistical value.

❖ 5 ❖

A Change in Dynamics

I have detached a corps of twelve hundred men
⊣ *...chiefly consisting of...light infantry, of course* ⊢
commanded by the Marquis De la Fayette

While Major General Nathanael Greene concentrated in the Carolinas, Washington sensed an opportunity in Virginia. This opportunity was more emotional and political than military, the capture of Benedict Arnold, the American traitor. Arnold now commanded enemy forces in the state.

On February 20, 1781, Washington made another crucial command decision. He ordered Major General Lafayette to take "command of this detachment which you will [march] to the Head of Elk," in Maryland. He further instructed that he "must act [on] your own judgment," as circumstances would permit, and immediately upon arrival to open "correspondence with Baron de Steuben who now commands in Virginia." Lafayette was not to alert Arnold of the intentions. However, Washington ordered, "if he should fall into your hands, you will execute [him for treason] in the most summary way" and, "keep me regularly advised of your movements and progress."[1]

Benedict Arnold was the objective, but his capture was more than satisfaction of Washington's personal anger. It was a warning to other Continental Army officers who might decide to sell out and join the enemy. While Lafayette's secret purpose was to capture the traitor Arnold, his stated reason was to join Nathanael Greene.

French Admiral Detouches, commander of French naval forces in Newport, Rhode Island, agreed to send ships into Chesapeake Bay in an effort to contain Arnold and prevent escape by sea. Washington wanted more than ships; he also wanted French troops, but conceded, "it is not probable that land force[s] will be sent." But the French were cautious. They wanted assurances of adequate support in Virginia. An attempt to capture Arnold required close land support, otherwise naval forces were vulnerable to a surprise British attack. In an effort to enlist state help, Washington sent advance word to "the

Commanding officer in Virginia to assemble" militia and make arrangements for "the arrival of the fleet."

With arrangements for Lafayette's move underway, Washington informed southern commanders of his decision to send additional forces south. "I have detached a corps of twelve hundred men," he wrote to Baron von Steuben. This force consists "chiefly of" light troops commanded by Marquis de la Fayette.

Lafayette's move into Virginia clouded the Baron's command position. Lafayette outranked the Baron by virtue of commission date. Washington's letter to the Baron was a delicate effort to inform, but absent was a clear explanation of the chain of command. At the time, Steuben reported to Nathanael Greene. He was fifty-one and Lafayette was less than half his age at twenty-three. Carefully, Washington emphasized cooperation, not authority. You should "make such arrangements [and] take such a position as you judge will be conducive to the success of the operation," he informed Steuben. "The Marquis will open a correspondence with you for this purpose."[2]

In a determined effort to inform individuals whose assistance was critical for success, Washington sent a series of dispatches by special couriers. The French navy "has dispatched a Ship of the Line of 64 Guns and three Frigates" to the Chesapeake Bay to find and destroy "the Fleet under the direction of Arnold," Washington notified Governor Jefferson. In order to assist them, "I have put a respectable detachment from this Army in motion. It is commanded by Major Genl. the Marquis de la Fayette." Washington explained the combined allied move, but stressed need "of your Excellency's assistance." I have requested Baron von Steuben to inform "you in every case where your" help is needed. Then he offered information to placate Virginia sensitivities by defining the chain of command. "The Marquis de la Fayette, who is the senior Officer, will take command upon his arrival."[3]

Lafayette's move into Virginia was a complex, risky, and dangerous action. Participation of French naval forces required a command and control process able to concentrate separated land and naval forces against the enemy. The essential ingredient was a communication network that operated with unprecedented security, speed, and efficiency. An absolute necessity was fluent French and English translators in American and French headquarters.

Without Virginia's help success was hopeless. Moving forces carried few provisions; they depended on provisions to be supplied along the travel route. Each state's legislature had to provide for a logistical supply base.

On February 27, 1781, Washington wrote a long letter to " Major General Nathanael Greene." By this time, the attempt to capture Arnold was not feasible and Washington explained the plans. He tried to keep Greene informed on the latest progress and developments of the war, but distance and time of communication transmissions made the task nearly impossible. Events in the

Etching by Alonzo Chapel.

Major General Baron von Steuben.

war changed dramatically, sometimes daily. By the time communications reached Greene, the information was often weeks and even months out of date.

Greene's isolation concerned the commander-in-chief and one way to reduce the sting of ignorance was to keep Greene informed as much as possible. Washington was well aware that the future of the southern states and their association with the patriot cause were in Greene's hands. "Amidst the complicated dangers with which you are surrounded, a confidence in your abilities is my only consolation," Washington assured Greene. "I marched a detachment from here under the Marquis De la Fayette, [to cooperate with our allies] in Chesapeak Bay against Arnold." But before the trap was closed, British naval reinforcements arrived and the French navy lost their superiority. This prevented "the execution of my project; but the Marquis still continues his march to make best of the circumstances." The separation of Lafayette's detachment weakened Washington's main army. "You will easily imagine the situation in which I am left" with the departure of this detachment.[4]

When Lafayette arrived in Virginia he was the senior Continental Army commander in the state. In this capacity, he not only replaced the Baron's authority, but, in the chain of command, von Steuben was Lafayette's subordinate, a touchy personal issue for the Baron's ego.

A multitude of difficulties faced Steuben during his command in Virginia. Some citizens viewed him with almost the same distaste as they did the British. "The Barons Situation is very disagreeable," a Steuben aide wrote to General Greene. "The Virginia Line gave him the greatest Trouble." They continually applied "for leave of absence." Greene had expected Virginia to send reinforcements to the Carolinas. Governor Jefferson issued the orders through newspapers, but his orders made little impression on Virginia's militias; there was no means of enforcement or penalty, if orders were ignored. "Had the Baron ordered them" to Carolina it would have no effect, the aide explained. Under no circumstances would they leave the state. "The Baron wishes to be with you. He would rather Obey in an Army than command in Virginia."[5]

Steuben tried to instill order and discipline into Virginia military forces, but when he did, they simply disbanded. On February 27, 1781, a frustrated and angry Steuben informed Greene of the serious difficulties in a command dependent on Virginia militia. In reality, the Virginia governor lacked control and did not intend to enact legislation for change. Cooperation from the generals in Virginia's state forces was nonexistent. For the most part, they acted independently with little direction from the governor. Steuben was forced to discharge militia under his command, because when ordered, they refused to leave the state while "a Body of the Enemy" remained in Virginia.[6] The state's military affairs were deplorable, with no indication of improvement

Lafayette headed into this turmoil and discontent. Although not evident at the time, the move to Virginia served as a pivotal influence on later allied success. Lafayette and his forces provided a pilot study that identified potential disasters. These would have crippled a large-scale movement of forces before the Marquis tested the waters. Lafayette recognized the need for communication and one of his first actions was to create a network. Shortly after receiving the command, he wrote to Governor Thomas Jefferson: "[I realize] an Opportunity to Gratify the High Sense I Have of My Personal obligations to the State of Virginia." Lafayette was no stranger to Virginians; at the Valley Forge encampment in 1778 his division was composed "entirely" of Virginians.[7]

With great eagerness, Lafayette began operations. He informed Washington that his detachment was "thus far well furnished with Provisions" and, "The troops have the Greatest Zeal, and preserve the Most Strict order in their March."

On March 1, 1781, Washington notified Lafayette that the French had agreed to cooperate in a joint effort. "Count Rochambeau and The Chevalier Des-touches [intend] to operate in Chesapeak Bay with their whole fleet and a detachment of 1,100 french troops, grenadiers and Chasseurs." But, he cautioned, "You know the infinite value of secrecy in an expedition circumstanced like this."[8] The enemy had penetrated "the country with great rapidity."[9]

The military situation in Virginia remained chaotic. Governor Jefferson lacked accurate muster rolls and was unable to determine militia strengths, needs, or distribution. His frustration was evident in a series of letters written between February 20 and March 1, 1781. Instead of using the threat to invoke martial law and build a resistance, Jefferson viewed government's role as much less autocratic and restricted the calls for militia to as few counties as possible.[10]

On the march to Virginia, Lafayette's detachment moved through several states and he maintained continual contact with the respective state officials. He informed Governor Sim Lee of Maryland that his command was at the "Head of the Elk" and with "Great Disappointment" is "Now Detained for Want of Vessels."[11] Earlier the Maryland legislature issued warrants impressing all vessels and crews in the Severn River and Baltimore for the purpose of transporting forces, but as Lafayette later found in Virginia, there was no means for enforcement.[12] Until transportation arrived, Lafayette's move stalled at the head of the Elk River.

Further south, despite disappointments and difficulties, Baron von Steuben informed Greene of his reaction to Lafayette's appointment. "[Do not think] my D[ea]r General, that this Idea, however mortifying, will in the least relax my zeal in the affair: on the contrary I hope the Marquis will find everything prepared for his arrival."[13]

While the Baron seemed reconciled to his relationship with Lafayette, his disdain for Virginia politicians exploded in a letter to Governor Jefferson on March 8, 1781. "I had the weakness to write to Genl Washington and Marquis De la Fayette [assuring them] everything was ready for the Expedition." He further complained, "My credulity is punished at the expense of my honor, and the only excuse I have is my Confidence in the [Virginia] Government."[14] Bitter and angry, he described examples of Virginia's failures "in procuring supplies and horses," with the consequences. If the state lacked powers to furnish "what is indispensably necessary" then this "Expedition must fail," wrote Steuben. He felt he had no choice but to, "suspend giving any orders till I receive your Excellency's answer to this, which [I will send to] the Marquis and the Commander of the French fleet, [so] they may not engage too far in an enterprise [with] no prospect" for success.[15] The Baron's frank assessment, blaming politicians for not carrying out their responsibilities, did not endear him to Virginians, but he did get attention. The next day Jefferson shot back in a pique, "We can only be answerable for the orders we give [and] not their execution. If they were disobeyed from obstinacy" or lack of enforcement laws, "it is not our fault."[16] Steuben's shock at Jefferson's reply can only be imagined. The Governor demonstrated little understanding of demands in a wartime environment.

While events in Virginia vibrated with emotional and chaotic intensity, Washington and Rochambeau engaged in strategic planning sessions at a conference on March 6, in Newport. The meeting was a spectacle of splendor. For the first time Washington was introduced to officers and men of the French army and navy, in a display of military protocol with, "the highest honors known to the Articles of War."[17] After the ceremonies concluded, Washington and Rochambeau discussed, "arranging the campaign of the year," but the real accomplishment was Washington's presentation to the French Army.

The world had changed since the war began in 1775 and Washington developed plans to harness the change. No longer just a rebellion with the mother country – the conflict was now a world war. Not all countries at war with Britain were allied with Americans. Spain was an ally of France, but not officially with the United States, although the Spanish supplied materiel, money, and military forces on land and sea. Washington understood the importance of Spanish operations in Florida; they forced a redirection of British military assets which might otherwise be used against Americans. "I am obliged by the interesting intelligence which you have been pleased to communicate [to hope nothing] will again prevent the progress of [a Spanish] expedition against Pensacola," Washington wrote to Francisco Rendon, Spanish representative in Philadelphia. "Our whole attention is turned Southward" and a "successful blow in that quarter may give a total change to the face of affairs there."[18]

Although Washington was encouraged by activities against British global interests, his attention focused on the southern theater. He sent additional reinforcements to Lafayette. The detachment came from the Pennsylvania Line, commanded by Brigadier General Anthony Wayne. In January, these same Pennsylvanians had mutinied, and sending them south into unfamiliar territory minimized temptations to mutiny again. After receiving notification to expect reinforcements, Lafayette wrote immediately to Wayne and explained the transportation difficulties in a move south. Lafayette's detachment was still stalled at the Elk River. "As soon as Vessels Come I will embark and take as [few vessels] as Possible, [so] that a Number of transports May Be left for Your Troops," he informed Wayne.[19] Several days later, Lafayette reported that "thirty boats" had arrived with "others" on the way.[20]

Lafayette's move had a great deal of flexibility. Initially the secret mission was to capture Arnold, but with that no longer possible, the mission was to continue south and join Greene's forces. In the meantime, an alternate plan developed. But first, in an attempt to engage Greene in the alternative, Washington requested comments. The alternative called for Lafayette to join "with the Generals of the french fleet and troops" and plan operations to "Relieve your Army and the Southern States," he informed Greene. When Washington wrote the letter, Lafayette expected to join Greene and wrote, "I am Happy [my troops] will Be under your Sole Command, and while I Stay in your department I Have (General Washington Excepted) no orders to Receive But from You."[21] In Washington's alternative plan, a cooperative effort with the French allies, Lafayette remained directly under the commander-in-chief's authority, but in certain unspecified geographical locations, he could report to Greene. By any consideration, it was a messy organizational situation, but it worked. Neither Washington nor Greene expressed reservations. Both realized Lafayette's tactical situation was dynamic and he needed authority to make decisions based on local situations in the best interests of the war effort. Lafayette recognized his responsibility in the information network and made every effort to keep Greene informed, even when discharging a mission under Washington's command.

Lafayette was a respected officer in the Continental Army, but his fellow countrymen had reservations. The French military culture had none so young, except French Royalty, with equal rank. Washington assumed Lafayette's nationality and political connections provided influence with Rochambeau and other French military officers; they did not. On occasion, some officers mocked him. "[Malicious] people were very wrong to say M. de Rochambeau pays my youth the honor of envying it," Lafayette wrote to Chevalier de La Luzerne, in a subtle hint at the lack of respect. Luzerne, French Minister to the United States and a friend of Lafayette's family, was in Philadelphia as a French representative to the Continental Congress on Franco-American affairs. Lafayette wanted to keep on the good side of the French minister and explained the plan to move his detachment down the Chesapeake Bay where he expected to meet French forces sent by Rochambeau.[22]

After writing to Luzerne, Lafayette sent another letter to Washington, raising a number of personal issues. Pride and reputation were always important to the Marquis. The delay at the Elk River presented some anxious moments. With a vivid imagination, Lafayette suspected the French might initiate a major assault before his detachment arrived. He wanted desperately, as a matter of honor, to represent America in any assault against British forces. "Comte de Rochambeau thinks His troops Equal to the Business," Lafayette wrote to Washington. "[They] Alone May display their zeal, and shed their Blood for an expedition which All America Has so Much at Heart." He worried that his opportunity to share in the glory of battle was fading. "I Heartly feel, My dear General, for the Honor of our Arms, [that] it would Be derogatory," if his detachment was denied "some share in the enterprise." Lafayette's pride and ego were on fire. A self-serving appetite for glory governed his feelings, but he was a volunteer, not paid. He used personal funds to benefit the Continental forces under his command. His only reward was recognition and acknowledgement, intangibles especially gratifying when leading an independent command.

Still in a writing mood, Lafayette unleashed a barrage of letters to various state governors where his detachment planned to travel, all filled with requests for logistical support. Governor Thomas Jefferson responded to the transportation demands. It is "out of our Power" to acquire a number of boats, he replied. "Some armed vessels of public and some of private property," were available but bottled up until "the Command of the Waters is again taken from the Enemy."[23] Two days later, Jefferson responded to the request for other supplies with excuses. Procurement was difficult because no Virginia organization existed to accommodate the demands of a war. It was not, Jefferson emphasized, because the people lacked interest in the cause. "Mild laws, a People not used to war," a lack of provisions, and no means "of procuring them render our orders often ineffectual." Jefferson's passive attitude added to tensions building between the Continental Army and the Virginia legislature's failure to enact laws to expeditiously create a military support base. A sense of urgency simply did not exist in legislature's effort to mobilize the population for war. Compounding chaos was an enemy who expanded intrusions into the very communities expected to deliver military support. Jefferson hoped Lafayette appreciated the "Circumstances" and would "ensure me your Cooperation in the best way."[24] While the governor appealed to Lafayette for understanding, his anger was directed at von Steuben. The Baron had written a letter excoriating the "Virginia Government" for not meeting their "assurances."[25] The Baron did not mince words. His combat experience left little sensitivity for others, especially politicians who seemed full of excuses.

As Lafayette struggled to address these challenges, the most uplifting and heartening news arrived in a private letter from the Compte de Vergennes in Paris. "The King has just made his decision regarding the assistance of all kinds to be given to the Americans for the next campaign," Vergennes wrote.

Lafayette sensed by the letter's tenor that Vergennes was excited. "I shall not give you the details, because I am transmitting them to M. le Chevalier de La Luzerne," in Philadelphia. "I do not doubt [he] will inform you." Vergennes felt certain that "Mr. Washington will be satisfied with the efforts we are making for the support of the American cause." The General should be assured, "we place the most complete confidence in his zeal, his patriotism, and his talents." "[We] shall with great pleasure see him finally achieve the glory of having delivered his country and assured its liberty."[26]

Uplifting as the news was, Vergennes conveniently avoided mentioning certain negative aspects. No second French division was planned for America and the King refused to guarantee a loan request from Congress for "25 million livres." But the good news included agreements to send forces under the command of Admiral De Grasse from the West Indies with a "subsidy of 6 million livres" from the King. The king also sent instructions "to Rochambeau to consider himself [completely] under Washington's orders." Without this unity of command an allied success was questionable. The availability of Admiral De Grasse was a pivotal event in the war.

On March 8, 1781, Washington informed Lafayette that the French fleet in Newport sailed on "a fair Wind this Evening about sunset," and that, "You may possibly hear of their arrival in Chesapeak before this letter reaches you."[27] Three days later, Washington sent further intelligence: the British fleet left New London, Connecticut, on March 10, 1781, "with their whole force" and was on their way to the "Chesapeak." Washington expected the French to arrive before the British.[28] A confrontation with the French fleet seemed inevitable.

Lafayette was delighted. At last he was at the center of operations, coordinating actions between Allied land and sea forces. "I have just arrived [at Yorktown and] await with much impatience the pleasure of seeing you," he wrote to Baron von Steuben. "My arrival is the result of a new arrangement." He promised, "I shall inform you of the very important objective that causes me to arrive ahead of my detachment."[29]

When Jefferson learned that Lafayette was in Virginia, he wrote to congratulate the Marquis on his safe arrival. Enclosed in the letter was a list of supplies "actually procured;" they will go "this evening, most of them in waggons to General Muhlenburg's, Headquarters." Jefferson sent other exciting news; boats were available to bring the rest of Lafayette's detachment south.[30]

Lafayette's next challenge was working with Baron von Steuben. He wondered how the Baron, who had ruffled feathers in Virginia, would react to a subordinate position. As a morale boost, he requested Washington to inform the Baron that he (Lafayette) had "Been much satisfied with his preparations."[31] On March 21, 1781, Washington wrote and praised the Baron. Praise from Washington was important to subordinate commanders, especially when they operated in distant and lonely commands under extraordinary hardships. Rarely did Washington criticize a subordinate commander for taking action, even when it failed. His approach – to support and not criticize – produced a cadre of officers, rich in *esprit de corps*.

Meanwhile communication flowed with more effectiveness. But occasionally lack of information presented political and military repercussions. Both the French and British fleets were at sea heading for the Chesapeake. Lack of intelligence on either fleet caused concern about deployment of allied land forces.

The lack of intelligence regarding the Battle of Cape Henry on March 16, 1781, had near disastrous consequences. Lafayette expected the French fleet to arrive soon in the Chesapeake Bay and his tactical plans included joining forces. Indications that something was amiss arrived from Governor Jefferson. "I am anxious to hear from you [about] the appearance of this British fleet," he wrote to Lafayette. Jefferson heard from "a Capt. Reeves" that "there was a partial engagement [by British forces with] the French Fleet off our Capes in which neither party sustained the Loss of any vessel or other considerable damage."[32] The Cape Henry engagement had a different outcome than reported in Jefferson's rumors. The French and British navies had engaged for about an hour and a half with both sustaining heavy damage, but neither was victorious.

In addition to the naval engagement, Washington, Jefferson, and Lafayette were unaware that a major military land action had occurred in North Carolina on March 15, 1781 – the Battle of Guilford Court House between forces of General Greene and British General Cornwallis. While technically a defeat for Greene, the price of British victory influenced the war's outcome.

As late as March 25, 1781, Lafayette informed Washington of uncertainty about the Cape Henry outcome. "I wish it had been in My power Not to Make Your Excellency A Partaker of our Anxiety Until I Might Have Known on What Side Victory Has Been."[33] The next day, he reported, "From My Late Intelligences I am led to Suppose that our Allies are Gone to Cape Fear" and the "first Engagement was in their favor and I am Sorry," but apparently "they did not pursue their Advantage." Then he cautiously added, "The Return of the British fleet to the Chesapeak destroys Every Prospect of an operation Against Arnold," and "Since the British fleet Have Returned and think themselves Safe in the Bay, I entertain very little Hopes of Seeing the french flag in Hampton Road."[34] Confusion abounded. Lafayette was unaware that the French Fleet withdrew after the Battle of Cape Henry and sailed back to Newport, Rhode Island, for repairs. With a new British fleet in Virginia, an effort against Arnold was impractical.

Arrival of the British Navy from New York brought 2,000 additional forces under the command of General Phillips who immediately took command of all British troops in Virginia.[35] As an alternative, Steuben proposed an expedition against General Cornwallis in the Carolinas.[36] "Cornwallis withdrew on the twenty-third toward Cross Creek, leaving behind all our wounded from the last action [Guilford Court House, North Carolina] ...General Greene is pursuing the enemy, but he is not very strong," Steuben informed Lafayette. Earlier, Greene had requested help, but still smarting from experiences with the Virginia militia, the Baron replied, "I no longer trouble myself with defending this state with militia. I await only the first letter from General Greene to join him."[37]

Lafayette faced a dilemma; with Arnold no longer the object, what was the next course of action? He had no reason to stay in the area. Either he moved south under the command of Nathanael Greene, or north under Washington's command. Either option removed any perception of his separate command.

The Continental Army was spread over three major geographic areas: Washington in the north, Lafayette and Von Steuben in Virginia, and Greene in the Carolinas. Washington continued to suffer communications problems. As late as March 29 he had no report on the naval engagement at the Capes. "I have not received any intelligence from Southward," he informed Rochambeau. "I should have heard [by now] unless a dispatch should have miscarried." He could only "judge...your Excellency's anxiety by my own, and shall [send] the most instant communication of what I may receive."[38]

Washington's concern was well founded. On March 31, he informed Rochambeau of intelligence received the previous evening, of the French fleets failure against the British, and described it as, "A circumstance in which the Winds and Weather had more influence than valor or skill."[39] Washington notified the president of Congress of, "the Naval engagement on the 16th inst: The good conduct and bravery exhibited by our Allies [entitle] the warmest thanks of the public, for tho' the plan ...has unluckily failed, they deserve the highest applause for the boldness of the attempt to carry it into execution."[40]

Washington described General Nathanael Greene's encounter at the Battle of Guilford Court House, North Carolina on a positive note. He informed Rochambeau, "Lord Cornwallis will find his efficient force greatly diminished by the Number of Killed and wounded and...encumbered with the latter, he will experience such embarrassments as to retard...all his future movements and operations."[41] Guilford Court House, while a tactical defeat for Greene, was a strategic disaster for Cornwallis, impairing his army for the balance of the war. British losses at Guilford, added to Cowpens, sowed the seeds for the eventual Allied victory at Yorktown.

After defeating Greene, Cornwallis headed to Wilmington, North Carolina. From there, with a new strategy, he intended to move toward Virginia and attack Continental Army supply depots. His decision to go into Virginia was one of the most fateful moves in the war. Cornwallis assumed Greene would follow him to conduct harassment activities. Confidently, Cornwallis expected another opportunity to destroy the third Continental Army's Southern command. Instead of shadowing Cornwallis, Greene, in an audacious move, headed into South Carolina.[42] It was a brilliant geopolitical strategy, effectively reclaiming the Carolinas and Georgia for the Patriot cause. Greene appealed to Lafayette to bring his detachment south. Greene sensed that a "very critical situation [existed] in the Southern States...[with] fatal consequences." Greene expected "the enemy [to] push their operations" in southern Virginia and northern North Carolina. An action which will necessitate "you to March your force Southward by Alexandria and Fredricksburg to Richmond...from which you can cooperate either with me or the militia in the lower Country."[43] Lafayette delayed sending men based on Washington's previous orders to keep his forces intact, but he did send "field pieces and Ammunition."[44]

Washington suffered a deep disappointment at the loss of an opportunity to capture Arnold and the French navy's defeat at the Battle of Cape Henry. He felt they had come so close to getting the traitor only to have circumstances change in a matter of hours. But he avoided any blame. "I am certain that the Chevalier de Touche exerted him-self to the utmost to gain in the Chesapeak," he wrote to Lafayette. There is "honor upon the Chevalier and the Marine of France."[45] Choosing words carefully, Washington avoided any insinuation critical of Lafayette's actions. "As matters have turned out it is to be wished that you had not gone out of the Elk. But I never judge of the Propriety of measures by after events. Your move to Annapolis, at the time you made it, was certainly judicious," Washington wrote.[46] "I imagine the detachment will be upon its march this way, before this reaches you." In a sudden shift, the next day, April 6, Washington changed directions. "I have attentively considered...what...importance it will be to reinforce Genl. Greene as speedily as possible," because "there can be little doubt but the detachment under Genl. Phillips...will ultimately join, or, in some degree, cooperate with Lord Cornwallis."[47]

Washington delivered, in clear and concise language, orders for the Marquis to head south:

> Private inconveniences must give way to the public good, and you will therefore immediately, upon the receipt of this, turn the detachment to the southward. Inform General Greene...you are upon March to join him; and take his direction as to your route when you begin to approach him. Previous to that, you will be guided by your own judgment.[48]

Washington explained his sudden change in orders. There was "uneasi-ness...among" some "Field Officers upon the appointments" of foreign offic-ers to field commands. They protested "to me upon the subject, and I gave them the true reason, which was...the Regiments...were so extremely thin of Field Officers" that appointments of foreign officers were necessary. "I have heard nothing of the discontent lately, but should I find it revive again...I shall be obliged, for peace sake to further review the appointments of Foreign Of-ficers."[49] In the reply to Washington, Lafayette complained of difficulties involved in moving his detachment south, but he stressed a willingness "to Move either way as Soon as possible."

❖ 6 ❖

The Power of Persuasion in Communications

We fight get beat, rise and fight again.
We have a bloody field; but little glory

With the capture of Benedict Arnold no longer a viable mission, Washington's orders to move south all but dissolved Lafayette's separate command. Serving under Greene was the least preferable of three options. He had nothing against Greene; in fact, they enjoyed great camaraderie during those cold bleak days of the Valley Forge Encampment in 1778. But if he could not remain in Virginia, he preferred to return north under Washington's command, although it probably meant losing his field command. Washington's orders were clear – head south and place himself under Greene's command.

The British sent significant land and naval forces to reinforce their hold on Virginia and they now stepped up military operations. With Cornwallis heading north from the Carolinas, the enemy appeared to undertake a new southern strategy: split the southern and northern colonies.

Lafayette sensed an opportunity. His impression was more intuitive than calculated, so convincing others was the challenge. He speculated that the new British strategy exposed them to vulnerability, at least for a short period of time. He considered the circumstances with Cornwallis heading north into Virginia, leaving only a few regular forces behind to defend the Carolinas. Couriers arrived almost daily with rumors and information about the British Army's move to Virginia. What did it mean? If Cornwallis was coming, how many troops did he have, and where was General Greene? Lafayette knew Cornwallis did not make such moves without considering opportunities and consequences; he was an excellent tactician and exceptionally skilled at designing traps for an unsuspecting opponent.

Cornwallis made no secret of his destination: the Chesapeake Bay to join British forces in the area with expectations of re-supply by sea. The senior commander in Virginia, he would receive manpower replacements for the terrible cost of the Battle of Guilford Court House. At first Lafayette was con-

cerned about the increased British forces; he already suffered from insufficient manpower. Then came additional intelligence. Greene, much to
Cornwallis' surprise, did not follow, but headed into the Carolinas to confront
depleted British forces deployed over a large area in relatively small units.

At headquarters, Lafayette and staff studied maps. It was obvious
Cornwallis had made a bold move, because success depended on the British
navy protecting the army from any assault by sea. The only weakness in his
plan was the prospect of an assault by significantly larger forces from both
land and sea; a prospect Cornwallis dismissed as remote. At the time no significant opposing forces were in the area. He hoped his move would draw
Greene into action. Then he would arrive in the Chesapeake area after destroying the third Continental Army's southern command. Cornwallis anticipated that opportunities for curtailing armed patriot action in the south were
never better.

Virginia lacked military capability on the scale required to check increasing British activities. The state had a few experienced commanders, including Generals Weedon, Nelson, Muhlenburg and George Rogers Clark, but they
commanded forces which operated as relatively independent units. An effective central command was nonexistent. No effective organization could supply reliable information on the size, operation, or actions of the disparate units.

Quickly, Lafayette initiated communication exchanges with the most pivotal individual, the governor of Virginia, Thomas Jefferson.[1] In a desperate
attempt for help, Jefferson appealed to foreign powers. "The extreme distress
of this State for Arms and military Stores...embolden me to ask your
Excellency's permission to...to purchase either from private or public Stores
within your Government," Jefferson wrote to the governor of Hispaniola.[2]

Simultaneously Jefferson made administrative changes. He informed
Lafayette of a new Commissioner of the Virginia War Office, Colonel William Davies. The appointment provided an experienced Continental Army
officer who acted immediately to install logistical improvements. Strategically, Jefferson understood Virginia's military significance, but he was suspicious of northern intentions, especially supplying Virginia with military
assistance. He did not believe Northern interests would make sacrifices for
Virginia's salvation. Jefferson felt, under threatening circumstances, the North
would abandon Virginia and the rest of the south. "We suppose one half of
the enemy's force in the United States" is in the south. "Georgia and South
Carolina have long been theirs, and North Carolina [is] convulsed by the ravages of two Armies [and] her Citizens are too much engaged in saving their
families and Property to join the American Army," he wrote to the French
Minister in Philadelphia, "While our Northern Brethren [with] infinitely superior [forces, have] Access to foreign Supplies, [and] all the Arms and Mili-

tary Stores of the Continent." In addition, they had "the protection of almost the Whole of the Continental Army, with the very important Addition of the Army and fleet of our Allies."[3] Jefferson described Virginia's threat from "Northwestern Savages," requiring Virginia to assign "two to three thousand men" to its defense. Despite suspicions of northern intentions, Jefferson believed that Virginia could defend herself if "our Citizens [were] Armed, but we have not as many Arms as [our] enemies."[4]

"The Northern States are safe: their independence has been established...our Enemies have transferred [attention] from that Quarter [and plan] nothing further [in the north] than A Diversion," while they assault the south. "It would be unfortunate indeed should it again be proposed to lose a Campaign on New York," exhausting their resources, sacrificing "the Confederacy" by giving up "Provinces in the South for towns in the North."[5] Jefferson described existing sectional differences between North and South in a country united, but without a national understanding. While complaints consumed the first part of the letter, he concluded by offering a southern military strategy. Jefferson concluded that the British Army depended on the navy for survival. "If they [the British] can be prevented" from moving by sea, "flying on the Wings of the wind to relieve...New York, this week" and "Portsmouth the Next, in Charleston the third," the "war would be totally changed." If the British army "at Portsmouth [Virginia]" was deprived of naval support, "they might be immediately blockaded by Land, and must fall in a due course of Time without the Loss of a Man on our part."[6] Jefferson's unheralded letter made an impression. Behind the scenes, where strategy was developed, Thomas Jefferson's suggestions, whether intentional or not, were incorporated into the next phase of allied operations. While the British divided military assets to protect specific cities and seaports, the allies had an opportunity to decide where to concentrate forces against any one target. The allies most difficult challenges were logistics and finance.

Lafayette was frustrated by the French fleet's inability to blockade Arnold. "Arnold was ours," he wrote to Alexander Hamilton, "but while the fleet failed in their attempt at Arnold, I think they Have Exerted themselves for the Common good, and this has been a Comfort in our Misfortune."[7]

Despite his relatively pessimistic letter to Hamilton, Lafayette presented a more positive view to Washington. The "Great want of Monney, Baggage, Cloathing, Under which both officers and Men are Suffering [make] it Very Inconvenient for the troops to Proceed Immediately By Land," but he quickly added, "I Have However Hurried on Preparations and will Be able to Set off to Morrow Morning."

On April 10, 1781, Baron von Steuben informed Lafayette of intelligence from, "Genl. Greene...in which he expresses his sorrow, That the Troops under your command had not marched southward." Steuben then reported three pieces of information confirmed by Greene. First: Cornwallis was moving his troops away from General Greene and heading to the coast at Wilmington, North Carolina. Second: Greene did not intend to pursue him, but was heading for South Carolina. Third: the arrival in Virginia of British reinforcements from New York, amounted to "1,500 to 2,000 men."[8]

Then, completely unexpected, uplifting news arrived. Lafayette was elated; Washington changed the orders. "Whether General Phillips remains in Virginia or goes further southward he must be opposed by a force more substantial than Militia alone," Washington wrote. Lafayette was instructed to "open a communication with Genl. Greene" and inform him of the situation in Virginia, "and take his [Greene's] direction as to marching forward to join him, or remaining there to keep a watch on Phillips."

On the surface, the order strengthened the official chain of command by supporting Greene as the senior commander and leaving the decision to him regarding Lafayette's deployment. But he delegated to Lafayette the task of describing the military situation in Virginia to General Greene. Washington suspected Lafayette would rather remain in Virginia than move south to join Greene and, aware of Lafayette's persuasive abilities, he offered an opportunity to convince Greene of the need to remain in Virginia. Washington also replied to Lafayette's previous complaints about logistical problems: "The difficulties which you will experience on the [scarcity] of provisions and transportation would have been common to any other Body of Troops. They will I know be great, but I depend much upon your assiduity and activity."[9] Essentially, Washington's message was: *stop the complaining; you wanted a separate command and this is the responsibility that goes with it.* Next, Washington referred to the situation in New York by saying that he "had the most distant prospect of such an operation [against New York]. I should have looked upon your detachment as essential to the undertaking, but I can assure you, without entering into a detail of reasons (which I cannot commit to paper) that I have not at present an Idea of being able to effect such a matter."[10]

On April 17, 1781, Lafayette wrote to General Greene and, just as Washington expected, presented a masterpiece of persuasion, tempered with military realities. He informed Greene of communication difficulties involved answering "Letters." Your previous correspondence was, "directed where I was not," mainly because of frequent moves. He informed Greene that General Phillips arrived in Virginia with reinforcements and of the desperate need for Continental Army units to counter Phillip's presence, "Without Which Your Situation Might become Very Critical." Lafayette suggested that if left unchecked, British actions in Virginia could drastically curtail supplies and reinforcements going to Greene. He lamented about manpower and supply deficiencies, including poor morale and a high rate of desertion. "I Have Borrowed from the Merchants of Baltimore A Sum on My Credit which will Amount to About two thousand Pounds [which] will procure a few Hatts, Some Shoes, Some Blanketts, and a pair of Linnen over alls, and a Shirt to Each Man," he wrote. "With these Precautions I think our Present detachment will Be Preserved in Good order." About manpower he reported, "I Will Send to You an Exact Return." He added, "we Have about thousand men Rank and file and a Company of Artillery."[11]

He acquainted Greene with the rapidly changing military situation involving Phillips and Arnold. The enemy's combined force at Portsmouth, Virginia, was "between 2500 and 3000 men," he reported. Using forced marches Lafayette arrived in Fredericksburg, Virginia, and expected "to Receive Some farther orders and Intelligences from You." If not, he would head to Richmond, and upon hearing, "Something of General Phillips will act to the Best of My judgment Untill I Receive from You More positive orders." He reported moving "towards Phillips" and if he executed "Such Motions as would be a disservice to You I will Make it My Business to…Check Him as far as it could be done." He added, "Going farther Southward would Be attended with Real and Imaginary Inconveniences," but "These Remarks…Are far from throwing the Least objection to our Marching Southerly if a junction [with] your forces Appears to You of Some Advantage." Finally, in an emotional appeal Lafayette requested, if it could be done in the "public Good…With propriety, I know You will Be Glad to Gratify Me. General Philip's Battery at Minden killed My father, I would Have No objection to" remaining in Virginia and observing his plans.[12]

Lafayette's persuasion made it difficult for Greene to refuse without a compelling reason. His desire to remain in Virginia satisfied a personal agenda, but was based on sound military judgment. The next day, after sending the persuasive letter to Greene, Lafayette reported positive news to Washington. "Desertion Has Been lessened," he noted, and the "Merchants of Baltimore [loaned me] about 2000 pounds" which bought clothes for the troops. In a "letter from Baron de Steuben Dated Chesterfield Courthouse," he reports, "General Philips Has at Portsmouth 1500 or 2000 Men added to the force under Arnold." Lafayette estimated "His whole Army Amount to 2500 men which oblige me to [march towards] Frederis Burg [Fredericksburg] and Richmond where I expect to Receive orders from Gal.[General] Greene."[13]

Lafayette's decision to remain in Virginia gained unexpected support from the Comte de Vergennes, in Paris who on April 19, 1781, notified Lafayette of new support. In a personal letter, Vergennes requested that, "You may tell General Washington the King has decided to underwrite a loan of 10 million livres tournois, floated in Holland, and payable to the United States." He also reminded Lafayette, "His Majesty will have given or procured for the Americans by the end of this year 20 million, [French Pounds]," Vergennes wrote. "The extraordinary means with which the king provides the Americans, sir, lead[s] him to hope...they will put [great effort] into operations they undertake during the next campaign." Vergennes begged Lafayette to inform Washington, "His Majesty has the greatest confidence in his experience, his activity, and his patriotism." But there were limits. "I hope that if the war continues beyond this campaign, as seems rather likely, we shall not be approached again with such requests," he warned. "It would be totally impossible to satisfy them. France is not an inexhaustible mine."[14]

Lafayette continued appealing to anyone who supported his zeal to remain in Virginia. With an exceptional flare for persuasion, Lafayette notified Governor Thomas Jefferson, of his intention "to hasten By forced Marches to the Support of Virginia," but requested the governor to supply desperately needed "Shoes and Cloathes of Every kind."

Virginia's vulnerability to increased British intrusions gave Lafayette an opportunity to pressure Jefferson into advocating support for his detachment to remain in state. He kept the Governor aware of orders "of our Going to the South ward," emphasizing the military situation building south of Virginia had priority, in spite of the "Vast and Immediate Danger which threatens this State." While not directly requesting Jefferson to influence Washington or Congress, the governor had no doubt of the desperate need for Lafayette's "Detachment" in Virginia.

Baron von Steuben supplied additional support for Lafayette's cause when he reported the enemy intended to operate "offensively very soon." At the time, the Baron commanded some Virginia militia units, but hardly in sufficient force to oppose the enemy offensive. The only action open was removing "public Stores to Some distance" to avoid enemy capture.[15]

On April 21, 1781, Washington complicated Lafayette's situation further by explaining that the, "situation in the Southern affairs would not permit me to recall your corps to this army," but, "My friendship for you makes me desirous of having you near me," because, "there will occur frequent occasions in cooperative measures [with our allies] in which it would be of the greatest utility [to] consult you." Washington did not request Lafayette to "return personally to Head Quarters," but offered an option; return without his "Detachment" or remain with his corps.[16]

In a letter to his friend, Minister Luzerne in Philadelphia, Lafayette revealed personal objectives in clear terms. "The general [Washington] writes" that "there are things he would like to tell me but does not dare confide to paper," and the attack against New York appears "to be very far off." My personal desire is, "I would rather stay in Virginia than go to Carolina."[17]

Luzerne influenced distribution of financial assistance to Americans and was a close friend of General Rochambeau. Although exhibiting a preference to remain behind the scenes, he was the single most influential French national in the United States. Within a ten day period between April 12 and 22, Jefferson and Lafayette independently wrote letters to the French minister, championing Virginia as a geographical area of military opportunity.

April 22, 1781, was eventful for the Marquis: Washington sent two letters; one private, the other routine. Both revealed important information and clarified some confusion. The routine letter acknowledged receipt of previous Lafayette communications. Washington was concerned about the "temper of your detachment," especially "desertions." The commander in chief described subtle supply difficulties experienced by other units on long marches "at a great distance from their states [they] are almost entirely neglected," and many were often "lost on the way." We must "compensate these detachments for the loss of state supplies by giving them a larger proportion" from Continental stores. "I will embrace the first safe opportunity to give you a full view of our affairs [so] you may regulate your future correspondence with your Court accordingly."[18] This was a rare acknowledgement of Lafayette's influence in the French Court and an indication that the Marquis's value to the American cause was more than military participation.

Washington's routine letter was revealing, but his private letter was explosive. He explained that the reasons for considering Lafayette's return to "American head Quarters" were "chiefly of a political nature;" and that he expected "great advantages will be derived from your being wherever the French Army and the American head Quarters are." Washington expressed his wish for Lafayette's return, but he wanted "to make things as agreeable to you as the nature of the service will admit"[19] The decision was Lafayette's. Washington, a keen judge of his subordinates, knew Lafayette's desire to retain a *de facto* separate command was the most likely choice. Lafayette answered, "I Had Rather Remain in Virginia than go to Carolina. This I mention Because orders Are to Come from General Greene," but if orders came "to go more Southerly I will get there as fast as I Can."[20] Lafayette's Virginia ambitions were further aided by British actions when a force under Generals Phillips and Arnold captured Petersburg, Virginia, with little more than token resistance, causing panic in Virginia militias and politicians.[21]

"As soon as we get [wagons, my] detachment will Rapidly proceed to Richmond, and" when we arrive will "Be Ready for Serious Operations," Lafayette informed Jefferson. If "the people" are "Willing to Afford us" supplies, "We might Have Advanced More Rapidly." As soon as I make arrangements, I "Shall Myself Hasten towards Richmond where I Can Get

Intelligences Relating to the Situation."[22]   Indirectly, Lafayette scolded
Jefferson for lack of assistance, but made every effort to reach an accom-
modation with the governor. "I will to morrow Evening Be at the Bowden
Green or Hanover Court House where I Shall Be Happy to hear from Your
Excellency."

Jefferson and the Virginia legislature issued orders to state forces, but
never specified enforcement. "I have ordered [the militia] to go to you, [but]
some have no arms," Jefferson wrote to Steuben. "We have found that men
of those Counties where the Enemy are cannot be kept in the Field; They desert
and carry off their arms. It seems reasonable [they] should be permitted to
go to their homes [to] take care of their families, and property."[23] Jefferson
continued to resist enactment of martial law to keep an army in the field for
defense and public safety.

"A Thousand militia under Major General Baron de Steuben and General
Mulenburg" engaged the enemy and they "behaved very Gallantly," Lafayette
advised General Greene. In "a few hours," he expected to be only "twenty
miles from Richmond. The Enemy are more than double our force." Their
command of the sea "gives them great advantages," he wrote.[24]

Finally, Greene replied to Lafayette's "long polite and interesting letter
of 17th April." While not commenting directly on his efforts to remain in Virginia, Greene wrote, "My force and my Talents are unequal to the conflict,"
but "It is my wish...your detachment should halt at Richmond until necessary
or further information [indicates] other measures necessary." If General
Philips should continue to engage in "offensive operations," Greene ordered
Lafayette to assume "command in that State and conduct...Military operations
as circumstances shall dictate to be proper," and added, "We fight get beat,
rise and fight again. We have a bloody field; but little glory."[25] Lafayette's
persuasion worked. He was to remain, at least for the present, in Virginia.
He had satisfied ambition without offending Greene or openly violating the
chain of command.

On May 1, 1781, Greene wrote to Washington of his decision to keep
Lafayette in Virginia: "I am greatly obliged to your Excellency for or-
dering the Marquis to the Southward. I propose to halt him in Virginia"
until he felt there was better understanding of the enemy's intention.
"Baron Stuben will join [me]." After his problems with the Legislature
of Virginia, he could not be as useful as in the past. Greene instructed
Lafayette to keep Washington "advised of all matters in that quarter, [be-
cause] it is too far [to march here] and then be sent back again."[26] Greene
reinforced Lafayette's position as an independent command. But Lafayette
was aware that his detachment of fewer than a thousand men could do little
more than harass a British force of three thousand.

Lafayette wrote to Washington, "tell me Some thing More about your Coming this Way. How Happy I would Be to See you. As you are pleased to give me the choice, I frankly Shall tell My wishes. If you cooperate with the french Against [New York], I wish to Be at Head quarters." If action is planned "in Virginia I will find Myself very Happily Situated," as long as "My detachment Remains in this State," He did not wish to leave. "I Have a Separate and Active Command tho' it does not promise great glory."[27] No subordinate had more influence with Washington and Greene than Lafayette. Financial reality required a significant infusion of French assistance. A despondent Lafayette, with his French connections, was not what Washington needed.

Organizations and Structure, Relief and a Unity of Command

I have struggled to the utmost of my ability, to
keep the Army together; but all will be in vain,
without…assistance of the States

Back in July 1780, news of the French arrival in Newport did not arouse public support. Lafayette, after returning from France, had presented the forthcoming arrival as an example of the French King's strong support for the United States and independence from Great Britain, but some Americans had deep reservations about French intentions. New Englanders, less than two decades before, had experienced brutal, vicious depredations from the French and their Indian allies. Many Americans harbored bitter memories of French and Indians performing atrocities during the War (1756-63). Additional animosity was spurred by religious differences. France, decidedly Catholic, and the United States, decidedly Protestant, were vulnerable to religious misunderstandings; included in the suspicion was France's Catholic ally, Spain. This past papal foe, roaming freely on American soil as a comrade in arms, was not an easy acceptance for many Americans.

As soon as he arrived, Rochambeau realized the need to deal with a serious public relation's problem, especially after the initial shunning by Newport citizens. American sensitivities, rooted in past relationships, needed massaging. Fortunately, General Rochambeau presented French forces as friends and sincere allies. After spending the summer building fortifications and arranging for supplies, in November Rochambeau's forces went into winter camp.[1] The French worked hard to engage in a harmonious social intercourse with the civilian population. Rochambeau insisted his soldiers present "such a favorable impression upon the Government and people of Rhode Island" that Americans responded with earnest accommodation for their allies. The winter encampment passed in a routine and uneventful manner with the French and Americans passing time getting better acquainted. Only one event marred a rather enjoyable period. On December 15, 1780, Admiral De Ternay, commander of the French navy at Newport died. Admiral Destouches succeeded him.

May 6 was a fateful day for the American cause. The Vicomte de Rochambeau, returned from France, arrived in Boston harbor on the French frigate *Concorde* with discouraging news concerning future of French support.[2] Accompanying young Rochambeau was Admiral de Barras who was to replace the deceased Admiral de Ternay. When the two departed from France they were unaware of Admiral de Ternay's death. Now Admiral de Barras replaced Admiral Detouches as commander of French naval forces in North America.

There were high expectations by both General Rochambeau and Washington for a sizable increase of French aid. Instead the Vicomte encountered official rejection for assistance on the scale requested. Although discouraged and disappointed because the amount of assistance was denied, the Vicomte did not return empty handed.

In a twist of perceptions, Washington's view of Vicomte's return differed considerably from General Rochambeau. Rochambeau was bitterly disappointed by what he considered paltry support from French authorities, even a personal snub by some plotting ministers at the royal court to taint the general's reputation. But Washington was ecstatic; the trip resulted in an infusion of cash to bolster the Continental Army and provided financial support to begin the eventual march south.

The Vicomte brought cash as part of a six million grant awarded the Americans with instructions from the French council explaining the refusal to support the increases proposed by his father. He also carried significant communications concerning the sailing for North America of the French fleet under the command of Admiral de Grasse.

In contrast to Washington, a stunned General Rochambeau felt betrayed. He did not consider the assistance offered as adequate and the explanations sent "were so vague and poorly conceived," that he "dismissed them completely from his mind."[3] The King did not agree to the extent of the support requested to implement the "conclusions reached at the Hartford Conference," between Washington and Rochambeau.[4] Reinforcements would be sent, but limited. The reason offered was "the English would lose no time in sending an equal number [and] the more troops we have in North America the more difficult will be their means of maintenance."[5]

While Rochambeau's initial perception was depressing, upon further evaluation the news offered encouragement. After receipt of the so-called bad news, came a realization they received "a free subsidy" of six million "Tours livres [French pounds]." Admiral de Barass brought a partial payment with the balance to be brought by Admiral de Grasse. In addition, "To crown his generosity" the King borrowed "ten thousand Tours livres" for the United States. In Paris, French minister Vergennes estimated "that in two years the sums advanced were equal to twenty-four millions."[6] The information of "superior naval forces [to arrive in] July or August," commanded by Admiral de Grasse, while encouraging, was uncertain.[7]

Despite the good news, Rochambeau was still furious at what he considered "so small and so problematic aid." High-ranking French officers who he considered friends, "treated him badly in their letters" and behind his back, they criticized Rochambeau's "lack of charm, his attention to details, his [poor] sense of economy, and above all his distrustfulness."[8]

Rochambeau's suffering over the reduced support issue was not shared at Washington's headquarters. The news and money that arrived was a blessing; it eased the Continental Army's financial burden, but angered Congress, because they eagerly expected to control the finances. The King intentionally bypassed Congress and placed the money under Washington's control. Adroitly, Washington moved responsibility for the money to the French Minister, Luzurne, in Philadelphia. Although Congress was unable to get direct control over the money, anger at the authority placed in Washington was appeased.

While Rochambeau and his officers considered the effect of reduced assistance on the prosecution of the war, Washington confronted additional potential disasters. Supplies dwindled to a precariously low level; shortages of everything required to keep an army in the field spread through the entire Continental Army. On May 8, Washington informed the Board of War that he had sent all the clothing, muskets, and "Cartouch Boxes" he could spare "to the southward."

The next day Washington reached out to distant sources. General William Heath received orders to scour "several Eastern States" and procure "supplies for the Army." Emphasizing Heath's influence in New England, Washington wrote:

> ...The present critical and alarming situation of our Troops and Garrisons for the want of provision, is (from the nature of your command) so perfectly known to you: and your personal influence with the New England States is so considerable, that I could not hesitate to commit to you, a *Negotiation*: on the success of which, the very existence of the Army depends.[9]

On May 10, Washington notified the New England States on the purpose and urgency of General Heath's mission. "I have struggled to the utmost of my ability, to keep the Army together; but all will be in vain, without [your assistance]." He hoped that, "this representation may be received in the serious light it is meant and deserves" and that he not suffer "from the dreadful consequences which must otherwise inevitably follow in a very short time."[10]

Lack of supplies was not the only source of discontent. Washington reminded delegate John Sullivan, previously a brigadier general in the Continental Army, of necessary organizational reforms required to establish " the principles of promotion in the Army" necessary to stop disputes:

> ...a stop thereby be put to those disputes which keep it in a continual state of distraction and discontent, are the reasons for my troubling you again on this subject and praying, that some decision my be come to by Congress. It is much easier to avoid disagreements than to remove discontents; and I again declare, that If my differing in Sentiment from the opins. of the Comee. on some points has been the occasion of delay, I would, rather than have the matter lie over a moment, yield a free assent to all their propositions; for any principle is better than none.[11]

Washington continued his letter with the following lament:

> My public letters to Congress will have informed you of the Situation of this Army, and I have no scruple in giving it as my decided opn. that unless a capital change takes place soon it will be impossible for me to maintain our Posts, and keep the Army from dispersing.[12]

Lack of hard currency was a primary cause of the Continental Army's supply deficiencies. Unfortunately, the French Army's availability of hard currency caused fewer available provisions for the Continental Army, and a spiral of inflation compounded the situation.

Depreciation of Old Continental Currency[13]
(Currency Required to Purchase $1.00 Specie)

	1777	1778	1779	1780	1781
(January)	1.25	4.00	8.00	42.50	100.00

The Vicomte's arrival with money brought temporary solution to some of Washington's immediate problems. But financial and logistical challenges still faced Lafayette in Virginia, and Nathanael Greene in the southern command. While Lafayette deflected some pressing shortages in his detachment by using personal funds, Greene enjoyed no such luxury.

Shortly after arriving, Admiral De Barras wrote to Washington. "I have the honor to announce to your Excellency my arrival.... I am very impatient to have the honor of making an acquaintance with you, and to assure you that I have nothing so much at heart as to render myself serviceable to the King and to the United States."[14]

Soon after the Vicomte arrived, Washington heard rumors that he carried significant news. At first, Washington was unaware of Rochambeau's disappointment at the amount of French aid. But in Washington's situation, any financial aid was welcome. He sent congratulations to Rochambeau "on the safe return of the Vicount de Rochambeau, who I hope is the Bearer of agreeable intelligences." Anticipating important news, Washington quickly offered to meet him "at any time which you shall please to appoint."[15] As a courtesy, Washington sent a copy of his Rochambeau letter to Minister Luzerne in Philadelphia. Rochambeau was so distracted and angry by the news from Paris that he neglected to inform Washington of his disappointment.

Three days after the "dismal information" arrived, Rochambeau wrote to the Secretary of War in Paris that his son had returned, "quite unaccompanied," with satisfactory news. Adding, "Whatever may come of it the king must be served," he intended "to begin this second campaign, using as best I can the very limited [means]" in his possession.[16]

In the meantime, Rochambeau requested a meeting with Washington, who was delighted and proposed they meet on May 21 at Wethersfield, Connecticut. Washington would bring Genl. Knox and Genl. du portail. He looked forward to "meeting your Excellency and the Count de Barras."

In other correspondence, Washington replied to Admiral Destouche's letter, announcing "the arrival of the Count de Barras to take command of His Majesty's Fleet" in Rhode Island. Washington, always sensitive to personal issues between senior commanders, avoided commenting on any potential adverse relationship between Destouches and De Barras. "You judge very rightly in supposing that the term of your command will not be looked upon as mispent. You may be assured, Sir, that America will ever retain the most grateful remembrance of the exertions you have made in her behalf." Washington added a personal note, "As to myself, I shall...be happy [for any] opportunities of testifying [to] the high sense I entertain of your merit."[17]

On May 17, 1781, Washington informed the president of Congress about "Count de Rochambeau's...dispatches [arriving] from the Court of France." Rochambeau had requested an interview, he wrote, and they were to meet in Wethersfield, Connecticut, in four days where he hoped, "we shall be able, from the intelligence received, to settle a definite plan of Campaign." The entire allied effort languished in a mode of inaction. Politically, Washington knew that continued public support hinged on successful demonstration of allied activity. The major hurdle, even with a plan, was money.

On the night of May 19, Washington arrived in Wethersfield. Rochambeau and his party arrived two days later. The conference began on the 22nd.[18] Rochambeau's late arrival was caused by the unexpected appearance of a British fleet off Newport, Rhode Island, forcing Admiral De Barras to remain and keep an eye on the enemy.[19]

Before departing for Wethersfield, Washington received intercepted correspondence from London indicating a major British assault was planned in the south. The new enemy strategy was to hold the allies north of the Hudson

River and prevent reinforcements from reaching the southern states. The London government expressed impatience with British commanders in America. They felt the war dragged on too long; it should have been over long before. "Very extraordinary" that General Clinton "should let the rebellion last so long," especially with "the precarious state of the finances of Congress," wrote a disgusted British minister. This intercepted intelligence was the source of long discussions among the allies.

This latest intelligence caused a rethinking of allied strategy. Sending reinforcements south, assisted by the French army and navy, was a serious opportunity. Initially, Washington wavered; he "had dominant in his thoughts an expedition against New York," Rochambeau reported later. "He [Washington] considered an expedition against Lord Cornwallis in Chesapeake Bay" an alternative only after "we were quite certain of our inability to accomplish the former," an assault against New York. At the time, Washington strongly favored an attack on the city, but Rochambeau was reluctant; his strong inclination was a move south. Extensive and detailed discussions followed, with many questions and answers posed in writing. Staff members held a number of deliberations. Both Washington and Rochambeau expressed strong reasons to support their positions, but neither ruled out the other's. Finally, an unenthusiastic Rochambeau conceded to Washington's desire for an assault on the city. Later, Washington wrote in his summary of the meeting, "The French and American armies [were] to form a junction [and then] move down to the vicinity of New York, to be ready to take advantage of any opportunity [that] the enemy may afford." A realist, Washington expected unpredictable events, so he qualified his comments about New York. When Admrial De Grasse arrived, the combined Allied forces, "may proceed" against the city or "be directed against the enemy in some other quarter as circumstances shall dictate."[20] This was the first indication that Washington entertained serious considerations for opportunities other than New York.

At Wethersfield, the accomplishments included agreements on alternatives and flexibility in operations for the next campaign. A series of plans and priorities developed mainly based on existing and anticipated conditions, but with recognition that contingent events might alter operations. Washington had moved from his rigid position for an assault on New York. Although the city was preferred, if conditions changed the plan was flexible. New York was the agreed upon objective under existing conditions, but moves against the city were flexible and designed to take advantage of opportunities that might arise elsewhere. From a strategic perspective, the conference demonstrated Washington and Rochambeau's determination, along with staffs, to cooperatively prepare complex military operations. On May 23, 1781, the conference concluded with Washington and Rochambeau returning to their respective command headquarters.[21] Dispatches describing the priority against New York fell into British hands, further convincing General Clinton that New York was the real Allied objective.

When Rochambeau returned to headquarters, he was surprised. "French vessels were [preparing] to sail for Boston." Expectations were high that the British planned a surprise attack on Newport Harbor. Rochambeau used all his persuasive powers to convince a skeptical Admiral de Barras to remain. After some tense moments, De Barras agreed. "No one is more interested than I in the arrival of M.de Grasse. He was my junior in the service and has lately been raised to lieutenant-general," de Barras informed Rochambeau. "As soon as I am apprised of his arrival I shall hasten to join him and place myself under his orders. I will serve through this campaign, but not a second one."[22]

Immediately Rochambeau attempted to communicate with Admiral De Grasse, but the process was slow. The French used fast frigates, which sailed periodically with communications between North America, the continent, and the French Islands in the West Indies. But always, exchanges met with many challenges; weather, capture, and a myriad of other time delays. In carefully written comments, Rochambeau revealed his preference to operate in the Chesapeake, but was cautious in explaining the action, because of Washington's passion for New York.[23] He "suggested…an expedition against Cornwallis in Virginia [was] more practicable and less anticipated by the enemy."[24]

Despite Rochambeau's effort to coax attention to the Chesapeake, he expected De Grasse to exercise his "own ability to judge the practicality of an attack on New York," but Rochambeau added a convincing argument; the previous attempts to gain entrance to New York harbor failed because of "the difficulty of securing pilots even with liberal offers of money."[25] As an incentive for the Americans Rochambeau urged De Grasse "to intercede with the Governor of Santo Domingo" for additional troops "and a loan of 1,200,000 francs." A prompt reply was requested so allied armies could "proceed by land as expeditiously as possible and join him [De Grasse] at any part of the Chesapeake."[26]

At this time in their relationship, Rochambeau respected and admired Washington, but also observed some of Washington's military inexperience. Washington exhibited little experience in naval matters. Basically an army man, he viewed the navy primarily as a tactical support force for army activities. While recognizing the importance of naval superiority, Washington was not experienced in strategic planning to harness the combined potential of land and naval forces on a grand scale. Rochambeau accepted Washington's experience in several areas vital to military planning, especially topography associated with a move south. Washington's main concern, for good reason, was losing men through desertion, but with pay and provisions desertion rates could significantly drop.

Meanwhile, extensive surveillance of British deployment in and around New York supplied manpower details. Enemy forces were reported as 9,997 rank and file fit for duty, plus Loyalist regiments which probably bolstered the size to 10,500.[27] The British overestimated the Allied forces at over 20,000. In reality, the Continental Army on the Hudson and around West Point numbered scarcely 3,500. French forces approximated 4,000 at Newport, Rhode Island.[28]

With little fanfare, but with a stroke of administrative genius, Washington designed a cataloguing process that impacted allied communications for the rest of the war. On May 25 he appointed Lt. Colonel Richard Varick his recording secretary at headquarters to employ the number of clerks necessary to classify correspondence into six sections with details on how to be filed and arranged. The process described information registration, cataloguing, and security issues. Washington's written communications needed a recovery process for expeditious follow up and cross-referencing. The effectiveness of his communications cataloguing process was a secret weapon and essential in exercising a successful command and control process. The files required easy mobility, not an easy task in the 18th century. Communications were the foundation of military moves, transmitting strategy and tactics to distant outposts. A masterfully designed cataloguing process assisted Washington's gifted aides to write most of his correspondence.

Events associated with allied plans caused Washington ever-expanding daily duties, some personal, but others had far reaching consequences. On a personal note he revealed "my whole attention has been occupied by a variety of concerns," including a request to Doctor John Baker for a pair of "Pincers to fasten the wire of my teeth," and added, "I now wish you to send me one of your scrapers, as my teeth stand in need of cleaning (the British intercepted this letter).[29] Challenges with far-reaching consequences involved continual changes in the Army's rank and file. Washington described in General Orders:

> As a considerable proportion of the troops in this Army will consist of recruits [who are] little accustomed to military service, and [with little time to train] them in the duties of their profession, the General [Washington] is extremely solicitous that [officers] should be wholly occupied in disciplining and forming them.

All officers were ordered to devote themselves to training and the Adjutant General was to oversee "the Exercising and manoeuvring of the troops so far as [his regular] duties," would allow. The Orders further stated, "The Commander in Chief will judge for himself [the] attention which shall have been paid to this order."[30]

In earnest, the allies engaged in the tedious task of planning the next campaign. Then came information bolstering the Allied cause. On March 22, 1781, John Jay, American representative in Spain, informed President Samuel Huntington "that he has obtained a loan in Spain for 150,000 dollars."[31] Immediately an American agent was appointed and sent "to reside at Havanna" and assist any American traders with advice.[32] More welcome news arrived; Virginia delegates in Congress informed Governor Thomas Jefferson, "Authentic Accounts have arrived here that" Spanish General Bernardo de Galvez "has entered the Bay of Pensacola with a considerable sea and Land force" making "good his landing" against British forces. There "is little doubt...that important place will soon be in the hands of Spain."[33]

Support from Spain brought welcome relief. Spain, an ally of France, was not officially allied with the United States. The relationship between Spain and the United States was tenuous. While cordial at best, with few exceptions, the relationship never developed the same personal warmth shown to the French allies. Fortunately, Spain and the United States had a common ally and a common enemy. Most Spanish financial assistance came through France. Some Spanish assistance went directly to individual states, especially Virginia. Spanish assistance, during the American War of Independence, was crucial, timely, and effective. A delegate from North Carolina reported two ships arrived at Boston "with about three thousand suits of clothes from Cadiz," and, "Mr. Jay has transmitted a full detail of his negotiations at the court of Madrid. They do great honor to his abilities, and promise a favorable issue."[34] Virginia delegates in Congress informed Governor Thomas Jefferson "that about three thousand Suits of Cloathing are safely arrived at Boston from Spain, which our Friend the King of Spain has Enabled our Minister [John Jay] at Court to procure."[35]

But French aid drew most Congressional attention. "We have received dispatches from France. The second division is not to be sent," wrote a delegate to Major General Nathanael Greene. He indicated, however, that there were additional naval forces on the way, "and a powerful diversion is intended in the West Indies. [We are to receive] a subsidy of six millions of Livres...part will come in cloathing &c and part to be a fund under the direction of the Comr-in-Chief."[36]

Financial circumstances had taken a positive turn. In May 1781 the Marquis de Castries, Minister of the Marine in Paris, wrote a perceptive letter to Lafayette summarizing the French perspective, in monetary terms, of contributions to the American cause. He noted that Lt. Col. John Laurens, representing Congress, was in Paris seeking enlargement of French financial support. De Castries offered to assist and made certain Laurens was aware of Lafayette's importance and the value of his recommendations. De Castries

Painting by unknown artist.

18th Century Spanish officer in New Spain.

"was sorry not to be able to confide [in Laurens because of] events that are to take place," and he felt "it is dangerous to inform him with to much precision of the dispositions we intend to make." Candidly, De Castries revealed, "We had a difference of Opinion, Mr. Laurens and I on the most important objective of your army's operations." De Castries shared Rochambeau's opinion that New York "would require stronger forces than those you could use to attack it."[38] He further stated, "Although Colonel Laurens did not obtain everything he requested; he should be satisfied with his negotiations." Laurens had received, "The equivalent of twenty million livres in silver money, or merchandise," along with other considerations "we add twenty million to" American support, a sum that "will…suffice for the army you have ready for action." De Castries understood, "how the poor state of troop's clothing and arms affects the opinion other troops have of it." He was convinced that "If all the resources being sent to you reach you, you will have abundance." Then he added a more ominous French concern:

> I do not wish to end my letter without telling you about the abominable speculation going on, [prohibiting] us from transferring funds through letters of exchange…more than 25 percent is lost in the exchange from France to America. There must be some money-grabbers who deserve to be pursued, and if [they are Frenchmen] they must be brought to justice.

Bills of exchange often suffered from a variety of exploitations; commissions were charged to cash them, as well as inflationary pressures placed on the goods acquired. Americans never appreciated the amount of French aid that was sent. A fair amount of supplies were captured and never reached the destination. Many circumstances contributed to a high shrinkage of French aid from origin to destination, not the least of which was American graft, pilferage, and an inefficient logistical support system. On a more personal tone, De Castries expressed, "I am pleased that my son has joined you and is working to your glory as far as he is able as your aide-de-camp."[39]

Washington acknowledged appreciation for the recently arrived Spanish aid. "These Things are of such immense Importance to all our Plans," he wrote to Major General William Heath. "In my last [letter] I mentioned forwarding the Clothing which [has] lately arrived from Spain, I request you…expedite this business, that it may not be stopped a Day on the Road from leaving Boston to its Arrival in Camp."[40]

✤ 8 ✤

Virginia Agonies – Support in the Shadows

 *I see just 900 Continental troops and some militia,
sometimes more and sometimes less but never enough*

Together with their staffs, Washington and Rochambeau faced the arduous task of transforming concepts into strategy and tactics. It was a very complex effort. Success depended entirely on a unity of action, exercised over hostile topography by widely separated land and sea forces, a challenge of unprecedented magnitude.

Included in the complexity was language. Plans demanded descriptions in French and English. Any mistakes or misunderstandings in translation had potentially catastrophic consequences during the action phase of tactical operations. While the number of allied translators, fluent in both French and English, were few, the quality of their work was extraordinary.

Complexities associated with designing this campaign dwarfed any previous experience of the war and past allied experiences were hardly encouraging. Neither Washington nor Rochambeau spoke or read the other's mother tongue; each relied on staff members to interpret and explain sometimes difficult semantics. Communication exchanges flowed with increasing frequency between American and French headquarters. While allied headquarters staffs concentrated on reducing operational tactics to writing, the military situation in the south changed.

Always fluid, military dynamics in Virginia started to change on a daily, even hourly basis. Lafayette sensed his location was at the center of changing enemy strategy. He wrote of his situation in a letter to Minister Luzerne:

> My situation, Monsieur le Chevalier, cannot help being a bit confusing. When I look to the Left, there is General Phillips with his army and absolute command of the James River. When I turn to the right, Lord Cornwallis's army is advancing as fast as it can go to devour me, and the worst of the affair is that on looking behind me I see just 900 Continental troops and some militia, sometimes more and sometimes less but never enough not to be completely thrashed by the smallest of the two armies that do me the honor of

visiting. Last night General Phillips was in Brandon, south of the James River thirty-five miles from here, and made me fear for Richmond again. The other day Lord Cornwallis made his entrance into Halifax, eight miles from here, and at the rate his lordship is going I expect to see him at any moment making his entrance into my camp. General Greene is in front of Camden. He had a long-fought engagement with Lord Rawdon, but having had only vague reports, I see only that the Camden entrenchments will not be carried so quickly, and since General Wayne is still far away, I have no help to hope for except...from my legs, of which I expect to make suitable use.

What tries my patience the most is the dearth of all things, the total lack of resources, the slowness in getting things done that one is forced to experience in this part of the continent.[1]

Strategically Lafayette was in the center of a communications network. Geographically, he was positioned to relay information between allied headquarters in the north and General Greene to the south. In addition, he was near the governor and legislative power of Virginia. His ability to exchange information in two languages was a major advantage, especially if French forces arrived in the area. While confused about the enemy's intentions, Lafayette was unaware of their confusion.

In early April, Cornwallis wrote to his superior, General Sir Henry Clinton, in New York. "I am very anxious to receive Your Excellency's commands, being as yet totally in the dark as to the intended operations of the summer." Then Cornwallis suggested a strategy. "I cannot help expressing my wishes that the Chesapeake may become the seat of war – even, if necessary, at the expense of abandoning New York. Until Virginia is in a manner subdued, our hold of the Carolinas must be difficult if not precarious."[2]

In the letter, Cornwallis did not state intentions to move into Virginia, only recognition of its strategic value in holding the Carolinas. Later he wrote, "It is very disagreeable to me to decide upon measures of such consequence to the general conduct of the war, without an opportunity of procuring your Excellency's [orders]. [But] the delay and difficulty of conveying letters and the impossibility of waiting for answers, render it indispensably necessary." He described "dangers and distresses of marching some hundreds of miles in a country chiefly hostile, without one active or useful friend, without intelligence, and without communication with any part of the country." He found the "situation in which I leave South Carolina adds much to my anxiety." This lack of effective communication exchanges hampered British military efforts during the war. On his own, he made the fateful decision to invade Virginia. His comments suggest that British difficulties with communication, intelligence gathering, and loneliness of separate commands seriously constrained implementation of an effective strategy. Clinton received Cornwallis' letter on May 22, 1781, four weeks after it was written.[3]

As Clinton and Cornwallis tried to overcome communication difficulties, Lafayette worked to improve allied communication. His location and limited forces forced him to prioritize tactical moves. The enemy could bring a general engagement; Lafayette could not. "This disadvantage and my inferior numbers force me to maneuver away when they approach, but still remain within Striking distance," he wrote to Baron von Steuben.

Lafayette's need for timely and accurate intelligence was critical for survival. The British were experts in conducting stealthy surprise attacks on unsuspecting American forces. Swiftly, Lafayette improved his intelligence capability. He ordered Von Steuben to send White's Dragoons to headquarters. Dragoons provided the speediest and most effective units for intelligence gathering. He notified the governor that "an immediate Supply of Wagons and Boats [is needed or] I am exposed and crippled in Every one of My Movements."[4] Lafayette increased pressure on all sources that might assist his tactical situation, including Governor Jefferson.

For information, Lafayette was not limited to North America. The Comte de Vergennes wrote to Lafayette on May 11, 1781, from Versailles. Although the letter did not arrive for several months, it contained further information regarding Lt. Colonel John Laurens' activities before he left Paris for North America. Laurens had converted some of the money "given by His Majesty into arms, ammunition, and clothing." There was other welcome news. "We are awaiting the result of the proposal for a loan in Holland for a sum of ten million," Vergennes wrote, but, "It cannot be made in the Americans' name, and the king [is the] principle borrower. I beg you not to let General Washington be unaware of that point." Vergennes criticized Laurens' manner in approaching the French Court. "I know he is complaining rather indiscreetly," about the lack of more assistance. "I foresee [that] he will make every effort to get at least his chief [Washington] to share his sentiments."

With his direct approach for aid, Laurens ruffled French feathers. Unsophisticated, he was accused of political immaturity. Vergennes cautioned Lafayette that, "France is not inexhaustible.... We are doing a great deal for the Americans, but they must do their part." Vergennes insisted that Americans must do more on their own. "That will be the best means of obtaining a quick peace."[5] He mentioned another difficulty, the lack of accurate information. "We are awaiting with great impatience...news from your area. Only through the English newspapers [we learned] there was a naval battle near the Virginia Capes [but we do not know] whether our troops landed or what became of M. Destouches."[6]

Precisely when Lafayette received Vergennes' letter is uncertain; it was dated May 11, 1781, at Versailles, France. Needing at least 40 days to reach Lafayette, it likely arrived toward the end of June. On April 26, 1781,

London's *Daily Advertiser* printed a letter from Admiral Arbuthnot to the "British secretary of the Admiralty" describing a British version of the situation in America. "The Rebel Militia…will speedily disperse; the Count de Rochambeau must seek another Opportunity" to visit Virginia, he predicted. "The Rebel Campaign is [in a confused state and] I flatter myself these events will be productive of very solid Advantages to his Majesty's Service," boasted the admiral.[7] While this report was inaccurate, as a propaganda tool Arbuthnot's letter discouraged the French who were in a quandary about continued investment of their time, talent, and treasure.

Lafayette possessed several traits that made him successful as an intelligence source. He was innately curious and a prolific writer with an appealing style. American politicians and most high-ranking Continental Army officers were convinced Lafayette enjoyed significant influence in France, especially at the Royal Court. The French, in turn, were impressed by his rank and closeness to Washington. His influence in America increased when the French provided additional aid. He had demonstrated bravery in battle, loyalty to Washington, and political astuteness in both military and civilian situations. Added to this was his geographical location, which quickly developed as the military epicenter of the war.

Earlier, on May 14, 1781, Benjamin Franklin acknowledged Lafayette's communication skills:

> You are a very good Correspondent, which I do not deserve, as I am a Bad one. The Truth is, I have too much Business upon my hands, a great deal of it foreign to my Function as a Minister, which interferes with my writing regularly to my Friends. But I am nevertheless extreamly sensible of your Kindness in sending me such frequent and full Intelligence of the State of the Affairs on your side of the Water, and in letting me see by Your Letters, that your Health continues, as well as your Zeal for our Cause and Country.[8]

On another matter, Franklin offered his version of the John Laurens episode. "I hope by [this time] the Ship which has the honour of bearing your Name is safely arrived," he wrote. "She carries Cloathing for near 20,000 Men, with Arms, Ammunition &c," and "Col Laurens, will bring a considerable Addition if Providence favors his Passage." Fortunately, John Laurens was not on the *Marquis de Lafayette*. The ship was captured on May 3, 1781, and all its cargo seized as contraband.[9] "I think it was a wise Measure to send Col. Laurens here, who would speak knowingly of the State of the Army," wrote Franklin. His visit "has been attended with all the success that…tho' not with all that was wished." Laurens, he stated, "fully justified your Character of him, & returns thoroughly possess'd of my Esteem." But he acknowledged that wouldn't please him "so much as a little more Money would have done, for his beloved Army." The

French "Court continues firm and steady in [doing] everything it can for us. Can we not do a little more for ourselves?"[10]

Despite intense efforts to improve communication, Lafayette found progress slow. With headquarters in the north the challenge was time; a process was needed to decrease time of deliveries. In the south, communication with General Greene was appalling. Both Greene and Lafayette were constantly moving to avoid superior enemy forces. Movement made expeditious communications particularly difficult. At times, routine exchanges required more than thirty days. Under current southern military dynamics, with almost daily changes, tactical cooperation between the two was unworkable. "I am so remote from Northern intelligence...circumstances happening so frequent [affecting] the safety of Virginia and North Carolina...I am embarrassed...what advice to give you or to Baron Stuben," Greene informed Lafayette. But Greene realized the situation had changed when Generals Cornwallis and Phillips joined. "[Keep] me constantly informed of the situation," Greene wrote, and "send copies...of all official reports" to Congress and General Washington. "Don't be sparing of Expresses as it is [important for us] to be well informed of our situation as well as the enemies."[11]

In a selfless and unheralded command decision, Greene changed the organization to strengthen Lafayette. He ordered Baron von Steuben "to put his troops at Lafayette's disposal" and "prevent the junction of Cornwallis and Phillips."[12] The organizational change was a self-sacrificing move by Greene, who desperately needed reinforcements, but also sensed the military opportunities developing in Virginia. The Baron received the letter after the British intercepted it.

Lafayette's immediate problem was Governor Jefferson's passive reaction to requests for raising militias and troops in Virginia. "I shall candidly acknowledge...it is not in my power to do any Thing more than [to inform] the General Assembly that unless they can provide [enforcement], it will be vain to call on Militia," wrote Jefferson. Reluctantly he offered to "do something by Reprimands to the County Lieutenants."[13]

The governor's reply indicated the absence of state initiatives to provide a platform for control and enforcement. At no time during the war was Jefferson's lack of tactical military experience more apparent. Resistance to aggressive action by Virginia's executive and legislative bodies was a critical flaw in the state's ability to support the war effort.

Jefferson did recognize an urgent need to improve communications, and asked Lafayette to maintain "very frequent Communication between yourself and the Executive." In order to expedite exchanges, Jefferson "directed the State Quarter Master to station a Line of Expresse Riders from your Camp to Charlottesville...to communicate your Wants," assuring "nothing in my power shall be wanting to supply them." Jefferson sensed Lafayette's unusual ability for information diffusion. "Interesting Events will always be acceptable whenever you shall have time to add them to a Letter or make them the Subject of a special one," Jefferson wrote, adding that he intended "to do myself the pleasure of calling on you at your Quarters tomorrow morning."[14]

With Baron von Steuben's forces under his command, Lafayette turned attention to another Continental force moving south commanded by Brigadier General Anthony Wayne. Lafayette and Wayne had a long association since the days of the Valley Forge encampment. "I am By General Greene directed to take Command of the troops in [Virginia]. [And] let You proceed to the Southward, [unless I have] an opportunity to fight Phillips to Advantage, [then] He desires me to keep you for a time with us," Lafayette informed Wayne.[15]

Need for speedier communication continued to be a significant influence on the Continental Army's effectiveness. Allied forces were deployed in relatively small units over vast distances and varied geography. Each unit was subject to destruction by an aggressive enemy, especially in the south. Enemy forces appeared to consolidate as Cornwallis moved towars Phillips, while the Americans remained dispersed in relatively small size units. "My detachment [is to be] Stationed in Virginia where I am to take Command of the troops," Lafayette informed Steuben. "I Beg, my dear Sir" for an account of your manpower size, situation and location.[16]

In an effort to deny the enemy access to foraging opportunities, Governor Jefferson notified "Various County Lieutenants, [to] order all Cattle and Horses" removed that fall "within twenty Miles of the Enemys Camp." If the owners do "not perform this within…a reasonable Time [you are to order the] proper Officers and men…to carry such Horses and Cattle to the Marquis Fayettes Headquarters for use of our Army [after] having them duly appraised."[17]

Lafayette faced more than supply problems. "The Baron von Steuben is sixty miles from here and will march south with 400 recruits. He is so unpopular in Virginia," Lafayette candidly informed the Chevalier de La Luzerne.[18] Steuben's unpopularity resulted from disputes with Virginia field officers about arrangements for the Virginia Line.[19] The gruff old drillmaster was aghast at the loose militia discipline associated with Virginia units. Original intentions were to send the Baron south to join Greene in the Carolinas, but as the situation changed, the Baron was needed in Virginia.[20]

Some of Lafayette's correspondence involved family members. "It is centuries since I have had news from you," Lafayette wrote his brother, Vicomte de Noailles, who served on Rochambeau's staff.[21] "[Our] affairs in Virginia [are] not very brilliant…. Until new orders come I am destined to command in this state. The various departments give me more trouble than Lord

Cornwallis." Without funds, he told his brother that, "we are spending immense sums, and [are still] short of everything. [None] of my friends in the north give me any news," Lafayette wrote. He was convinced there was a fine line between either an opportunity or a potential military catastrophe in Virginia. "If more is not known about our situation I fear I shall be judged severely, even unjustly."[22]

Lafayette sent relentless appeals to Jefferson, citing lack of supplies, especially horses. "Your Excellency will be sorry to hear that all the fine Horses in the Country are falling into Enemy's hands." Jefferson received one dispatch after another; the governor had second thoughts about his request "to communicate your Wants." With the Marquis located so near, the stream of wants was endless. "Your orders to impress [are limited to] twenty miles, and unless [you] give a warrant for 50 miles we cannot get a single Horse," Lafayette complained. The enemy has "so many Dragoons that it becomes impossible to stop or reconnoiter their movements."[23] As for manpower, "No Rifleman, no arms, and few Militia" had arrived. The Culpeper Militia tried to join them, he claimed, "but were prevented, [because you] had not called for arms." He also told Jefferson they needed "Your Excellency...order Riflemen to join us. Without them and [horses] we can do nothing."[24]

Lafayette made certain Jefferson was informed and unable to claim ignorance of supplies needed to carry out Virginia's defense. Belatedly, Jefferson responded to the impending threat and informed various County Lieutenants that "Lord Cornwallis from Carolina and a Reinforcement of 2000 Men from New York" have joined the "hostile Army" in Virginia. They "crossed the James River [and we must] bring a very great Force into the Field," if Virginia was to be saved. "Every Man who possibly can...come armed with a good Rifle and those who cannot [with] a good smooth Bore if they have it." They could expect a duty "in the Field two months from the Time of their joining the Army. [I] urge you to the most instantaneous execution of these Orders." Until reinforcements were placed in "the Field the whole Country lies open to a most powerful Army headed by the most active, enterprising and vindictive Officer who has ever taken up arms against us."[25]

Finally, Jefferson was energized. As "soon as the other Branch of the Legislature is convened I believe they [will] strengthen you with Cavalry to any Amount you think proper and with the horses you think necessary," he informed Lafayette. The militia has been called from "our best rifle Counties." Instructions were to, "rendezvous at Charlottesville and there expect your Orders." At last Jefferson reacted aggressively to the impending enemy threats. "I sincerely and anxiously wish you [are able to] prevent Lord Cornwallis from engaging you till you [are] sufficiently reinforced and...engage him on your own terms."[26]

Immediately, Lafayette responded to Jefferson's action, especially "Resolves Respecting the Impress of Horses." The latest intelligence went to the Governor and described General Greene's successes. The "posts of Fort Motte, Orange Burg, Fort Watson, Fort Granby Have Surrendered to General Greene's army." He included some optimistic news about events in Virginia. "To my great Satisfaction the Virginia Recruits and the Virginia Militia will Remain in this State," and not be sent further south. "New Levies" and "the Pennsylvanians" would remain in Virginia, as well as Baron von Steuben's forces. Badly outnumbered, to his relief, Lafayette's command was growing.[27]

Meanwhile, the British intensified activities and Lafayette sent orders for the Baron to remove stores ahead of an expected British advance.[28] As soon as the increasing British threat was apparent, Lafayette adjusted and maneuvered his forces.[29]

Brigadier General Anthony Wayne sent Lafayette good tidings. His force of "1000 Combatants...9 Officers 90 Non Commissioned Officers & mattrosses with Six field pieces," was to arrive the next day and take "the most direct course for Fredericksburg, unless the Manoeuvers of Lord Cornwallis should render an other Direction more advisable."[30]

Fate intervened on May 12. General Phillips died of fever and Benedict Arnold took command. The next day Arnold tried to contact Lafayette, but Lafayette refused.[31] While Arnold temporarily took command, Washington's intelligence indicated that Phillips' replacement was Major General James Robinson from New York. Events indicated the British intended to send additional forces to Virginia, an action Washington hoped to prevent.[32]

With the British change in commands and their apparent effort to intensify the war in Virginia, Lafayette's tactical approach and response required continued adjustments. But in the north at Washington's headquarters, changes occurred with significant impact on Lafayette's future operations, slowly at first, and initially without clear direction.

One outcome of the Wethersfield conference was a new infusion of energy in allied activities and Washington, with his penchant for information diffusion, informed key subordinate commanders of the latest developments. An "attempt upon New York" was considered "preferable to a Southern operation," he wrote to Lafayette. "We have rumours [the enemy is] about to quit New York altogether." If they did, he noted they would probably follow them into the "Southern States." But Washington's concern for security prevented him "from mentioning many matters I wish to communicate to you." The British confirmed Washington's caution by intercepting the letter.[33]

✤ 9 ✤

Cornwallis and Clinton – Adrift in Isolation

⊲ *Another such victory would ruin the British army* ⊳

As the allies engaged in a unity of effort to finalize operational plans for the next campaign, a new British strategy changed the war's direction. In contrast to allied unity, the British command was rife with clashing egos at the highest levels, including constant interference from London.

The relationship between British Generals Clinton and Cornwallis was contentious and constrained opportunities for effective unity of effort. They loathed each other. Although Clinton was the senior commander, the mutual distaste assured they operated in separate commands. Added to the Clinton and Cornwallis contention was disdain between Clinton and Admiral Arbuthnot, commander of the British navy in North America.

Years later, Cornwallis described how this contributed to British failures in Virginia. He was convinced Clinton had forwarded communications to London in a manner that distorted Cornwallis's decision for "the march into Virginia."[1]

Clinton fanned the acrimony when he requested to be replaced. He realized Cornwallis would probably succeed him, but kept the request confidential without notifying Cornwallis. Later Clinton suspected Cornwallis was informed by sympathetic political sources in London. Clinton justified his action of not informing Cornwallis by insisting, "the crowds who usually followed my steps would soon change the object of their homage and swell His Lordship's [Cornwallis] train."[2]

British Minister for American Affairs, Lord Germain, denied Clinton's request, and ordered him "to retain Command." When informed that Clinton's request was denied, Cornwallis felt slighted and concluded, "he was not slated for the command." Everything involving the two seemed to increase tension in their relationship.[3] By now Clinton despised Cornwallis and accused him of "fermenting discontents" in the army "against its commander in chief.[4] Whenever he is with me, there are symptoms I do Not Like," Clinton wrote.[5]

Admiral Arbuthnot, commander of the Royal Navy in North America, was another senior officer subjected to Clinton's wrath. Unfortunately for Clinton, the admiral commanded ships that the British army depended on for supplies and transportation. Clinton was convinced Arbuthnot was "a sinister villain plotting behind his back." Increasing Clinton's paranoia surrounding the admiral was General Cornwallis's cordial relations with Arbuthnot.[6]

On August 8, 1780, a month after the French arrived in Newport, Admiral Arbuthnot requested a meeting with General Clinton.[7] Clinton accepted, expecting "to settle any plan of cooperation that can be agreed on in the present situation of the enemy."[8] After Clinton traveled 120 miles to attend the meeting, he discovered the Admiral had "put to sea [with the entire fleet] that very morning."[9] Furious, he complained, but Arbuthnot dismissed the complaint by answering that he had written earlier, "I am preparing to weigh to cruise for the enemy...I do not think it proper to delay a moment."[10] Clinton was convinced the admiral was unwilling to cooperate on military matters.

While the Allies planned the next phase of operations, the three British commanders maintained the friction in their personal relationships. Clinton was so outraged he wrote to London strongly suggesting either his or the admiral's removal.[11] Eventually Lord George Germaine replied that Arbuthnot was "to relieve Sir Peter Parker in Command at Jamaica" and be replaced in North America by "another flag officer." But Lord Germaine, soured by Clinton's complaints, continued, "should you...desire to return home, His Majesty [will permit] you to resign the command of his forces to Lord Cornwallis."[12] Although Arbuthnot was replaced, Germaine's reply was no endorsement of Clinton. Patience in London for his complaints disappeared. There was increasing London sentiment that Clinton should expend more effort prosecuting the war. Turning his command over to Cornwallis was not an act Clinton savored.

Earlier in the war, the two had worked together to accomplish a significant victory at Charleston, South Carolina. The British captured the entire southern Continental Army under the command of General Benjamin Lincoln. Cornwallis envisioned a separate command and remained in Charleston after Clinton returned to New York.[13] Before departure Clinton was confident that "Georgetown and almost the whole country between the Pedee and Savannah had submitted without opposition."[14] In reality, he considered Cornwallis' command more exile than opportunity. To Clinton, the war in the south was over and he returned to New York in search of additional laurels.

The British victory at Charleston yielded a large amount of contraband, but not without internal consequences. Disagreement developed between the British army and navy over shares of prize money. The "Admiral [probably Arbuthnot]...was not inclined to admit the army to any proportionate share."

The navy divided "among themselves three-fourths" of the prize money "while the poor soldier...got nothing." The total amount of contraband was nearly 40,000 Lbs sterling.[15]

On June 10, 1780, Cornwallis assumed command at Charleston.[16] A week before departing, Clinton drafted instructions virtually yielding Cornwallis an independent command. He instructed Cornwallis to pacify South Carolina, then move north to "recover" North Carolina. Later, Cornwallis claimed Clinton left him without sufficient means to carry out the instructions. Clinton argued Cornwallis had adequate forces including 6,000 men and by October, 1780, the force increased to 11,306.[17]

Three months after American forces surrendered at Charleston, Cornwallis received unbelievable intelligence that another Continental Army, commanded by Major General Gates, was approaching. Delighted for an opportunity to achieve another victory with his independent command, Cornwallis headed immediately for Camden, South Carolina.[18] By August 16, 1780, both sides prepared for battle and Cornwallis' victory was complete. The British effectively destroyed the second Continental Army southern command in three months.[19]

Despite Cornwallis's total victory, Clinton was concerned when he learned of the action. He noted his "mortification [at] the return of an army which he had...three months before...so completely annihilated." The return of a second southern Continental Army in so short a time was unexpected, especially after Clinton was convinced all effective resistance in the south was over. The rebels' ability to field a second command was a troubling prospect for the General.[20]

Cornwallis viewed the situation from a different perspective. He was convinced "rebel" aid coming from the north was the only reason rebellion was still alive in South Carolina and Georgia. "It may be doubted by some whether the invasion of north Carolina [is] prudent," Cornwallis wrote to Clinton. "I am convinced it is...if we do not attack...we must give up both South Carolina and Georgia."[21]

On Sept 8, 1780, Cornwallis moved toward Charlotte, North Carolina. The objective was Hillsboro, North Carolina, but illness dogged his army. Almost immediately, Patriots skirmished with Loyalist forces along the Catawba River west of Charlotte.[22] Cornwallis resumed the march on September 25, with cavalry in advance to gather intelligence and scout the area for armed resistance. With reckless, almost arrogant action, the cavalry galloped into Charlotte and met a withering fire from American Patriots.[23] Embarrassed, the British cavalry commander dismissed the action as "a trifling insignificant skirmish." More embarrassing was the thought of significant resistance in the south, so far inland; especially after British intelligence reports indicated a collapse of Patriot resistance. This relatively unknown action extracted severe consequences on Cornwallis's communication capability. In an army already weakened by sickness, he lost irreplaceable horses and scouts.[24] In his memoirs, Banastre Tarleton, the British cavalry commander, reluctantly admitted, "The King's troops did not come out of this skirmish unhurt."[25]

Cornwallis marched into the interior, away from coastal harbors where supplies were more easily provided by sea. Shocked, he found a different reaction from the population than expected. The "counties of Mecklinburg and Rohan were more hostile to England than any others in America. The vigilance and animosity of these surrounding districts checked the exertions of [our forces]," wrote a British officer. They "totally destroyed all communications between the King's troops and the loyalists in other parts of the province...intelligence [about] the continentals [is] totally unattainable."[26]

While Cornwallis marched through the Carolinas, Clinton and Arbuthnot suffered another prickly episode. The Admiral informed Clinton that he had appointed three ships to act as "victualers" for the British army in New York. The ships were assigned to bring supplies to the city from military supply depots in Halifax and Charleston. Clinton had requested such assistance. Two days after informing Clinton of plans to assign ships for army use, Arbuthnot requested "500 head of cattle for use of his fleet" from New York supplies until he could replenish them from the other depots. Clinton complied with the "requisition as far as [he] was able." Clinton expected ships to sail immediately and replace provisions given to the navy, but soon discovered the Admiral had ordered three army supply ships back to Halifax before they were unloaded. In a fit of anger, Clinton vigorously protested.[27] Only mildly concerned, Arbuthnot replied that he regretted the ships were sent back to Halifax, but otherwise exhibited no interest.[28]

While Clinton faced challenges in New York, Cornwallis' problems escalated. In a series of disasters between November 1 and the end of 1780, every element of Cornwallis' invincible forces – regulars, provincials, and the only Loyalist militia he ever counted on were defeated, not by American regulars, but by Patriot militia."[29] The tide of war turned against him. After leaving tidewater regions to march inland, Cornwallis suffered increased vulnerability to larger scale harassment by Patriot groups. He soon learned that the British Army without naval support was an easier victim than anticipated.

Clinton's reaction to Cornwallis' situation was the "unpromising turn, which our affairs took." What worried Clinton more was that matters showed no inclination to improve. Unfortunately "furnishing the enemy with plausible pretenses for crying victory, [encouraged] the whole country to flock to rebel arms," Clinton wrote.[30]

Cornwallis' command suffered more small wounds and was forced to return to a safe haven along the coast where the navy could provide supplies and reinforcements. But first he left North Carolina and headed to Winnsboro, South Carolina, in the north central part of the state, which he selected for winter quarters. Clinton was so concerned about Cornwallis' tactical situation that he ordered reinforcements under the command of Major General Leslie south to join Cornwallis.[31]

Logistical problems plagued Cornwallis' forces, and they barely survived, a devastating experience.[32] The fit for duty numbers decreased, effective communication exchanges "worsened," and his intelligence gathering capability "collapsed." Cornwallis' fighting capability was reduced to a fraction of its previous potential.[33]

The lack of logistical support and diminishing forces forced Cornwallis to leave Winnsboro and South Carolina on January 7, 1781. Meanwhile, Continental Army Major General Nathanael Greene arrived in Charlotte, North Carolina, to construct a third Southern Command. Cornwallis decided to go after Greene. With sound reasoning, but false assumptions, Cornwallis moved north to attack. One big mistake was his false assumption that Loyalist forces intended to join and help dampen Patriot morale, which was encouraged by Greene's presence. Cornwallis' tactical objective was to prevent Greene's paltry army from becoming a serious threat. With Greene defeated, Cornwallis felt control of North and South Carolina was an easy task.

Adding to Cornwallis' good humor was intelligence indicating Greene had split his forces and sent Brigadier General Daniel Morgan in a separate westerly direction – a military blunder, Cornwallis felt, offering an immense opportunity to smash both rebel forces. In his optimism, Cornwallis ignored the fact that his forces were actually split in three. While retaining the main British force under his direct command, Cornwallis sent his best cavalry officer, Banister Tarleton, to challenge Morgan. The third force commanded by General Leslie was still on the march to join Cornwallis.

Cornwallis' forces traveled through Patriot country where rebel militia delighted in attacking British foraging parties, supply trains, intercepting dispatch riders, and generally disrupting communications between his separated forces. Even with all these threats Cornwallis could not ignore an opportunity to inflict what he considered Morgan's certain defeat.[34]

Cornwallis sent a detachment north to the Cape Fear River in North Carolina with the objective of using waterways to transport supplies, effectively splitting his army into four. Around the same time, an express dispatch was sent to Clinton in New York requesting an order to send a force from Virginia against Greene's rear. Clinton responded by sending Benedict Arnold from northern Virginia on harassing raids, hoping Greene would divert troops and go after the hated traitor, while Cornwallis chased Greene.[35]

As Tarleton rode toward Morgan, communications with Cornwallis were unreliable. It was difficult to keep timely intelligence flowing between the two camps when both constantly moved.

General Leslie reached Rocky Mount, North Carolina, on Jan 14, 1781. Two days later Cornwallis arrived at Hillhouse's Plantation where he waited for a junction with Leslie. Cornwallis expected momentarily to receive Tarleton's report of Morgan's defeat. He was already planning ahead.

On Jan 17, 1781, Tarleton, in full pursuit, reached Morgan.[36] Morgan arrived at Hannah's Cowpens, South Carolina, on Jan 16, 1781.[37] The next day Tarleton attacked; the outcome was a resounding American victory. Even more shocking was the extensive British manpower loss, something not easily replaced. "I fear about four hundred of the infantry are killed, wounded, or taken," Cornwallis reported to Clinton. "It is impossible to foresee all the consequences that this unexpected and extraordinary action may produce."[38] More important than the devastating effect on British morale, the defeat ended any possibility of a significant Loyalist force rising to join Cornwallis.

On Jan 18, 1781, General Leslie joined Cornwallis a few hours after Tarleton reported his defeat. With Leslie's arrival and Tarleton's return Cornwallis had about 2,400 men. At 8:00 a.m. on Jan 19, 1781, Cornwallis made a tactical decision – he started after Morgan in a desperate attempt to regain some reputation and free Morgan's captives. Faulty intelligence started him on the wrong road, but on January 21, 1781, Cornwallis learned that Morgan was only a day ahead. "I shall march tomorrow with 1200 Infantry & Cavalry to attack or follow him [Morgan] to the banks of the Catawba," he wrote. When Cornwallis reached the Little Catawba River, Morgan was already across.

At the beginning of Cornwallis' chase, serious delays were caused by burdensome baggage wagons and cannon. To increase speed, Cornwallis left the wagons and guns behind. Once free of baggage, he tried to catch Morgan by forced marches, but torrential rains made roads and streams almost impossible to travel or cross. Finally, Cornwallis reached the river, but was forced to stop and wait for the baggage to catch up.

Rains made the river impossible to ford. Cornwallis had failed miserably in a desperate effort to catch Morgan and now considered the consequences. On January 25, he notified a subordinate officer, "My situation is most critical. I see infinite danger in proceeding, but certain ruin in retreating. I am therefore determined to go on, unless some misfortune should happen.[39]

For three days, Cornwallis remained at Ramsour's Mills, attempted to re-provision his impoverished forces, and tried to avoid being the prey rather than the hunter. Cornwallis was aware that American forces in the area increased at alarming rates. Isolated in hostile territory, far from reinforcements, he adopted a defensive maneuver. For the foreseeable future, his objective was to avoid the fate of General Patrick Ferguson at Kings Mountain the year before. Desperate to gain mobility and speed, after the baggage arrived he burned most of his wagons and finally departed on January 28, 1781.[40]

On the other side of the Catawba River, Morgan observed the enemy. After the river receded, Cornwallis crossed the Catawaba on February 1, 1781,[41] and again unsuccessfully pursued Morgan. Morgan reached Guilford Courthouse and awaited the arrival of Greene.[42] Cornwallis was 12 hours late reaching the Dan River after he crossed the Catawaba. By then Greene and Morgan had joined and were safely in Virginia.

Cornwallis' unsuccessful pursuit had a devastating effect on the British Army. They were worn out and nearly out of provisions. Realizing the futility of his actions, Cornwallis decided to turn back into North Carolina and headed to Hillsboro, the capital.[43] With illusionary expectations, Cornwallis waited for reinforcements from a large body of Loyalists, which did not materialize, to his chagrin. In the meantime Greene sent forces into North Carolina to engage in harassment activities.[44] When Cornwallis departed Hillsboro on February 25, 1781, Greene's forces were less than twenty miles away. Greene avoided an action, while Cornwallis made every effort to engage, still convinced he would decisively defeat Greene. Both armies suffered extreme hardships during extensive maneuvering, but the British toll was irreplaceable.[45]

When Clinton received notification of the Cowpens defeat, he wrote prophetically, "I am most exceedingly concerned [by] the unfortunate affair of the 17th January. From the account...I confess I dread the consequences."[46] At the time Clinton was unclear of Cornwallis' situation. His headquarters filled with rumors of Cornwallis' advance into Virginia in pursuit of Morgan and Greene. The rumors all favored the British by suggesting disastrous results for the Americans.[47]

Greene took a position at Guilford Courthouse on March 14, 1781, with forces superior in number to Cornwallis.[48] Informed that Greene outnumbered him, Cornwallis was still confident British forces would inflict a crushing defeat, and effectively end organized rebel resistance in the south. Determined and arrogant, Cornwallis headed toward Greene. In the ensuing battle, Cornwallis demonstrated great tactical maneuvering and won a victory at Guilford Court House against Greene, but he paid an excessive price in manpower with further depletion of his army. The victory proved a strategic disaster. "Another such victory would ruin the British army," wrote a British politician.[49]

It was now March 18, 1781, and Cornwallis began an agonizing move from Guilford Court House to Cross Creek at the head of the Cape Fear River. For unknown reasons, he still expected Loyalist assistance which never materialized. In Cross Creek "Provisions were scarce." Almost immediately he left and headed down the west side of the Cape Fear River, reaching "the evirons of Wilmington, North Carolina on April 7."

At Guilford Court House Cornwallis had faced the third American southern command in a year. In reports to General Clinton, he described his "satisfaction of informing...our military operations were uniformly successful; and the victory at Guilford, though one of the bloodiest of this war, was very complete." In tactical terms Greene had destroyed Cornwallis' ability to carry out further effective military operations in the Carolinas. After revealing the battle's details, Cornwallis abruptly changed the subject. "I am very anxious to receive Your Excellency's commands." He was "totally in the dark [of] the intended operations of the summer." My own wishes are that "the Chesapeake may become the seat of war, [even] at the expence of abandoning New York." Cornwallis was convinced, "Until Virginia is [under control], our hold of the Carolinas [is] difficult if not precarious."[50]

The distance between Cornwallis and Clinton effectively resulted in separate commands. Differing on a wide range of issues and priorities, each officer saw the war unfolding from a different perspective and with different opportunities. Although Clinton was Cornwallis' superior, there was no practical way for him to control British tactical operations in the south. Each man's strategic views were shaped by local conditions; the other's situation was remote and sometimes misunderstood. From a British perspective, prosecution of the American war had reached a critical stage and the two senior British commanders held very different views on future military operations. Also in the mix was disparity about the military value of the Carolinas and New York. Cornwallis favored retention of Carolina and Georgia seaports, while implementing a tactical operation to subdue Virginia. Clinton was convinced the rebellion would collapse in a few months and the key to success was to hold New York.

Communication difficulties minimized British attempts to execute a comprehensive military plan. The ability to respond to tactical opportunities and concentrate forces required communication heavily dependent on the British Navy, a communications conduit along the eastern seaboard. But the personal relationship between Clinton and Arbuthnot constrained such cooperation. They neither liked nor trusted each other. The personal animosities between the three senior British commanders severely restricted employment of an effective unity of command. When they did work in unity, it was usually too late.

Cornwallis complained that Clinton's orders did not reach him in a timely fashion and he never knew what was expected until too late. But Cornwallis learned to use delays in communication exchanges as an excuse to justify executing his preferred strategy and tactics, even if different from Clinton. Any orders from Clinton questioning tactical moves could easily be designated out of date by the time they reached Cornwallis. "It is very disagreeable to me to decide upon measures so very important, and of such consequence to the general conduct of the war, without Your Excellency's directions," he wrote Clinton. "[I find] the delay and difficulty conveying letters [then] waiting for answers," make it extremely difficult to carry on operations. "I have experienced the dangers and distresses of marching...hundreds of miles in a country chiefly hostile, without one active or useful friend, without intelligence, and without communication with any part of the country. The situation in which I leave South Carolina adds much to my anxiety."[51] Cornwallis did not indicate a move into Virginia, but the next day, April 24, he notified General Phillips of his march to the Chesapeake to assume command of British troops.[52] Later when Clinton found that Cornwallis was in Virginia at the expense of the Carolinas and Georgia he described the move as, "the fatal resolution of abandoning both Carolinas to their fate and flying into Virginia."[53]

Clinton had little doubt the rebellion was in "its last gasp" and if the British escaped any serious setbacks they could expect "the most decisive victory." He was convinced the French suffered financial difficulties and would "not assist beyond 1781."[54]

For almost a year Cornwallis operated as an independent command. He made strategic and tactical decisions based on his judgment without any superior officer providing input.[55] On April 25, 1781, Cornwallis "left Wilmington, [North Carolina] with one thousand four hundred thirty-five rank and file present and fit for duty." On May 10, 1781, he reached Halifax, North Carolina, and on May 13 he crossed the Roanoke River a few miles below the Virginia Border.[56] Cornwallis still did not notify Clinton of his progress. He sensed that Clinton did not approve of abandoning the Carolinas for his trek into Virginia, but he was convinced Clinton did not grasp the geo-politics involved. With arrogance reinforced by a lengthy independence, he marched into Virginia. Later he explained, "The delay and difficulty of conveying letters, and...waiting for answers," justified his move.[57]

After Cornwallis moved into Virginia, he headed toward Petersburg, arriving there on May 20, 1781. Five days before, General Phillips had died and was replaced by Benedict Arnold, someone Cornwallis did not respect as a senior officer. Shortly after Cornwallis took command, Arnold left for New York to join Clinton.[58] With the junction of the two British armies and some reinforcements Cornwallis had, "seven thousand effectives."[59] This was more than enough, Cornwallis felt, to justify his move north to consolidate forces. He was convinced he now had an army to subdue Virginia, cut the rebellious colonies in half, and defeat any attempt by enemy forces to challenge his intentions.

On May 20, Cornwallis received a letter from Clinton addressed to General Phillips dated March 14, which indicated Clinton was fully aware that disastrous communication exchanges influenced British fortunes of war. He told Phillips he "will see that the want of intelligence has again lost us a fair opportunity of giving a mortal blow."[60]

Cornwallis now began the final and most inglorious chapter of his military career in North America.

❖ 10 ❖

Opportunity from Action

*The injury done my Country, and the chains of
Slavery forgeing for posterity, calls me fourth to
defend our common rights, and repel the bold
invaders of the Sons of Freedom.*

Washington's method of operation with distant commanders was effective: they were on their own, but not alone.

After Continental Army Major General Nathanael Greene reached Virginia in November 1780, he spent a short time reviewing the military situation. He found chaos, confusion, and incompetence dominating a dismal military scene. Under the deplorable circumstances, he expected little, and he worried about the effect of failure on his personal life:

> I cannot contemplate my own situation without the greatest degree of anxiety. I am far removed from almost all my friends and connections; and have to prosecute a war in a Country in the best state, attended with almost insurmountable difficulties, but doubly so now from the state of our finances and the loss of public credit. How I shall be able to support myself under all these embarrassments God only knows. My only consolation is, that if I fail I hope it will not be accompanied with any peculiar marks of personal disgrace. Censure and reproach ever follow the unfortunate. This I expect if I don't succeed; and it is only in the degree not in the entire freedom that I console myself. The ruin of my family is what hangs most heavy upon my mind. My fortune is small; and misfortune or disgrace to me, must bring ruin to them.[1]

But Greene's despair did not translate into less effort; he continued on to North Carolina.

To his shock and dismay, Greene found the military situation in North Carolina even more distressing than Virginia. Everything in Carolina was strange – the people, the culture. It was a foreign land inhabited by persons who might as well be Europeans, except for one redeeming feature. They spoke a version of English he could understand, although at times, local expressions were difficult to comprehend.

"On my arrival here I find nothing but the Shadow of an Army in the midst of Distress," he informed the governor of North Carolina.[2] He sent a more depressing account to his wife Catherine:

> My dear
>
>   I arrived here the 2d of this month and have been in search of the Army I am to command; but without much success; having found nothing but a few half starved Soldiers who are remarkable for nothing but poverty and distress. But I am in hopes matters will mend. I am in good health and good spirits; and am unhappy for nothing except the seperation from you and the rest of my friends. Pray write me where you are, and how you do. It will give me great pleasure to hear from you. My love to all friends. Yours aff
>
>   N Greene[3]

His first full report from North Carolina indicated shock and despair at the appalling conditions. At one point, he considered the situation beyond repair, and described the situation to Washington:

> Nothing can be more wretched and distressing than the condition of the troops, starving with cold and hunger, without tents and camp equipage. Those of the Virginia line are literally naked, and a great part totally unfit for any kind of duty, and must remain so untill clothing can be had from the Northward. I have written to Governor Jefferson not to send forward any more untill they are well cloathed and properly equipped.
>
>   As I expected, so I find the great bodies of militia that have been in the field and the manner in which they came out, being all on horse back, has laid waste all the Country in such a manner that I am really afraid it will be impossible to subsist the few troops we have; and if we can be subsisted at all, it must be by moving to the provisions, for they have no way of bringing it to the army.[4]

Greene was also concerned at the lack of support from the local population. He continued his report by noting, "The inhabitants of this country are too remote from one another to be animated into great exertions; and the people appear notwithstanding their danger, very intent upon their own private affairs."[5]

The partisan forces in the field were divided into two groups, those "whose cases are desperate" after they lost their homes and the others who were only "allured by the hopes of plunder."[6]

Washington sensed the agonizing despair in Greene's report, but could do little except offer appreciation for Greene's efforts. The weight of this lonely command rested solely on Greene's shoulders. "Your difficulties I am persuaded are great – they may be insurmountable – but you see them now through a different medium than you have ever done before." While "your friends...expect everything from your abilities," Washington wrote, "[they] know full well the deranged situation of our southern affairs." Assuring that no one expected the impossible, he added, "I therefore think that you have nothing to apprehend on the score of public dissatisfaction – on the contrary, that you may gain, [and not] lose in your military reputation."[7]

Earlier, in 1775, Greene wrote to his wife Catherine explaining what compelled him to serve:

> My Dear Wife   Providence, June 2, 1775
>
> I am this moment going to set of for Camp, haveing been detain by the Committee of Safety till now. I have recommended you to the care of my brethren; direct your conduct by their advice, unless they should so far forget their affection for me as to request anything unworthy of you to comply with....
>
> I have not so much in my mind that wounds my peace, as the seperation from you. My bosom is knoted to yours by all the gentle feelings that inspire the softest sentiments of conjugal Love. It had been happy for me if I could have lived a private life in peace and plenty, enjoying all the happiness that results from a well-tempered society, founded on mutual esteem....
>
> But the injury done my Country, and the chains of Slavery forgeing for posterity, calls me fourth to defend our common rights, and repel the bold invaders of the Sons of Freedom. The cause is the cause of God and man. Slavery shuts up every avenue that leads to knowledge, and leaves the soul ignorant of its own importance; it is rendered incapable of promoting human happiness, piety or virtue; and he that betrays that trust, being once acquainted with the pleasure and advantages of Knowledge and freedom, is guilty of a spiritual suicide. I am determined to defend my rights and maintain my freedom, or sell my life in the attempt; and I hope the righteous God that rules the World will Bless the Armies of America, and receive the spirits of those whose lot it is to fall.... I commend you and myself; and am, with truest regard, your loving husband
>
> N Greene[8]

Washington made every effort to keep Greene informed, but over such a distance it was rarely satisfactory. Once Lafayette reached Virginia, he served as an information conduit between Washington and Greene, and the speed of communication exchanges improved from deplorable to poor.

On June 21, 1781, Washington updated Greene on a variety of military situations, including the meeting with Rochambeau and the decision to assault New York. But first he addressed some of Greene's personal concerns revealed in previous correspondence. "The difficulties which you daily encounter...with your small force are a credit to your reputation." If he withdrew "from south and even North Carolina," Washington assured, "it will not be attributed to either your lack of ability or effort...the true cause [will be a] want of means of support." As far as the defeat "before Campden, after it seemed in your favor... I hope you will have found the enemy suffered severely," as they reported in a New York paper.[9]

At Headquarters in New York, Washington and Rochambeau exchanged a series of pivotal letters. Intelligence flowed to Washington from Lafayette and was immediately relayed to Rochambeau. "Lord Cornwallis had formed a junction with General Arnold at Petersburg," Lafayette wrote, and "a number of Transports had arrived in Hampton Road." He assumed they "were the same which sailed from New York the 13th. of May." Lafayette's steady supply of intelligence encouraged Washington to press for action. "The strides which the Enemy are making to the southward demand a collection of our force in this quarter," and a start of our operations, he wrote to Rochambeau. "I know of no [action] so likely to afford relief to the southern States in so short a time as a serious menace against New York."[10]

While acknowledging other possibilities under contingent circumstances, Washington still expressed enthusiasm for an attack against New York. His two most compelling arguments were that the British garrison was weakened by forces sent to Virginia and second, that a concerted effort against New York would certainly relieve pressure on the Continental Army's southern command by forcing reinforcements to return to New York. But Washington soon found any campaign faced a major hurdle, lack of money. No one with stature and experience administered the army's financial affairs.

The French, dismayed by the lack of financial administration, insisted that Congress appoint Robert Morris the Superintendent of Finance. Previous financial affairs were contaminated by incompetence and corruption. Washington knew future military activities depended on proficient financial management. Without the right person and organization, military financial affairs were certain to collapse. Such an obvious state of finances convinced the British that the rebellion was about to dissolve.

Washington accepted Morris as the right individual. "My hand and heart shall be with you, and as far as my assistance will or can go, command it" and "I will aid your endeavors to the extent of my abilities," Washington wrote.[11]

An earlier Congressional appointment also had impact. On September 22, 1780, Timothy Pickering "assumed the duties of Quartermaster General with the main army." Lack of funds had contributed significantly to the mutinies Washington faced in January 1781, and made Pickering's job impossible.[12] His problems were not only a lack of funds, but organization, and he used the rest of 1780 to complete the Quartermaster Department's reorganization.[13] Finally, rudimentary management organizations existed for finances and supplies. In additional moves, Congress strengthened the army's line organization. Washington issued General Orders and announced a number of Resolves passed by Congress, including procedures for promotions within the

Continental Army.[14] Washington was delighted and considered the promotional resolves a big step forward. Although not everything he wanted, previously unclear issues, which had spawned contentious encounters between officers and states, were clarified.

Good news continued to arrive. An excited Washington received, by express courier, intelligence of Admiral de Grasse's arrival in the West Indies on the way to North American waters. He immediately notified Rochambeau, requesting any further information the general received, about arrival time and fleet size. With all this good news descending at one time, Washington reexamined the ramifications of De Grasse's arrival. "Accounts from Virginia are exceedingly alarming," he wrote to Rochambeau. "The enemy [has] concentrated their force [and] are marching thro' the State almost without control." Unfortunately, "the Body of Men under the command of the Marquis de la Fayette [is] too small to give effectual opposition."[15] But Washington still held out hope that an immediate attack on New York was the fastest way to alleviate British pressure in the South.

In an irony of perception, Rochambeau viewed Washington's justification as a strong case to bypass New York and directly attack the south. Despite his tactical zeal for New York, Washington maintained a strategic vision and continued to send reinforcements and materiel south. "Sensible of the pressing exigencies of the Southern States, [I have ordered] seven Battalions of Infantry [and a] Corps of Horse and Artillery to be raised" and sent to Virginia, he wrote to a Virginia congressional delegate. He wished it were "in our power to give more immediate and powerful assistance. I will still attempt to use the means intrusted to me [and] expel the Enemy, from every part of the United States possible."[16]

Once news of Admiral de Grasse's arrival was confirmed, the entire allied high command sensed opportunities to change the war's direction. But opportunities only existed for a limited time, and required financial and material support.

Although Timothy Pickering was appointed Quartermaster General, the prime mover was Washington. Pickering realized that only the commander-in-chief had sufficient influence to move states and Congress to action and he was perfectly content to work under Washington's umbrella. With grim determination the commander-in-chief personally dissected logistical problems. But he recognized the need to engage his Quartermaster General. His objective was to prepare the ground for Pickering's influence. Anyone contacted by the Quartermaster General should accept that he represented Washington's desires. He ordered Pickering to assemble transportation. If "there is anything in my power which [can hurry] this…necessary business, I wish to be informed." All measures would be taken to help. "I wish you [to inform me how] Arms and accoutrements" are to be transported "to the Southward." This matter is "of the greatest consequence to the Southern States, which are in danger of being over run for the want of Arms."[17] Stockpiles of supplies existed for the Continental Army, but a lack of transportation denied deployment. Movement of Allied forces en masse created an unprecedented demand for transportation vehicles.

Washington focused on acquiring provisions and transportation. He urged General Heath in New England not to "relax your [efforts] until the great objects of Your Mission are fully accomplished." The plan of the next "Campaign is now settled upon the presumption of [success, and] a failure in the smallest degree" will place "us in the deepest distress." General Heath's influence in the New England States helped Washington pressure state legislatures. "As to summer Cloathing, I request you to make known to the States, that almost every article in the public Store [has] been sent...to the Southern Army," Washington wrote. Without those stores the troops are "literally naked." In desperation, Washington ordered Heath to forward a "quantity of Cloathing (about 2000 Suits)" which had arrived "at Boston from Spain." To make certain nothing was pilfered, the shipment would go in original and unopened packages to the Quartermaster General for transport. With unusual attention to detail, Washington ordered Heath, if "teams cannot be procured [for everything], at least 1000 Suits compleat with the same number of Hats and a proportion of Serjeants Coats must be sent on; the Coats, Waistcoats, and Breeches should be divided by their size, into three distinct parcels, [and] marked accordingly. I expect your personal attention on this matter."[18]

Next Washington contacted Governor Thomas Jefferson, who earlier had tried to get Washington to come south and aid his mother country, Virginia. Washington acknowledged enemy action in Virginia was "very alarming," but "my presence is essential" here for operations with allies. He informed Jefferson of enormous drawbacks to moving a sizable military force from the north to Virginia. Without "command of the Water it would be next to impossible for us to transport the Artillery, Baggage, and Stores so great a distance." All these issues were raised previously with Rochambeau, but now Washington unloaded on Jefferson. Losses would approach "at least one third of our force by desertion, Sickness, and the heats of the approaching Season even if it could done." For Washington the only acceptable military rationale to move south was for the British to "evacuate New York and transfer the whole war to the Southward." Without sea power Washington argued, the only possibility for them to relieve pressure in the south was by a "diversion" against New York.[19]

In the meantime, Brigadier General Anthony Wayne's forces arrived in Virginia, after a difficult and tedious march with both incident and drama. Washington congratulated Wayne, but questioned a rumor about the "good

Order and Discipline." A story circulated at Headquarters of another mutiny in the Pennsylvania Line at York Town (Pennsylvania), before they journeyed south. The slightest suggestion of mutiny in the Continental Army received the commander-in-chief's immediate attention. Washington still suffered aftershocks from the January mutinies. The rumor was true. Some soldiers refused to continue and prodded others to join their refusal, but without hesitation Wayne shot, bayoneted, and hanged the mutineers; then he marched the "Line by Divisions around the Dead." The next day the Pennsylvanians marched south "Mute as Fish."[20]

On June 9, 1781, Rochambeau's forces moved to join Washington for a possible assault on New York City.[21] When the French left Newport, in a display of camaraderie and friendship, its citizens saluted them with a memorial. "We reflect with the deepest feelings of gratitude upon the harmony and friendship which has existed between the army and citizens of this town, which were the natural results" of the wisdom "which your Excellency has shown in his conduct on all occasions," expressed by the citizens of Newport to Rochmbeau.[22] The fraternity, frivolity and deep feelings of the departure took on a ceremonious air when "the officers, the soldiers, American men, American women, all mixed together in a dance. It was the Festival of Equality."[23] Initial skepticism by the citizens of Newport had turned to near adulation when they departed for New York. General Rochambeau and the whole French army had worked to build a favorable American perception. A man of many talents, Rochambeau's sensitivity toward his American allies was a catalyst promoting Allied unity later during the Yorktown campaign.

As Washington and Rochambeau built a closer relationship, a danger of clashing egos was always present. A crucial by-product of their association was the evolution of mutual respect. Each man actually liked the other and developed an uncanny appreciation of the other's temperament, position, and responsibilities. Once established, their relationship, although challenged at times, was the bedrock of allied success. For the balance of the war this unique relationship drove events, contributing to the success.

Rochambeau never shared Washington's passion for an assault on New York. Even during the beginning of serious discussions with Washington about joint Allied operations, the French General was obediently lukewarm when the subject of an assault on New York was raised. His official communications supported such an enterprise, but in private he expressed reluctance. Politics of command left Rochambeau a narrow path to maneuver between Washington's ardent desire for New York and the French general's reservations. Rochambeau applied slow persuasion to divert Washington. At one time during discussions, Washington casually expressed some qualifications that gave hope he might change interest in New York. At first he tried to change

Rochambeau's reservations by employing his own quiet persuasion. Washington not only was convinced New York was the most important target, it was inconceivable that any other option was more than a poor second. The two commanders jousted for position and influence to incorporate their preferences for the next campaign. While Washington reached a state of frustration from the passive resistance Rochambeau projected for New York, he had learned not to paint himself into a corner without some means of escape. The key in this debate was how to decide on one approach or the other without bruising egos. Rochambeau had observed Washington for almost a year and appreciated the limits of arguing with his commander-in-chief. From a propaganda view, it was essential that Washington appear as undisputed commander-in-chief of all allied military forces. Any apparent conflict within the chain of command, especially between French and Americans, projected a weak alliance, something demoralizing for morale and delightful for the enemy.

With intense interest, Washington observed and evaluated Rochambeau. The American cause depended entirely on continued French participation and the personal support of Rochambeau. Washington found Rochambeau no ordinary general. He demonstrated leadership charisma under the extreme difficulties of warfare in North America. In spite of occasional differences, Rochambeau never publicly challenged Washington or weakened the Alliance.

The pressing challenge was preparation of operational plans and to meld French and American forces into a tactical military operation. In May 1781, Rochambeau wrote to Admiral De Grasse and explained the situation in North America. He obliquely drew attention to the Chesapeake Bay area of Virginia, as an opportunity for a unified military effort. In the same correspondence Rochambeau evaluated New York as an opportunity with less than encouraging prospects.[24]

On June 12, 1781, Rochambeau notified Washington of a dispatch ready for transmission to Admiral De Grasse with notification "that your Excellency...desired my marching to the north river [to strengthen or even attack N Y] when the circumstances [are favorable]." Included was an estimate of garrison size in the city and Washington's preference for the assault on New York. He had informed the admiral "of the Enemy's naval forces and, it would be a great stroke to go to Chesapeake Bay" where the Admiral could do great things against the the enemy's naval forces there. Afterward, with favorable winds, the fleet could arrive in New York in two days. Rochmbeau notified De Grasse of the need for additional military forces and the desperate shortage of money, included to catch Washington's eye. Adroitly, Rochambeau requested Washington's review and asked if he cared to add anything to the dispatch.[25] "Your requisitions to the Count De Grasse, go to everything I could wish," Washington quickly replied.[26] But the correspondence reflected some change.

"Your Excellency will be pleased to recollect that New York was looked upon by us as the only practical object under present circumstances; but should we be able to secure...naval superiority, we may perhaps find others more practicable and equally advisable," Washington reminded Rochambeau. "I understand...you have in your communication to him, [De Grasse] confined our views to New York alone" but he suggested it would "be best to leave him judge, from the information he [receives of] the enemy's Fleet upon this Coast, which will be the most advantageous quarter for him to make an appearance."[27]

Some years later in his *Memoires,* Rochambeau admitted he advised the French Admiral to use his own judgment, but in his "private opinion [a] move against Cornwallis [was] the most practicable and least expected;" an opinion certain to influence De Grasse's sailing for the Chesapeake Bay. While there was no decision to abandon New York, a more flexible groundwork existed to allow an alternative: avoiding perceptions that Washington's only passion was New York.

Washington was deeply concerned about a French convoy of 15 ships sent ahead by Admiral De Grasse. The ships contained six hundred and ninety recruits along with all-important cash. Washington had no intelligence of their whereabouts. In fact part of the fleet had arrived at Boston on June 11, but the information had not yet reached Washington's headquarters. The rest of the fleet was dispersed by a gale, but arrived soon, and Washington breathed a sigh of relief.[28]

More good news arrived from General Greene describing success in the south, especially by partisan forces under his command. On May 14, Greene informed President Samuel Huntington detailing the actions and forwarded a copy to Washington. In a separate letter to the commander-in-chief Greene registered "distress" at Cornwallis's move north. "I hope to God our affairs may not be reduced to extremity in Virginia."[29] Washington was elated over Greene's successes and described them in General Orders of June 15. "These brilliant repeated successes which reflect so much glory on the Southern army will be attended with the most important consequences to those States." They "are a happy presage of our [ability] to expel the Enemy from every part of the Continent, with proper exertions." Now, an entirely new optimism entered Washington's correspondence.[30]

Immediately Washington sent the news of Greene's successes to Rochambeau, and included statements of a serious change in strategic focus. "The consequences will be important, but they would be more so, had we a sufficient force in [the south] to pursue the advantages we have gained." All of a sudden, the Chesapeake area dominated Washington's discussions. He wanted a French naval force – a "50 Gun ship [to] take a position with security in Chesapeak Bay, it would be of the utmost importance at this moment,

[and] would effectively prevent a reunion of the Enemy's forces." It would prevent "those in Virginia from receiving any supplies by water." They would suffer "great difficulties and distresses," he informed Rochambeau. Washington avoided a perception of interference, taking care to only "mention this as an Idea which has struck me, not as a matter which I would undertake to advise, unacquainted as I am with naval affairs." But Rochambeau determined that Washington's attention was shifting to Virginia.[31]

On June 15, Washington received word that Rochambeau made every effort to join him, as expeditiously as possible. In return he thanked Rochambeau for his "Zeal and Wish to join the Army under my Command," and revealed the latest intelligence of British movements around New York. "By Information received from the Enemy at N York It seems they are taking a position not far from East Chester," and "marking out an Encampment. This Movement I conjecture [is designed to cover] their Foraging Parties, which will probably at this Season be very busily employed." He offered new intelligence, just received, about a British fleet "bound for the Coasts of America" and if true, "the Enemy may give us much Trouble in the Southern Quarter, [unless] they are seriously opposed in Force, or their Intentions Diverted."[32]

More good news arrived from further south. On May 9, 1781, in British Florida a military action occurred with significant influence on Allied operations. Spanish forces commanded by General Bernardo de Galvez captured Pensacola. Galvez began operations in New Orleans and marched across the Gulf Coast, capturing the cities of Mobile and Pensacola. The British deployed land and sea forces against Spanish intrusions along the Gulf coast to protect commercial interests in the West Indies. Later, however, the British claimed General Galvez's success was against depleted regiments, "composed principally of Germans, condemned criminals, and other species of gaol-birds."[33] For the allies, however, Galvez's action diverted British military assets from reinforcing units to the North. "Sir: I wish the greatest pleasure [to] congratulate you on the success of His Catholic Majesty's Arms at Pensacola," Washington wrote to Senor Francisco Rendon, who represented Spain to the Continental Congress. He further added that a review "of the particulars will reflect much honor upon General Don Galvez and the troops under his command."[34]

Rochambeau's forces headed south for a junction with Washington. While the plan still was an attack on New York, the contingencies associated with Admiral De Grasse's arrival reduced the certainty.[35] Rochambeau reported his advance units were in Hartford, Connecticut, on June 22, and would remain there for several days, repairing vehicles and "to rest the young artillery horses and oxen."[36] Washington expressed "Pleasure [at] the progress you make in the march of the Troops under your command, and your Intention to come to my Camp in Person, from Hartford. Be assured, Sir I shall be very happy to see you whenever you arrive."[37] Washington reminded Rochambeau of the inherent dangers of acting on intelligence reports alone. "I informed you of the Intelligence I had received of the Arrival of a large Reinforcement from England, at Chesapeak Bay. I have good Reason now to believe" the information was not correct "having since received Letters from Congress, and others of much later date, in which nothing has been mentioned." Unfortunately, "My Intelligence from the Southward is too vague and uncertain to communicate to your Excellency."[38]

Rochambeau's forces continued south, arriving at Newton, Connecticut, on June 28 where they remained through June 30.[39] The French described Newton as a "capital of the Tory country [with] much poverty there among the inhabitants."[40] Washington sent an aide to assist and lead the French to his camp.[41] When the aide arrived, he revealed the Americans had already "started a campaign," wrote a French soldier. Rochambeaus ordered us forward "to serve in America as Auxiliary troops under the supreme command of the American generalissimo."[42] Washington informed Rocahambeau that, "It would have given me the greatest pleasure" to come to Newton, but he expected "His Excellency the Chev. de la Luzerne" to arrive any moment."[43] Luzerne, the French Minister, resided in Philadelphia and "exerted great influence on American affairs, especially in regard to [the French Alliance]."[44]

The General Orders of June 27 proclaimed, "The Commander in Chief has the pleasure of announcing to the Army the approach of the troops of his most Christian Majesty under the Command of his Excellency Lieutenant General Count de Rochambeau." Washington felt it unnecessary "to recommend to the officers and Soldiers of the American Army" how vital "is a cultivation of acquaintance and friendship with our generous Allies." He also hoped for "a nobler motive, Gratitude."[45]

In correspondence dated June 29, Washington finally acknowledged that his passion for an attack on New York had faded. "I am every day more and more dubious of our being able to carry into execution the operation...not only [because of inadequate] number of Men, but from information which I have just received from the Minister of France." The British had sent reinforcements "of between three and four thousand Men [to] Charles town [South Carolina], the remainder are intended for Augustine [Florida] and New York," Washington informed Brigadier General Henry Knox.

"My dear Marquis: The last letter I have had the pleasure of receiving from you is dated" June 3, 1781, Washington wrote to Lafayette. "I have since received a thousand rumors of your situation;" none of them seemed reliable. "I fear some of your letters have miscarried. [Based on your] usual punctuality, I am certain you must have written." The next letter, he hoped "will confirm the accounts which I have...that Lord Cornwallis had retreated to the south side of the James River." Previous correspondence, Washington wrote, had informed him of, "our general plan; particulars I dare not enter into [until] I am assured…there is no danger of my letters falling" into enemy hands.[46]

The approach of French forces to form a junction was an event Washington relished. The General Orders of June 30, 1781, expressed optimism and expectations. The "American Line [should be] as full and…respectable as" possible, Washington wrote. The "General is desirous of showing all the Respect in his power to those Generous Allies who are hastening with the Zeal of Friends and the ardor of Soldiers to share with us the fatigues and dangers of the Campaign."[47]

While Washington waited, the British made a move which rekindled his zeal to attack New York. Intelligence reports generated unusual excitement. "The enemy, by sending a detachment into Monmouth County in Jersey to collect Horses, Cattle and other plunder, have so weakened their posts upon the North end of York Island that a most favorable opportunity seems at this moment to present itself," Washington informed Rochambeau. A surprise attack, "if it succeeds, will be of the utmost consequence to our future operations…[I intend] to make the attempt on the night of [July 2]." Since his forces were too small to "maintain an advantage should we gain it, I must [request] your Excellency to put your first Brigade under march tomorrow Morning…the remaining Troops to follow as quick as possible."

Washington continued: "There is another matter which appears to me exceedingly practicable. [On] the same night that we attempt [to take] the Works on York Island," he wanted to use "the Duke De Lauzun" in Rochambeau's command, "provided his Corps can be brought up" in time. He intended to "surprise" a British "Corps of Light Troops" presently camped "at Morrisania." In order to succeed, he needed cavalry and "the Duke…will be joined by Col. Sheldon with 200 Horse" and shortly "by about 400 Infantry" who were "perfectly acquainted with the Country." He requested that Rocambeau "order the Duke [to] march tomorrow morning and to reach Bedford" no later than the evening of July 2. "I shall move down with the remainder of this Army towards Kingsbridge and shall be ready to form a junction with your Excellency below at some point," to be agreed upon later.[48]

"The success of the Enterprise" depended on "a Sudden Surprise of the Posts" at night. Although there was "a good Probability of Succeeding," Washington took precautions. "I have directed" Major General Benjamin Lincoln to personally survey "the Enemy," and determine "by any Means in his Power" what are "their probable Strength and Numbers." Then he was charged to estimate the "probable Success or Failure." If he obtained "Information of the Enemy's Position and Strength" and decided against "the Attempt on their Posts; he [is to] form a Covering Party [for] the Duke de Lauzun." He finished with, "[Your] Excellency may depend on being regularly advised."[49]

❖ 11 ❖

A First Unity of Action

The French army and we are in the most perfect harmony, it extends from the Commander in Chief down to the lowest sentinel

Washington needed a successful outcome in his first action with French allies, after the dismal failures of previous attempts at a unity of action. Americans, as a whole, were unconvinced of the benefits from a French association. Now came the first allied action, small as it was, with Washington in command of operations. Although strict secrecy was maintained to insure surprise, the action failed. But the failure served a purpose.

On July 2 Brigadier General Benjamin Lincoln landed amphibious forces at the northern tip of Manhattan Island; unfortunately the landing was discovered before operations were completed. The only success was an orderly allied disengagement. As usual Washington quickly emphasized benefits. "The operation of this day are over," Washington informed Rochambeau. "I am sorry to say, [the operation did not] succeed to my Wishes," but hopefully added a "very essential Benefit will result to our future Operations."[1]

To General Lincoln and the troops who carried out the assault, Washington wrote, how "extremely pleased with the regularity and order with which the late movement was performed." He did not remember "a march where discipline was more strictly observed."[2]

After the French arrived in Newport, the British worked incessantly for more than a year to fortify New York and its harbor. Well-trained engineers designed and constructed fortifications against both land and sea assaults. At the time, British forces in the city numbered about 14,500. Rumors circulated in both French and American camps that the city was impregnable. Washington considered the rumors exaggerations, but after Lincoln's failed assault he wanted to personally observe these so called "impregnable defenses." A better idea was to invite Rochambeau and his staff. At a safe distance, the group traveled over a long front facing the city. With powerful telescopes, they observed defensive construction. Shielded by trees and natural terrain, they noted observations with diagrams and comments for future reference.

French engineers in Rochambeau's party were impressed. The latest designs and fortification technology were employed in construction. Washington was surprised at the detail, size, and breadth of enemy defenses. Reluctantly, he agreed that any attempt on New York needed forces far greater than available at the time. Greatly disappointed, Washington's passion for an assault against New York cooled.[3]

"I shall be happy to receive your Excellency with your Troops...on the Day after Tomorrow," Washington informed Rochambeau.[4] The Americans had prepared a French campsite about four miles from the village of White Plains, New York. Washington looked forward to meeting French forces and "conducting" them to camp.[5]

On July 6 the French arrived, after "a march of 22 miles." Allied armies came "together for the first time under the immediate command of their American chief."[6] The march was punishing, the heat excessive. "It is impossible to be more uncomfortable than we were that day," a French soldier wrote. We had "more than 400 [drop] from fatigue, and it was only by frequent halts and much care that we brought everyone into camp."[7]

The sacrifice and determination of French troops was not lost on Washington; the "General Orders" of July 6, 1781, showed this. "The Commander in Chief with pleasure embraces the earliest public opportunity of expressing his thanks to his Excellency the Count de Rochambeau for the unremitting Zeal with which he has [marched] to form the long wished for junction between the French and American Forces." He requested that, "his Excellency the Count to Convey to the Officers and Soldiers under his immediate command the grateful sense he entertains of the Chearfulness with which they have performed so Long and Laborious a march at this extreme hot Season."[8]

The junction's effect on esprit de corps and morale was vital. While both armies tried to maintain strict military appearance, this was a first opportunity for the majority of private soldiers in each army to observe the other. Concern had been expressed that a junction might result in contempt or ridicule between the allies. Officers under Washington and Rochambeau led by example with mutual admiration, but much depended on impressions formed by the common soldiers. All eyes strained to observe one another. Festivities abounded with military music and polished military protocol.

"General Washington came to [our camp]," a French soldier wrote. "He is a very fine-looking man...in the highest degree." Impressed by Washington's manners, he noted, "[They] are those of one perfectly accustomed to society, quite a rare thing certainly in America." General Washington, "dined with us, and later we escorted him several miles on his return."[9]

Washington is "Brave without temerity, laborious without ambition, generous without prodigality [and] noble without pride...[and] virtue without severity," wrote another French soldier.[10]

Both French and American headquarters were relieved and overjoyed by the camaraderie. The juncture was a public relations bonanza with many public officials and civilians witnessing the great link of allied armies. The "junction was made with great acclimation on the part of the Americans," Rochambeau reported. "We have made 220 miles in eleven days' march. There are not four provinces in the Kingdom of France where we could have traveled with as much order and economy, and without wanting for anything."[11]

American private soldiers fascinated the French. One French soldier noted "[they] have no regulation uniform, only perhaps the officers and some of the artillery. Some regiments have little white...fringed hunting tunics – the effect of which is quite agreeable. They all wear linen pantaloons, easy and comfortable especially during great heat." As to appearance, "American linen uniforms are very satisfactory in every way and are kept quite clean. This neatness is noticeable particularly among officers."[12] A few days later, on a visit to an American camp, one French officer offered his impression. "I was struck, not by its smart appearance, but by its destitution: the men were without uniforms and covered with rags; most of them were barefoot." He saw, "children who could not have been over fourteen [and] many Negroes, mulattoes, etc."[13] "Three-quarters of the Rhode Island regiment consists of negroes and that regiment is the most neatly dressed, the best under arms, and the most precise in its maneuvers," wrote another French officer.

"The French army and we are in the most perfect harmony, it extends from the Commander in Chief down to the lowest sentinel," reported an American soldier.[14] "The Junction of the two Armies is formed at this Place, & has commenced with high seeming Cordiality & Affection, demonstrated by constant acts of Conviviality & social Harmony."[15]

Allied celebrations continued and Washington received a steady stream of military reports from the south, along with appeals for help from Governors Thomas Jefferson of Virginia and John Rutledge of South Carolina. Precisely when Washington decided to move south is uncertain, but the decision was kept secret to keep the British convinced that New York remained an allied objective.

Earlier, on March 29, 1781, Admiral De Grasse wrote to Rochambeau of his planned North American arrival; not earlier than July 15, 1781. The letter arrived on June 9 during the junction celebrations and Rochambeau immediately informed Washington. Rochambeau replied, recommending arrival in the Chesapeake as soon as possible, for once there, the Admiral could evaluate opportunities to strike a blow before proceeding to New York.[16] Previously, Rochambeau had informed De Grasse of the desperate financial situation and requested "a loan of 1,200,000 francs" from the governor of Santo Domingo. The Admiral and one of his officers pledged their properties of considerable value on the island of Santo Domingo "for a loan to the Crown." To his shock the loan was denied. In an act of good faith, "A Spanish director general" interceded and offered "a draft [for] a far greater sum in Havana without guarantee."[17]

Rochambeau implored De Grasse to expedite a favorable reply. He assured the Admiral they would "take the earliest opportunity to continue our march [together with] General Washington [over land to join you] at any stipulated part of the Chesapeake."[18]

More good news arrived from the south. "The enemy has been so kind as to retire before us," Lafayette wrote.[19] Washington replied, and congratulated Lafayette "on the favorable turn of Affairs" and reported on "General Greene's further successes in south Carolina." Then came Washington's real news: "I shall shortly…communicate matters of very great importance to you, so much so, that I shall send a confidential Officer [with the message]. In the present situation of Affairs, it is of the utmost importance that a Chain of Expresses should be opened between [here and our army in Virginia]."[20]

Political pressure for a southern campaign escalated. Governor Thomas Jefferson wrote "for the people of Virginia," and requested, "Washington to take command of the army in that State."[21] Richard Henry Lee, a Virginia legislator, proposed that the Continental Congress order Washington to Virginia "as the head of the federal union" and until a civilian government could be formed given "Dictatorial powers."[22] Washington replied, the "plan you have suggested as a relief [for Virginia] is…proof of your unbounded confidence in me." But, he said, the "obstacles [which] I cannot entrust to paper" were insurmountable. The "measures I have adopted will give more effectual and speedier relief to the State of Virginia than if I were was to March [there] with dictatorial power." The letter gave Washington leverage to solicit assistance from Congress. "The fatal policy of short enlistmts. (the primary cause of all our misfortunes; the prolongation of the War; and the source of the immense debt under which we labour) is now" seriously restricting our opportunities. "I am labouring under all disadvantages and evils" of these policies.[23]

On July 14, 1781, with all the pressure mounting for a southern campaign, Washington acknowledged in his dairy the futility of any attempt on New York: "Matters having now come to a crisis…I was obliged, from the shortness of Count de Grasse's promised stay on this coast" and the lack of any

French enthusiasm, "to force the harbor…to give up all ideas of attacking New York."[24] Whether intentional or not, Washington's reluctance to conduct a southern campaign provided leverage. He extracted from his allies, Congress, and the state of Virginia, basic support of finance, supplies, and legislative changes required for a viable effort.

In another move, Washington sent an Allied force of 5,000 to probe British defenses in the city suburbs of Kings Bridge. He was delighted by the outcome; it shocked the enemy and was a complete surprise. The British considered the probe a move in force against New York City. But after some initial skirmishing, Allied forces retired towards Dobbs Ferry. The action impacted British reaction, strengthening their conviction that it was the start of a major assault on New York. The probe at Kings Bridge froze enemy forces in New York, discouraging General Clinton from sending further assistance to Cornwallis in Virginia. Clinton was so confident of a major allied thrust on New York that he ordered Cornwallis to send forces to New York. Without reinforcements from Clinton and orders to send troops to New York, Cornwallis withdrew from an inland position and headed to the Chesapeake area where he expected assistance from the British navy.[25]

For the rest of July into August, Lafayette continued barrages of correspondence and urged Washington to come south to get Cornwallis.[26] Lafayette's intelligence reports forced Washington and Rochambeau to meet with regularity and review southern developments. With situations changing almost daily, they agreed "definitive Measures" for the next campaign should await the "Arrival of Count de Grasse." If the Admiral "should not think it prudent to [force] a passage of" New York harbor, then allied troops would head to Virginia.[27]

Then the lightning stroke – correspondence arrived from De Grasse to Rochambeau. De Grasse had "the sum of 1,200,000 livres" and assembled a force of:

3,000 men, 100 artillerists, 100 dragoons, 10 campaign cannons, seige cannons, mortars etc. They will be embarked on 29 men-of-war which will set out August 3rd to make the Chesapeake as soon as possible…. I will be obliged to you for employing me promptly and effectively in order that the time be sufficiently well employed…but I cannot leave you the troops longer; they are under the orders of the Spanish Generals who have need for them…. This entire expedition has been arranged following your orders and as it was impossible to communicate with either the French or Spanish Ministers I believed myself authorized to take over the responsibility in view of the common good; but I dare not change entirely the plan of their projects by transplanting such a considerable corps of men.[28]

De Grasse's news arrived so suddenly; the first response was stunned silence followed quickly by an explosion of joy. More good news arrived. On August 13, 1781, Washington informed Congress, "I have information that a Fleet of twenty sail entered [New York harbor] on saturday last. [My] informant was of the opinion they were from Virginia. I expect to hear from him again every moment, with a certain Account [of their origin].[29] Did Cornwallis really weaken his position by sending troops to defend New York City? No, but as Washington found later, the arrival was "a reinforcement of near 3000 Hessian Recruits" from Europe.[30]

Fresh intelligence arrived in steady streams. On August 14, 1781, decisive news arrived. Admiral De Grasse had headed to the Chesapeake, not New York. His planned departure from the West Indies was on August 13, and he scheduled his return for the middle of October.[31]

Admiral De Grasse's plans cast the final and decisive vote in favor of Washington and Rochambeau's Virginia campaign.

Virginia's Transformation

I am so convinced that my appearance on the other side of the James River will trouble Lord Cornwallis that I can hardly wait to set out.

While a work in progress, Virginia's transformation into a support platform for Allied armies was nothing less than miraculous. Change fell to a few dedicated and ingenious individuals who demonstrated determination, resourcefulness, and relentless pursuit of objectives to build Virginia into a Patriot platform. But change brought agony and tension. A frustrated Baron von Steuben reported difficulties in building an effective Virginia fighting force. He was unable to "assemble the necessary equipment as quickly as I would like," he wrote to Lafayette. There are arms, "but no cartridge pouches, and the state cannot supply me with any. Today I am expecting a little ammunition, some blankets, shoes, and shirts." He planned a "campaign five days from now," and stated, "I am so convinced that my appearance on the other side of the James River will trouble Lord Cornwallis that I can hardly wait to set out."[1] In reply, Lafayette sent an express courier to update the Baron on his own difficult circumstances. He knew Lafayette was aware of "the few Militia I have" and informed him that his regulars were slightly "above 800. The Enemy have 500 Horse and We 40." They appeared headed "towards Fredericksburg," but "our intelligence is very bad." With inadequate forces to seriously oppose enemy intrusions, Lafayette ordered the Baron to remove "Stores, and every other Article [to] a place perfectly safe." There was some good news. "The Governor has ordered riflemen to rendesvous at Charlottesville" where they would serve under the Baron's command, Lafayette informed him.[2]

Lafayette desperately needed reinforcements. He had reduced activities to nothing more than harassment, but even that was conducted with sparing enterprise. The primary objective was to avoid a surprise attack, so Lafayette kept moving his forces. Mobility left the British uncertain of his location and numbers. Reinforcements were on the way, but the arrival date was unknown. Finally, a message came. "We shall reach Leesburg this Evening, [after marching] thirty Miles in two days," wrote Brigadier General Anthony Wayne.[3]

Shortly after Wayne's message arrived, Lafayette received additional promising intelligence. General George Weedon, commander of Virginia state forces, "intended moving to-night with the small handful of men." Weedon and Lafayette were not strangers; they had served together at Valley Forge where Weedon commanded a Virginia Brigade. "I shall send out flour in the morning," he informed Lafayette. At the time, Weedon was engaged in "removing the stores," to avoid enemy capture. His immediate problem was lack of help. There was no one left, "but myself [to carry out] the smallest piece of business [or] direct the supplies for Genl. Wayne," he wrote to Lafayette. He also wrote that he was sending out parties to collect "all the horses" ahead of "the enemy's advance." For Lafayette this was additional welcome news.[4]

Panic and fear infected Virginia's Patriot population, as the British marauded without mercy or opposition. An account published in *The* (Boston) *Continental Journal and Weekly Advertiser* on May 17, 1781, described events to the southward:

> The papers received yesterday from the Southward, contain many accounts of the deprivations committed by British forces in the Chesapeake bay. Their chief employment appears to be the destruction of property, both public and private, and in distressing, as much as possible, all who appear to take any part in the defence of their country. Letters from that quarter say, that a considerable force has taken possession of Alexandria, where they were entrenching. Want of time and room obliges us to omit the horrid tales of British barbarity.[5]

As enemy actions increased, Patriot response grew slower and more feeble. Accumulating intelligence on British movements was nearly impossible. They moved with such frequency and speed that information was obsolete in a matter of hours. The lack of intelligence caused major tactical difficulties for Patriot commands.

"No letters from General Greene or from you, my dear Marquis, for six days," von Steuben complained. "Here I am with 550 men in this desert, with no shoes, no shirts, and what is worse no cartridge pouches. I write everywhere. I send express messengers everywhere, but I get nothing," not even information. "I beg you to send me news." The Baron felt ignored. "I don't know where you are, nor what has become of Cornwallis." He asked for news "about Wayne [or the] French Fleet? ...tell me something," he pleaded.[6]

Even worse complaints about information flow and intelligence came from Washington. The enemy – "it is supposed" – intercepted classified letters and after examining the contents, sent them back on a path to the recipient. Such information provided the British all sorts of opportunities to counteract Allied intentions. "Communication is so insecure! ...from one part of the Country to another [is] liable to such accidents," Washington wrote to Lafayette.[7]

While allied communication exchanges appeared in a state of chaos, Virginia's political climate boiled. Governor Jefferson's term of office ended on June 2, 1781, and Thomas Nelson, Jr., his successor, was elected on June 12.[8] The circumstances surrounding Jefferson's decision not to seek reelection are shrouded in obscurity. Whether he declined or was not offered another term is unclear.

Thomas Nelson, Jr., was born December 26, 1738, in Yorktown, Virginia. As a young man, he became a personal friend of Washington. Nelson signed the Declaration of Independence and later resigned his commission as captain in the Continental Army for personal reasons.[9] Washington's reaction to his election was near ecstasy. "I am much pleased with your choice of a Governor," he wrote to his stepson, John Parke Custis. "He is an honest man, active, spirited and decided, and will, I dare say, suit the times as well as any person in the State."[10] Washington congratulated Nelson. "Among your numerous friends, none will be found whose congratulations on your appointment to the Administration of the Affairs of Virginia, are offered with more cordiality and sincerity than mine."[11] Washington considered Nelson's military experience and knowledge a significant advantage over Jefferson.

Almost as soon as he took office, Nelson actively supported Colonel William Davies as commissioner of war. Davies was appointed on March 22, 1781, to invigorate the inept supply organization, but under Jefferson's term he lacked the vigorous support necessary to build an effective wartime administration. Davis faced insidious hurdles, such as the "mismanagement in the department of Commissary of provisions." He wrote, "The distress and oppression of the inhabitants in the vicinity of our Camp in consequence of the Commissary's deficiency, is too painful."[12]

William Davies was also a Virginian and well known to Washington, Greene, Lafayette, Baron Steuben and Nelson. Born in 1768, he was a lawyer and Princeton graduate whose father was, at one time, the University's president.[13] A fellow officer described Davies as possessing "an uneasy disposition, and less accommodating than could be wished." While at times demonstrating an abrasive personality, he had an effective administrative ability and got things done. Early in the war, he joined a Virginia Continental Army regiment and served at Valley Forge.[14] After Nelson's election, Davies performed tirelessly to improve all aspects of Virginia's supply situation. He demanded action and bluntly informed "The County Lieutenant of the War Office" at Berkley, Virginia, of the desperate need for "waggons and clothing" from that county; continuation of the war effort depended on their success. He needed "the earliest information on the subject" in order "to give the government any intelligence they may desire," and to send "assistance to the troops" commanded by "General Greene and the Marquis de la Fayette."[15]

On June 12, the same day Nelson was elected, a series of Executive Orders went to various county lieutenants. Acting governor William Fleming took the initiative to put Virginia on a war footing. He informed the lieutenants of "pressing Calls from the Marquis Fayette for [manpower]." The General Assembly voted "to give [Lafayette] all the assistance in their power." The Governor required them to "embody two thirds of your Militia under proper Officers and march them to join the Marquis in detachments of not less than 200." They expected "immediate...execution of this order as the preservation of the State may depend on the dispatch with which the army is reinforced."[16]

Fleming's executive orders strengthened construction of an Allied support platform. His orders were improvements over Jefferson's previous passive approach. But Fleming was hampered; existing legislation provided inadequate enforcement or punishment for ignored orders. On June 20, Governor Nelson moved convincingly to create enforcement legislation. He convened a special commission "to hear and determine all treasons [and] all offences against an Act of general Assembly." He insisted on "affixing penalties to certain crimes, injurious to the independence of America." Nelson ordered the commission to use an existing act of the General Assembly as a legal basis to impose enforcement and punishment for non-compliance. It gave wide discretion to the commission in decisions for specific penalties and provided enforcement authority.[17] The enactment of an enforcement provision at Governor Nelson's insistence advanced the process for a military support base. Another law enacted by the legislature enabled "the Commanding Officer...to declare Martial Law," in accordance with "the Continental Articles of War within 20 Miles of our Camp and within the same distance of the Enemys," Nelson wrote. Nelson informed Virginia's militia lieutenants of Lafayette's authority to enact the provisions of these laws. "I expect...his orders" will be carried out, Nelson wrote.[18] While only limited martial law with restrictions imposed by distance, it was a step forward.

In Nelson's first letter to Washington as governor he described Virginia's military situation. As the enemy invaded, "our force is limited, but rather than make no appearance we take the field with the few we can collect." The enemy "is superior to us" in most areas, and "with assistance of their Ships, make good their landing where they please, seldom at the place where they expect opposition." They did not appear to seek a major action, "not even Lord Cornwallis." All their "running up and down [into] different parts of the country may make a great noise in Europe," but when the "circumstances are known," Nelson wrote, he doubted if "British Commanders" would acquire "much military fame [or] we shall suffer so much disgrace as may at first be attributed to both."[19]

British incursions into Virginia increased with brutal ferocity in areas of Patriot sympathies. Nelson described the public's reaction: "They have made Whigs [Patriots] of Tories." On another subject Nelson informed Washington, "You could not have made the Militia of Virginia happier than by sending the Marquis to take the command here. They have great confidence in his bravery and conduct." Even "private Citizens are [pleased] with his affability and great regard for their Civil rights." His character is held in the highest estimation."[20] The governor generously praised Lafayette, but conspicuously absent was praise for Baron von Steuben. If earlier the Baron had enjoyed the same Martial Law as was now available, his situation might have differed, but one of the Baron's great weaknesses was an absence of political and public relation skills on a par with Lafayette.

Nelson's executive orders became frequent and stronger. In response to Lafayette's need for "several Pieces of heavy Cannon on travelling Carriages," he informed William Davies on July 31, 1781:

Sir,

The Marquis has urged so strongly the mounting several Pieces of heavy Cannon on travelling Carriages, that I must desire you to give the most pointed Orders for carrying this Business into immediate Execution. The Delay of a few Days my produce the most unhappy Consequences. I am sensible that the Public are not possessed of Materials for this Work; for which reason it will be necessary, disagreeable as impressing is, that Artificers, Tools, and every thing requisite be taken, wherever they are to be found, if not to be procured by any other means.[21]

✤ 13 ✤

The Baron and Lafayette Odyssey

The Baron's Conduct does great mischief and will do more if he is not recalled

Baron von Steuben's contributions to a successful Virginia campaign are substantial, controversial, and legendary. In late 1780, he went to Virginia with Major General Nathanael Greene. His assignment, under Greene's command, was reconstruction of a third Continental Army Southern Command. Steuben's association with Virginia military forces began in the Valley Forge encampment of 1778 where his training forged the Continental Army into an adequate fighting force. In those days his rough, gruff, no-nonsense approach of hands-on training made him the idol of Continental soldiers. Convincingly the army responded with a demonstration of much-improved fighting qualities at the Battle of Monmouth in June 1778. The Baron had no time for personal sensitivities during training sessions at Valley Forge. His results earned him widespread recognition and respect in Virginia military circles.

After Greene surveyed Virginia's situation, he realized the state's appalling military incapacity. Effective resistance to British intrusions by Virginia's existing military organizations was impossible. In an attempt to construct a military effort, the Baron remained as Virginia's Continental Army commander and Greene headed south to the Carolinas.

The Baron's reputation preceded him; his exploits training the Continental Army were legendary. At first, Virginians were delighted to have someone with his reputation and experience. But Southern culture and Virginia society presented challenges which the Baron had never experienced. Although lacking a magnetic personality, Steuben possessed an analytical mind and quickly determined a number of glaring flaws in the state's military situation. He had an uncanny ability to construct simple and effective improvements to complex problems. Unfortunately, he lacked personal skills to persuade a sea of incompetents to change their systems. Steuben faced incompetence with contempt and his abrasive personality was a lightning rod for the wrath of many Virginia political and military authorities.

"Unfortunately [the Baron has] become universally unpopular, and all ranks of people seem to have taken the greatest disgust at him," William Davies informed General Greene. They write "to Congress for his recall." Only a few had "raised all this clamour, but his usefulness here is over."[1] Davies knew the Baron well after serving in his command at Valley Forge. He was aware of the politics involved, when he characterized complaints as coming from a few, but their importance was overpowering. The cabal against von Steuben was well orchestrated. His detractors made Steuben a prime scapegoat for failing to stop a British assault against the Virginia Arsenal at Point of Forks and a June 4 raid against Charlottesville, which scattered the Virginia Legislature including a narrow escape by Governor Jefferson.

Joseph Jones, Virginia delegate in the Continental Congress, leveled a vitriolic attack against the Baron. Previously, Jones had tried to persuade Washington to come and take command of Virginia's military activities.[2] But he was determined to blame the Baron for failure of the state's military enterprise. With arrogance and rancor, Jones started his politics of personal destruction against the Baron. "We have 600 fine Men under Baron Stuben...he will not carry [them] into action, what are his Reasons I know not, but I can assure you his Conduct gives...universal disgust," Jones complained to Washington. People complain "that they are dragged from their Families at a time when they are most wanted," but the Continental soldiers "they have hired at a very great expence lay Idle." The Baron's "Conduct does great mischief and will do more if he is not recalled, and I think it behoves you to bring it about. I assure you it is the wish and desire of every Man that this event [should] take place. I believe him a good officer on the Parade [but he is the] worst in every other respect." While Jones aimed the nastiest complaints at the Baron, Lafayette was not immune from his attack:

> I like the Marquis much and so does every Body in the Country but is he not too young for such a command as he has, and of such great consequence to the American Cause and this great Country – would not St. Clair think you from his experience be useful here.[3]

Jones held a rank of major general in the Virginia militia with significant political influence throughout the state.[4] His assessment of the Baron came mainly from second-hand sources and a network of Virginians. Jones had close associates who considered Virginia military affairs their private domain. While unable to provide supplies or place the state on a sufficient war footing, they quickly criticized anyone who cast blame in their direction.

Lafayette did not help the Baron's situation when he wrote to Washington, "The Conduct of the Baron, my dear General, is to me Unintelligible. Every man woman and Child in Virginia is Roused Against Him." They even question "his Courage But I Cannot Believe their assertions. I must However Confess that he" commanded over "500 New Levies and Some militia." When the enemy approached with inferior forces, the Baron retreated "70 miles" and the new levies were so disgusted they deserted. "I do not know where to employ him without Giving offense."[5]

On June 20, Lafayette expressed similar private sentiments, condemning Steuben to Greene:

> ...Had the Baron Held 24 Hours Every one of the Articles Might Have Been Carried up as High as Albermale Old Court House where they did not venture. Instead of it He went to Staunton River 75 miles from the Point of Fork and Crossed it. General Lawson with the Militia left Him. His New levies deserted. All Virginia was in an Uproar against Him. The Ennemy Laughed at Him. And I Cannot describe to You what My Surprise Has Been – But I did not choose to Be too Severe in My public letter and Request this May Be private to Yourself.[6]

As Washington read the complaints, he sensed a cabal in progress with many of the same political taints the commander-in-chief had experienced at Valley Forge during the Conway Cabal in 1777-78. "The complaints against Baron de Steuben" were more unexpected than distressing, Washington answered Jones. "I always viewed him in the light of a good officer." When he forms "a junction with the Marquis, he will be no longer Master of his own conduct" and the claims "against him will cease."[7] Washington disappointed Jones with his curt reply, without criticism of the Baron's actions. As for Jones' innuendos against Lafayette, Washington wrote, "command of the Troops in that State cannot be in better hands than the Marquiss...[he] possesses uncommon Military talents, is of a quick and sound judgment, persevering, and enterprising without rashness." He has "a very conciliating temper and perfectly sober, which are qualities that rarely combine in the same person. [Some] men will gain as much experience in the course of three or 4 years, as some others will in ten or a dozen, you cannot deny the fact."[8] His characterization of Lafayette left little doubt of Washington's support for the young general.

Washington addressed Lafayette's criticisms of the Baron. While not mentioning him directly, he recognized a political necessity for action to benefit both the Baron and Continental Army. "What you say in confidence of a certain Officer shall be kept a profound secret, and [if necessary] I will contrive means of removing him from the quarter where he is so unpopular."[9]

While communications about him flowed, the Baron was not idle. On June 19, "25 Miles from Richmond," he wrote to Greene and commented on Nelson's election as the new governor. The Baron felt "a change of Administration may produce a Change of Measures, Gen [Thomas] Nelson is the new governor, and the Council is materially changed[;] from this we may have certainly more to hope than fear."[10]

In spite of improving circumstances, Virginia's Patriot cause remained in crisis and near collapse. Resistance against British incursions evaporated; only occasionally was there an isolated response. The British were determined to destroy all rebel resistance in the state. For the Patriot cause to survive, Virginia needed effective military mobilization.

Gone was the high level of enthusiasm that immediately followed the Declaration of Independence. Now, the common folk had doubt, despair, and to a large extent, disinterest. Even some of Virginia's leading patriots experienced "a deep sense of disillusionment." A doctor from "Hanover County" described "the low morale;" there was a great unwillingness "to fill draft quotas," he wrote. "The attention of the people of this state is very little taken up with the war at this time, or indeed for a year or two past." Local politicians suffered scorn; "many of those that are chosen are men of mean abilities & no rank." In an example of deteriorating valor, the doctor witnessed many of his neighbors going "eagerly to the invaders in order to be paroled" and therefore – they hoped – escape draft in the "service of the commonwealth."[11]

Freewheeling enemy activities humiliated Virginia's military authorities. Lafayette decided to counter the British. With some caution, he planned harassment operations to slow British ability to move with arrogance and impunity.

Other circumstances drew Lafayette's attention. "General Wayne will be four miles East of Richmond tonight," he informed the Baron. "This morning General Mhulenberg [was located] at the fork of the road, 8 miles above Bottom Bridge." The enemy marched at daybreak; Mhulenberg followed them at 7 a.m. And when General Wayne was positioned he would "gain a proper distance in the enemy's rear." Then came the Baron's marching orders. "You will...advance your troops six or seven miles this evening, and proceed in the morning [along] the Williamsburg road." If all went as planned, the separated forces would join, Lafayette wrote. "I am informed by Gen. Mhulenburg, that mounted rifle-men are of no use [because] the powder they received [is] damaged." Order "a sufficient quantity of good powder from the field commissary. It is essential [for] the remaining mounted rifle-men [to] lose no time in joining General Mhulenburg."[12] He also ordered the placement of a "horseman or two" at strategic positions along the road to bring him intelligence. Lafayette notified Wayne of the Baron's intentions "to move seven or eight miles to-night [and] form a junction with your troops" early the next day. "If the enemy are to be injured," he wrote, they had to be stopped by Muhlenburg's striking their rear.

Lafayette avoided a specific tactical plan; he intended to shadow the British from a prudent distance and probe for targets of opportunity. Success depended on a constant flow of accurate, timely intelligence between American forces. At the same, Americans attempted to intercept enemy intelligence, and generally disrupt their communications.

On June 23, 1781, with prodding by Governor Nelson, Virginia's General Assembly passed an act, and effectively declared martial law. The result was a dramatic improvement in the state's ability to respond quickly in changing military situations. While martial law improved military potential, some contentious issues remained between the Continental Army and local militias. Dealing with the enemy was a constant source of friction. Local "County Lieutenants" dealt directly with enemy representatives on a number of administrative issues, which sometimes placed the Continental Army at a disadvantage. No overall policy existed on issues associated with prisoner exchanges, passports, and flags of truce.

Later, after an initial shock from the enemy's successful assault against Point of Forks and the Virginia Capitol passed, the results were not as extensive as first claimed. "Our loss at the Point of Fork chiefly consisted of Old Arms out of repair and some Cannon, most of which have been since recovered," Lafayette informed Nathanael Greene on June 27.

Earlier, Baron von Steuben was severely criticized for not defending Point of Forks with his force of approximately 400, comprised, for the most part, of militia. Personal attacks against the Baron followed reports of large quantities of arms and ammunition. In fact, the Baron had removed most of the "proper arms" by wagons. He destroyed old arms and threw bits and pieces in the river. His refusal to stand and fight with a suspect militia was a sound military decision. Years later the Baron's actions were corroborated from archaeological finds of destroyed pieces at Point of Forks. What he left the enemy was of little use.[13]

The British, accustomed to Patriot resistance melting at the first shots, expected no change. With audacity and reckless abandon, enemy dragoons often charged Patriot forces in full expectation of their disappearance at the first sight of British steel. On June 26, 1781, at "Spencer's Tavern," the situation changed. Lafayette seized an opportunity to concentrate American forces against a British intrusion. Actually, the encounter began on June 18 when the British Army moved toward the Americans. The enemy attempted "to strike at a detached Corps commanded by Genl. Muhlenberg," but was unsuccessful. By June 19, Lafayette had reinforcements with the arrival of Generals Wayne and von Steuben. American light troops challenged the enemy and attacked in a series of skirmishes "near N. Kent Court House." At the time, General Cornwallis' main army headed toward Williamsburg with his flanks well covered by British cavalry. Lafayette shadowed Cornwallis during the entire trip. Finally on June 27, Lafayette "pushed forward a Detachment," and deployed "50 light Infantry" with dragoons. In a concentration of forces Wayne and von Steuben, along with Lafayette, attacked at "Spencer's Tavern." Although a draw, the Americans achieved a tactical success in exercising unity of command. Lafayette surprised the British who eventually withdrew until reinforcements arrived. The enemy counterattacked, but finally withdrew to Williamsburg.[14]

Lafayette, delighted, was especially satisfied by the level of cooperation achieved. The intelligence exchanged during the operation was effective, expeditious, and accurate. The Americans maneuvered, feinted, and probed against an enemy superior in numbers. Swiftly he sent favorable accounts to Nathanael Greene with copies to Washington and the Continental Congress. When the letters arrived, the recipients interpreted "Spencer's Tavern" as a victory – something Lafayette did little to discourage.

In spite of his flare for public relations, Lafayette had a "heady respect" for General Cornwallis' ability to execute tactical maneuvers and entrapments. Reinforcements from Anthony Wayne improved the opportunity for offensive operations, but predicting Cornwallis' intentions was a constant challenge.

Lafayette increased communications with Governor Nelson, a central figure influencing Continental Army's opportunities because Nelson controlled provisions. On July 1, 1781, Lafayette thanked Nelson for establishing "a Chain of Expresses" between this camp "and the Seat of" government. Ease of communications with Nelson was essential in Lafayette's tactical operations. But Lafayette faced a larger issue – one with immediate impact on fighting capability and only the governor had a solution. "Many men are Daily Deserting," he informed Nelson. "They were only Engaged for Six weeks and the Harvest Time Recalls them Home." Virginia's reservoir of manpower provided the only immediate resources for an effective challenge to British intentions.

Lafayette outlined steps of "absolute necessity" to save the state. First, order the "County Lieutenants" to court-martial any militiamen who lacked proper excuses and did not appear "when called for duty." Next, bring the militia immediately into the field. Without a large turnout, "the ground we Have obtained" from General Cornwallis would be forfeited. Then, offer "Severest punishment to civil officers who do not immediately" capture deserters and force the militia to the field.[15]

Governor Nelson's response was not as strong as Lafayette desired. To "The County Lieutenants" the governor wrote, "The Harvest time being over, I hope the militia which have been ordered into Service...will take to the field with the greatest alacrity." The enemy makes every effort to "gain Posts in this" state. Increasing our opposition at this time "will in all Probability," change the war's direction.[16]

In a report to General Greene, Lafayette vindicated the Baron for past accusations and personal attacks by his Virginia detractors. "What has been lost at Point of Fork is in a Great Measure Recovered." There was actually little lost, "including the Baron's popularity in Virginia."[17] How the Baron's popularity was recovered is not addressed, but Lafayette was embarrassed by his own earlier criticisms of the Baron.

In an effort to keep constant pressure on the enemy, Lafayette harassed them where opportunities appeared, especially near the rear and flanks of British operations. He recognized Cornwallis' tactical genius, but also knew that Cornwallis, despite his genius, occasionally made audacious moves that produced opportunities for an adversary with accurate intelligence.

Cornwallis masterfully dismissed failures and maximized successes, but he was well aware of his communications deficiencies. In a 1781 letter, after a series of failures, he wrote, "we have been precluded from all communication with the rest of the world, as though in the deserts of Arabia."[18] Conveniently, Cornwallis forgot to mention that he had decided to march through the backcountry of the Carolinas and Virginia where there was no protection from the British Navy. He soon discovered communications exchanges were constantly a target for Patriot interception.

On July 6, 1781, Lafayette engaged Cornwallis at the Battle of Green Spring, Virginia. A cautious Lafayette prevented disaster. A significant disparity in cavalry existed between Lafayette and the British. Both sides always needed horses, but British ground forces were not as widely deployed as American. While British cavalry was depleted earlier at the Battle of Cowpens, they effectively employed their remaining cavalry. Virginians strongly resisted surrendering horses to Lafayette or the British, but after learning that the only options were to supply horses to Lafayette or give up everything else to a marauding enemy, horse supplies improved.

On July 7, before smoke cleared from the field of battle, Lafayette wrote to a colonel in the Virginia State Regiment and described the Battle of Green Spring. "Last evening there has been a severe skirmish between a Detachment of 800 Men and the British Army. Our loss [was not extensive] in killed, more in wounded [and] almost none in prisoners." He requested that the colonel visit "the Wounded and [find] if they are in want of any thing." He directed that the officers and men "should know my orders are that every possible relief and refreshment be procured for them at [my expense]."[19]

Lafayette's attention to the needs of private soldiers was a hallmark of his leadership. It explains why this foreigner was popular and not subjected to serious resentment from officers and men. But he kept close attention on the British who were capable of a surprise counterattack. He ordered an officer, "You will be very alert to Night [and put] everything in readiness to move at the shortest warning." If attacked "Your Brigade" must deploy quickly into the woods and "defend the road." He told the officer to order "Pack [oxen] and Waggons" to the rear, and move "to Morrow Morning at 3 oClk" to relieve "Genl. Lawson."[20] On arrival, "you will take measures for the safety of our left flank. I imagine the Enemy " were crippled by the action yesterday and although he did not expect them to "venture against our Army, [we] must guard against possibilities."[21]

On July 8, Lafayette wrote to General Greene with a more detailed version of the Battle of Green Spring. The British had evacuated Williamsburg and Lafayette, unsure of their intentions, moved his forces toward them. Cautiously he moved to within nine miles, then dispatched "an advanced Corps, under General Wayne" to reconnoiter "the Enemy's situation." Wayne sent riflemen ahead to attack the enemy "Piquetts." Meanwhile, Lafayette carefully advanced cavalry to observe enemy actions; he received intelligence that Cornwallis had detached his baggage to a safe area and was deployed under protection of naval cannons. Lafayette moved forward and found Wayne "more generally engaged" than expected. Shortly afterward, "the whole British Army came out, and advanced to the thin Wood occupied by Genl. Wayne," whose force was "chiefly composed of Pensylvanians and some light infantry," totaling fewer than "800 Men." After a short skirmish, the enemy "greatly outflanked" them, and Lafayette sent Wayne "orders to retire half a Mile where [our] Light Infantry Battalions had arrived." The Light Infantry were ordered to form and they remained in this position for most of the night. "The Enemy retreated during the night to James Island," which they soon evacuated and crossed "over to South side of the River." The Americans occupied their ground on this side of the river. They left "A Number of valuable Horses...in their retreat...the Enemy's Loss has been very great, and [they tried hard] to conceal it."[22]

Typical of military engagements with mixed results, Lafayette and Cornwallis accounts differ. Cornwallis claimed he was on the way to Portsmouth, Virginia, with intentions to embark troops for Clinton in New York, when he learned of an opportunity to encircle Wayne. Lafayette's decision to stay close to Wayne allowed him to move quickly and extract Wayne before Cornwallis completed the encirclement. The British account gave no special acknowledgement to Lafayette's action and officially reported that, "darkness prevented" Cornwallis from continuing his advantage. One British officer claimed "Lafayette's army could have been annihilated if a detachment had been sent against him before dawn." Later Cornwallis argued it was the need to embark troops for Clinton which impeded pursuit of the Americans.

To the Americans, Cornwallis' planned encirclement was parried. Again Lafayette exercised a unity of action, using effective and frequent communication exchanges with constantly moving the separated state, militia, and Continental Forces.

On July 9, 1781, Lafayette offered a different perspective of the battle to his brother-in-law, the Vicomte de Noailles. "The skirmish at Green Spring was followed by [the enemy] retreat that left us in possession of everything on this side of the James River." Two cannon were lost, but "I consoled myself for the loss [by the capture of] some stores and the horses the enemy left behind." He was pleased to report that, "Lord Cornwallis treated the wounded that fell into his hands with every refinement and courtesy to our army. This devil Cornwallis is much wiser than other generals with whom I have dealt. He inspires me with sincere fear, and his name has greatly troubled my sleep...God grant that the public does not pay for my lessons."[23]

Lafayette studied a stream of intelligence reports on British activities in the area. He sensed an enemy that was changing strategy. Under certain circumstances, the British were vulnerable to an assault. But an assault required changing from defensive to offensive operations. At first, the thought of going on the offensive was preposterous when there was barely enough support to maintain minimum defensive operations. With the war in a virtual stalemate, opportunities did not always appear at favorable times. Lafayette was certain some audacious response was needed to stop the British in Virginia.

Between July 10 and 13, 1781, Lafayette wrote three letters to Governor Nelson detailing events. The letters contained updates on current military activities, but quickly addressed pressing issues, especially an unreliable performance of Virginia militia who were "vanishing daily." He vividly described a series of desperate problems including, "I would beg...to recommend that all the horses" needed for the cavalry and dragoons "be immediately completed." Intelligence indicated the enemy was headed "towards Petersburg," with some headed for Carolina or New York, Lafayette reported.[24] On July 17, after incessant prodding by Lafayette, the Virginia Executive Council finally authorized impressments of three hundred horses.[25]

The war's dynamic changed rapidly. Lafayette sensed an end to the stalemate. Even from the north, Washington signaled change. On July 13 he congratulated Lafayette "on the favorable turn of Affairs" mentioned in previous letters and that he had "reports of General Greene's further successes in south Carolina." Washington described details of the long-awaited junction with Rochambeau's forces, "a few days ago." After tantalizing Lafayette with preliminaries, the commander-in-chief excited Lafayette's imagination. "I shall shortly have occasion to communicate matters of very great importance to you, so much so, that I shall send a confidential officer" to you. "You will in the mean time [assemble] as respectable a Body of Continental troops as you possibly can and take every measure to augment your Cavalry."[26]

Something was planned, but what? Whatever the action, Lafayette believed he was involved. Washington further ordered, "In the Present situation of affairs it is of the utmost importance that [communications] by a Chain of Expresses should be opened between this Army and that in Virginia." With a reliable chain already established as far as Philadelphia, Washington directed that, if there were none to that city, "take measures for having it done."[27] Tantalizing Lafayette more was the order to establish "a communication with the Coast" and determine "whether any troops" were sent "by sea from Lord Cornwallis's Army." Washington felt it probable that if Cornwallis could not overrun "Virginia he will take a strong post at Portsmouth or Williamsburg and [send reinforcements to] New York or South Carolina."[28] Washington's correspondence arrived on July 30, indicating that under the best conditions exchanges required two weeks.[29]

Washington's information bolstered the Marquis' enthusiasm. Immediately Lafayette replied, sending a detailed report on British movements in Virginia and his opinion of future British actions, but he cautioned, "This State is So difficult to Be defended," especially for "one that Does not Command the water." On communications he reported, "There is a chain of expresses. But I shall See that it is More properly Conducted."

On July 25, Governor Nelson improved the military situation in Virginia further by shifting orders given to County Lieutenants. "The Militia from Spotsylvania must join the Marquis [and] County Lieutenants [are directed] not to deliver Cloathing" except by "order of the Commissioner of the War Office," whose orders were the only ones authorizing delivery of military stores.[30]

With determination charged by purpose, Nelson pressured change for Virginia's military climate. Enforcement was essential for violations or dereliction of duty. Nelson knew military discipline did not rest on statements, but on demonstration. On July 30 he directed Colonel James Innes, a member of the Virginia Board of War:

> Should any of the Militia persist in pleading their Paroles as an Excuse for not performing military Service, which I hope no one will be so ignorant or unmindful of his Duty as to do, it is necessary that he be proceeded against according to the Proclamation issued by the late Governour, which Proclamation has received the Sanction of the General Assembly. A strict Adherence to this Order of Government may in some Cases bear an Appearance of Cruelty, but the insidious Arts of the Enemy & the general Welfare render it indispensable. It is however my Desire that no Person be rigorously dealt with, whom there is a Prospect of bringing back to a better Sense of what is due to his Country.[31]

Washington's letters continued to tantalize Lafayette's imagination. In a letter dated July 30, "You will not," Washington wrote, "Regret your stay in Virginia." If the enemy moved part of his forces "from Virginia to New York," there was a good probability "that we shall also intirely change our plan of operations."[32]

But in Virginia, one unresolved thorny issue was authority. As increasing numbers of Virginia State and militia forces came to the field, simultaneously with additional Continental Army units, demands for supplies and provisions escalated. Demands from four growing interests competed intensely for the same provisions: the enemy, Virginia's citizens, the Continental Army, and Virginia's state forces.

Authority over provisions caused serious tensions between Continental and Virginia's State forces. An infuriated Governor Nelson informed Lafayette about the "Seizure of Stores, the Property of this State," by Brigadier Anthony Wayne. The stores were "intended for the use of our Troops now in the Field, which are in the greatest Want of them." The seizure could not "be tolerated, where civil Government is established" with procedures "for procuring Necessities for our Armies." Other violations were reported, which were "committed on the Property of Individuals by the Troops of the Pennsylvania Line." Nelson hoped the actions were not sanctioned by officers: but whatever authority sanctioned these actions, "as first Magistrate of the State & Guardian

Author's collection.

Archaeological finds from the vicinity Point of Forks, Virginia. The destroyed pieces of bayonets and musket barrels attest that General von Steuben left nothing serviceable for the enemy.

of the Rights of the People, it is my Duty to" prevent them. He reminded Lafayette that he was the "Commander in chief of the American Forces in the State of Virginia," with the "Power of examining" and "regulating the Conduct of all subordinate Officers."[33]

The governor leveled serious allegations against a general officer in the Continental Army. The dispute's suddenness was eclipsed only by its ferocity. Governor Nelson learned of the incident from a letter written on July 28 by William Davies. General Wayne had removed Virginia stores from a location in Chesterfield, Virginia, Davies complained. If "any officer of any rank whatever has the right to appropriate the stores of the State at his pleasure, at a time when our troops are in want of them, I think our situation must be truly deplorable," fumed Davies.[34]

On August 7, Lafayette replied to Governor Nelson. While attentive and respectful of Nelson's obvious anger, the Marquis maintained military protocol by first considering the officer involved. A copy of Nelson's letter was sent to General Wayne. "I hope His proceedings may Be Explained to the Satisfaction of Government and the People. I Hope Every officer in this army will Be Equally desirous with me to Preserve Harmony and Good order."[35]

Lafayette partially sidestepped the issue by directing the letter to Wayne. At the same time he attempted to diffuse the emotional content and affirmed a desire for harmony.

On August 9, Wayne replied with his version of the "seizure of certain articles of Clothing belonging to the State of Virginia."[36] He made no denial but described a different perspective:

> The situation they were found in, & the danger of being all embezzled or destroyed, added to the distressed Condition our people were in for want of shoes & Overalls (more than three fourths being totally destitute of the first article, & too many bare leged (rather too high up for a modest eye to view)) as well on the presumption that they were the property of the United States, Induced me to (order them to a more proper use than a part had lately been appropriated.
>
> However should they be the property of this state, they shall be delivered to the Governors Order. In this case 173 Veterans must inevitably be rendered unfit for service for want of these essential articles. It will therefore be my duty to send these troops into a safe position until shoes & overalls arrive from Pennsa. Humanity will also Induce me to direct Genl. Irvine not to advance his Detatchment until properly supplied with Clothing.[37]

Wayne continued by saying, "It was not without some pain that I perused the following sentence in [the Governors] letter [about] other excesses...said to be committed upon the property of Individuals, by the troops" of the Pennsylvania Line. He was convinced the officers did not "countenance" such actions.[38]

On August 11, Lafayette replied to Wayne and supported him, but suggested a compromise by offering back some of the confiscated items. Lafayette sent a copy to William Davies who replied and gave a lengthy justification of his views about the situation. But the real problem was not ownership; it was creation of a process to identify authority. A logistical unity of command was desperately needed to cope with demands of large mobile military forces in the field.

In spite of addressing logistical challenges, Lafayette did not lose sight of strategic opportunities unfolding in Virginia. "The position at Yorktown enables Lord Cornwallis to collect his forces and will make him formidable," Lafayette wrote to the French Minister Luzerne in Philadelphia. "Fortune will grow tired of protecting us and when I am quite alone, I shall be beaten," if something was not done quickly. "My God, why don't we have a squadron here," Lafayette lamented. "If the French Army could all of a sudden arrive in Virginia and be supported by a squadron, we would do some very good things."[39]

On August 15, Washington sent Lafayette the first confirmed intelligence of the Virginia Campaign. Admiral De Grasse was headed for the Chesapeake. "You will take measures for opening a communications with Count de Grasse the moment he arrives, and will concert measures with him for making the best uses of your joint forces until you receive aid from this quarter," Washington ordered.[40] The allied Virginia Campaign was about to begin, but was Virginia ready?

14

A Last Dance

My situation now becomes very critical

Lafayette's immediate task was developing Virginia into a platform for military support, while always keeping an eye on a relentless and resourceful predator. Survival of his command depended on Virginia's transformation, but at the same time, eluding an enemy snare of another army. The other army was commanded by British Lieutenant General Charles Earl Cornwallis, often referred to as the Earl and sometimes "His Lordship."[1]

On May 13, 1781, after extensive operations in the Carolinas, Cornwallis crossed the Roanoke River in North Carolina and marched into Virginia.[2] While in the Carolinas, he executed a series of tactical successes, but at the expense of irreplaceable military assets, especially manpower. The Battle at Guilford Court House, North Carolina, on March 15, 1781, was a tactical victory, but with human cost so great the British were unable to conduct another offensive in the Carolinas.[3] Although Cornwallis demonstrated superb "tactical leadership," the move into Virginia began the last phase of his military experience in North America.[4] The Earl learned a lot about Americans during his campaigns in the Carolinas, and they gained his grudging admiration. He was constantly surprised by their ability to absorb defeats and then rise to fight again. Like a cat, they had nine lives.

Cornwallis regarded his troops superior to any in the world, especially the Americans who rarely stood their ground against British swords and bayonets. Still, he was amazed by their uncanny ability to survive. Each time he faced them in battle, the outcome was a foregone British victory. But lessons learned in the Carolinas reduced his arrogance somewhat. The occasional rebel advantages were dismissed as irrelevant, insignificant skirmishes, or temporary setbacks in a larger picture of British successes. But realistically, Cornwallis accepted that his situation was precarious. He could not continue operating in the Carolina backcountry, while sustaining the current rate of losses. Even in victory, his forces were devastated by manpower depletion. Sooner or later he faced the prospect of annihilation from overwhelming rebel numbers. This gloomy forecast left Cornwallis with two options: head for the coast and receive reinforcements by the British navy or immediately force the rebels into a large action and decimate their army in a conclusive defeat. Or as he later decided, a third option was to combine the first two.

After crossing into Virginia, Cornwallis headed toward Petersburg and arrived on May 20.[5] He moved into Virginia on his own initiative. His immediate superior was Lieutenant General Sir Henry Clinton headquartered in New York City, but for the most part, Cornwallis ignored Clinton and operated as a separate command. Conveniently, communication delays served as explanations for his failure to consult headquarters on matters when he anticipated disapproval. Specifically, he blamed communication problems for the failure to exchange views with Clinton on the decision to abandon the Carolinas in favor of Virginia.[6]

When Cornwallis reached Petersburg he absorbed an army commanded by the American traitor Benedict Arnold. It was immediately clear the Earl had little respect for Arnold as a soldier or an individual. Shortly after Cornwallis took command, Arnold departed for New York.[7] At Petersburg, Cornwallis had seven thousand effectives, a respectable army by any account.[8]

In previous communications, Clinton sent orders to fortify "a naval [base] other than Portsmouth," in case it became "unsuitable."[9] After review, Cornwallis considered Clinton's instructions a constraint and countermanded them.[10]

On May 20, 1781, Cornwallis received a letter from Clinton written on March 14, 1781. The contents included information on a number of military matters already out of date. Clinton was aware of difficulties caused by communication delays, but blamed Cornwallis. He chided the Earl, saying, "you will see that the want of intelligence has again lost us a fair opportunity of giving a mortal blow."[11]

After reaching the Chesapeake area, Cornwallis' first project was to evaluate terrain and fortifications. He conducted a personal review of Portsmouth and determined the seaport "would not serve the navy's purpose." Cornwallis notified Clinton that he "favored Yorktown." But the Earl strained to launch his "respectable" force against the enemy, rather than lose time fortifying naval facilities. He developed his own strategy without considering input from headquarters. For the most part, input from Clinton was treated as more obstructionist than helpful.

When Cornwallis left the Carolinas, he was vulnerable to the charge of violating Clinton's orders. His defense against such an accusation was carefully thought out. Clinton's original orders were "to reduce the Carolinas." The Earl argued that a successful campaign in the Carolinas was impossible without first neutralizing Virginia. But intrusion into Virginia opened

Cornwallis to a charge of changing British military strategy in the south without Clinton's approval. A major campaign in Virginia at the expense of the Carolinas and failure to fortify a naval facility for British operations changed Clinton's previous operational mandate.

In June Cornwallis sent a subordinate commander, General Alexander Leslie, to reinforce Portsmouth while he proceeded "to dislodge Lafayette from Richmond." But Lafayette, tipped off to the Earl's intentions, left Richmond and headed north to a junction with Brigadier General Anthony Wayne. After a council of war with his officers, Cornwallis decided against pursuing Lafayette. He perceived Lafayette as more of an annoyance than a serious threat and someone to deal with later. For the moment there were more important objectives. He sent forces to destroy "magazines and stores," that supported the Continental Army. The large Virginia arsenal at Point of Forks was the main target. Cornwallis was convinced the arsenal's destruction would interrupt supplies to the Carolinas. A surprise attack presented a tempting opportunity to capture the commander, General Baron von Steuben. On June 4, British advance forces raided Charlottesville and almost captured Governor Thomas Jefferson at Monticello. Cornwallis reached Point of Forks on June 7, 1781, but Steuben escaped just before the British arrived, after methodically destroying everything he did not carry. He left nothing of value. But Cornwallis had achieved one goal: Point of Forks was out of operation.

Cornwallis used the next month to prosecute a vigorous offensive.[12] He conducted a scorched earth policy throughout the state in an effort to force Lafayette into a general engagement, where Cornwallis concluded he would destroy the American forces.

The pressure on Lafayette was immense, especially from Virginia politicians, to face the British. The Patriot press excoriated Cornwallis for his brutal activities. News "from the southward, contains many accounts of the depredations committed by the British forces" in Virginia, printed a newspaper. "Their chief employment is destroying property and terrorizing all who appear to take part in the defence of their country." Lack of "time and room obliges us to omit the horrid tales of British barbarity."[13]

Cornwallis' pressure to force Lafayette into action was working. The Earl knew the politics of his enemy's situation. But Lafayette wanted no part of a general action with Cornwallis' main force. The two were in complete agreement; a general action favored British tactics and almost assured an American disaster. Lafayette's force was not large, although it increased after General Wayne arrived. Inflamed Patriot public opinion demanded action. At the time, the British enjoyed complete freedom to waltz through Virginia's countryside.

Lafayette decided that the only prudent options were well-planned harassing operations with a minimum exposure to his forces. On June 25, 1781, he sent an advance force under Colonel Richard Butler towards Spencer's Ordinary, a small town midway between the James and York Rivers. Butler's force surprised a British rear guard, more interested in plundering than defending against an attack. Outnumbered, the British fled toward Williamsburg.[14]

Back at headquarters in Williamsburg, Cornwallis reviewed his recent accomplishments with pride. The enemy legislature was shattered and their supply magazines were in ruins. He had manpower to meet the enemy anywhere in Virginia. For Cornwallis the next opportunity was destruction of American forces. He was certain that with continued aggressive operations, rebel resistance in Virginia must collapse. It was a chance to demonstrate the value of active operations, improve his reputation with the ministry in London, and at the same time cast a shadow on Clinton's passive approach to waging war.

On June 26, Cornwallis' optimism was shattered by correspondence from headquarters in New York. Clinton was furious by the "move from North Carolina into Virginia." Sir Henry was focused on New York and suddenly found the Earl opening a campaign in the Chesapeake; an action without any support from Clinton and an entirely new military strategy. But Clinton suffered his own detractors – his passive approach drew ire from ministries in London, while Cornwallis' actions were received as a refreshing change. Clinton was in an embarrassing political situation. Lord George Germain, "secretary of state for the colonies" was impressed with Cornwallis and "disenchanted" with Clinton.[15]

The three-way discord between Clinton, Cornwallis, and the London bureaucracy minimized any effective unity of effort against the colonies. Clinton was convinced "the ministry itched to give Cornwallis the supreme command." In the meantime, Washington and Rochambeau's meeting at Wethersfield, Connecticut, convinced Clinton of an impending attack on New York. He ordered Cornwallis "to take a defensive station" and send reinforcements to New York.[16] On June 30, 1781, Cornwallis promised to send reinforcements when Clinton sent transports.[17]

Intelligence reports flowed into British headquarters and, along with closely observed allied movements, signaled New York was the target of a major allied effort. Believing a thrust on New York to be imminent, Clinton had no interest to begin a major campaign in the south. Compounding his aversion was the lack of "faith in the British admiral commanding in North America, Marriot Arbuthnot."[18] The Admiral's fleet was key to any movement of men and materiel and an officer Clinton neither liked nor trusted.

Cornwallis, as might be expected, disagreed with Clinton's northern approach. "It is natural for every officer to turn his thoughts particularly to the part of the war in which he has been most employed," he wrote to Clinton.

My responsibility was "the security at least of South Carolina, if not the re-duction of" resistance in North Carolina. The best way to accomplish this ob-jective was destruction of rebel support coming from Virginia. Until "Virginia was to a degree subjected we could not reduce North Carolina, or have any certain hold on the back country of South Carolina," Cornwallis argued. It was "impossible to maintain a sufficient army in either of these provinces at a considerable distance from the coast, while "the men and riches of Virginia" furnished "ample supplies to the rebel southern army."[19]

The contrast with allied operations was striking. In the allied camps, an effort to develop and refine an effective communication network was a pri-mary objective. Washington, Rochambeau, and their staffs worked to build harmonious personal relationships, based on trust and mutual respect, an es-sential in building a successful unity of command.

Back in Virginia, Lafayette expanded harassing tactics. On July 6, 1781, Cornwallis' forces fought a pitched battle with Wayne's troops at the Battle of Green Spring. The British surprised Wayne after planting false intelligence in the American camp. Fortunately Wayne reacted quickly to the surprise and delayed almost certain entrapment. Lafayette, luckily not far behind, arrived with reenforcements to extract Wayne. The British had won another battle, inflicting heavy American casualties. But Cornwallis' casualties reduced the number of reinforcements available for Clinton in New York and were forces impossible to replace.[20] Again Cornwallis demonstrated tactical superiority, but at a high price.

On July 8, Cornwallis began to receive a series of letters from Clinton. Communications between Clinton and Cornwallis were difficult before; now they were confused and contradictory. Clinton sent orders for Cornwallis to make a variety of moves, which were, under the best conditions, impossible and contradictory. Simultaneously, Cornwallis was to attack in Pennsylvania, establish a post on the Chesapeake, and send reinforcements to New York.[21]

Confused and disgusted, Cornwallis decided to send troops to New York. While embarking forces for Clinton, new orders arrived; Cornwallis was to keep the troops in Virginia and "hold Old Point Comfort which secures Hamp-ton Road" as a base of operations for the British navy.[22] Clinton's letters ar-rived with increasing frequency and the changing orders seemed bizarre.

The real insult to Cornwallis' ego was Clinton's stinging censure for the move into Virginia. On that issue he had to respond. On July 26, he wrote that the criticisms "were unexpected...they are undeserved."[23] He defended his actions and insisted there was no violation of any orders or instructions received. In a sense he blamed Clinton for lack of clarity and confusion in directions from headquarters. But he had the good judgment not to carry his independent command to extreme. He knew when to carry out Clinton's busi-

Watercolor by Don Troiani; Author's collection.

A Private of the Queen's Rangers,
1st American Regiment (Loyalist).
This regiment saw action at Yorktown.

ness, even if he disapproved. Cornwallis and local British sea commanders did survey Old Point Comfort and "unanimously" found it lacked potential for a naval station.[24] While not ideal, Cornwallis decided York and Gloucester were "feasible locations." He wrote to Clinton, explaining his decision, and headed for York. He arrived on August 2, 1781. The rest of August was spent building fortifications.[25]

As Clinton and Cornwallis debated the merits of New York or Virginia, Washington assembled allied forces, but without disclosing intentions. By August 19, 1781, the allied move was obvious when they openly headed south.[26] Although obvious to many, Clinton was not convinced of Washington's southern intentions until the end of August. Incredibly, despite "overwhelming evidence" indicating allied intentions, the British did nothing.[27]

On August 31, 1781, a dismayed Cornwallis discovered the arrival of a significant French Fleet. "There are between 30 & 40 sail within the capes," Cornwallis reported to Clinton. Every day more troubling intelligence arrived in the Earl's headquarters. He never expected events with such ominous consequences. To make matters worse, it was even more precarious than Cornwallis first imagined. After arriving at York, he had split his forces sending a sizable number to Gloucester on the other side of the York River. Soon he found the French had moved a large force up the James River and now occupied the territory to the south behind York Town. The irony was that if Cornwallis had fortified naval facilities at Old Point Comfort as Clinton suggested earlier, there was "maneuvering room" for any British naval forces coming to his aid. But with the French in force, they were in excellent position to block British attempts to relieve Cornwallis by sea. The Earl's intelligence indicated an enemy force of at least eight thousand opposed him.[28]

What to do next was difficult to plan; every time he considered a tactical move, new information arrived to alter the situation. A persistent option was to fight his way out of a strengthening encirclement. Previously, he had been the hunter, the expert in designing entrapments, but now, in a new experience, Cornwallis was the game. As he attempted to devise a plan, there was no indication that Washington and Rochambeau were marching with additional forces. Later on, Cornwallis indicated that if he had known the allies were coming, an attempt to fight his way out would have been the only option. But at the time, as far as he was aware, Washington remained engaged in an effort against New York City. To make matters worse, with his forces split, Cornwallis had few ships to support operations between York and Gloucester and nothing to challenge the increasing superiority of forces opposing him.

On September 5, euphoria erupted at British headquarters with the first good news in more than a month. An English fleet from New York was sighted off the bay and French ships immediately maneuvered to engage it. Still shocked by the array of events cascading against him, Cornwallis enjoyed a momentary respite with the English fleet's arrival and possibility of relief. British Admiral Graves arrived from New York with "nineteen ships of the line." Although unaware of De Grasse's strength, Graves, in a fit of arrogance, was "sublimely confident" of defeating the French. When Graves realized the opposition's size his confidence was shattered. The French and British navies initially engaged on September 5. After a week of maneuvering, the French were "safely anchored inside the Capes."[29] During the week, De Grasse received additional support when Admiral De Barras arrived from Newport, Rhode Island, on September 10.[30] During the naval engagement, Cornwallis learned there was a large allied land force commanded by Washington on the way.

Cornwallis, holed up in Yorktown, observed with trepidation results of the naval engagement off the Capes. The only hope for the Earl was a complete British victory; anything less and his forces were vulnerable to a series of allied actions. All placed him at a decided disadvantage.

Unfortunately for Cornwallis the engagement was considered a tactical draw, with little actual combat. In fact, it was a strategic disaster for the British. The result sealed Cornwallis' fate. For the allies, it was the most important sea engagement of the war. Finally, on September 13, British naval forces commanded by Admiral Graves departed for New York, leaving control of the Chesapeake Bay entirely to the French.[31]

"Discordant views" between Clinton and Cornwallis were not the only impediments to a British unity of effort; the navy was rife with its own contentions. Admiral Graves' official accounts of events in the Chesapeake do not indicate excessive discord, but later revelations of contention by subordinate officer Admiral "Sam" Hood were critical. British inability to dislodge the French navy or at least keep them from a significant station in the Chesapeake was indeed an allied accomplishment with little heralded attention at the time. Later analysis indicated how critical the French success was to the allied cause.

Earlier, on September 6, three British Admirals had met for a council on board the *London*. They were Admirals Graves, Hood, and Drake. Hood later described the meeting as "most inharmonious." Hood blamed Graves for not concentrating forces against the French, a tactic he considered guaranteed victory. After the events, Graves and Hood locked in a continuous series of recriminations, generated mainly by their egos.[32]

An ominous reality awakened both Clinton and Cornwallis. For Clinton it was a sudden realization that the allied army had frozen him in New York, while they marched south. Cornwallis' first jolt came with the French navy's arrival in force, deflecting any relief or escape by sea. Then the dreaded news arrived; a large land force under Washington was headed toward him. By September 17, Cornwallis realized the British navy had not broken the French hold of the bay.

Military opportunities for Cornwallis evaporated on a daily basis. Relief from Clinton in New York was remote. Back in the city, Clinton remained unaware of the naval engagement at "The Capes." Without intelligence revealing Admiral Graves' inability to protect British land forces at Yorktown, Clinton notified Cornwallis that he would arrive with about 4,000 men. Convinced that reinforcements were on the way, Cornwallis decided to wait rather than try to fight his way out of certain entrapment.[33]

Cornwallis received a letter from Clinton on September 15, 1781, with this notification: "Mr. Washington is moving an army southward, with an appearance of haste, and...he expects the co-operation of a considerable French armament. Your Lordship...may be assured that if this should be the case, I shall endeavour to reinforce [you] by all means within the compass of my power, or make every possible diversion in your favor."[34] By the time Cornwallis received the letter, allied forces were nearly a month underway. With this intelligence debacle, added to their contentious personal relationship, prospects for a British successful response diminished.

On September 29, 1781, Cornwallis received notification from Clinton that 5,000 men were to leave New York for the relief of Yorktown by October 5. Aroused, Clinton, in a near-panic effort, had responded to Cornwallis' precarious situation. It had finally dawned on him that a potential military disaster of enormous proportions was possible. Suddenly he faced a stark reality: a personal culpability both in a military and political sense with the events unfolding in the Chesapeake.

On October 3, Cornwallis acknowledged receipt of Clinton's letter dated September 25, 1781, and reported forlorn prospects:

> The enemy are encamped about two miles from us. On the night of the 30th of September they broke ground, and made two redoubts about eleven hundred yards from our works, which, with some works that had been constructed to secure our exterior position occupy a gorge between two creeks which nearly embrace this post. They have finished these redoubts, and I expect they will go on [with] their work this night...I can see no means of [you] forming a junction with me but by the York river, and I do not think that any diversion would be of use to us...I see little chance of my being able to send persons to wait for you at the capes, but I will if possible.[35]

Cornwallis accepted the inevitable outcome, as an experienced tactical commander. While not yet completely hopeless, the odds against his escape increased quickly.

On September 30, Clinton acknowledged that the outlook was dim, but tried to boost Cornwallis' hopes. Sincerely, he stressed that past animosities had not affected an effort on his part to rescue the situation. "Your Lordship may be assured that I am doing every thing to relieve you by a direct move, and I have reason to hope the assurances given me this day by Admiral Graves, that we [will leave New York] by the 12th of October...if the winds permit, and no unforeseen accident happens: this, however, is subject to disappointment." If, in the meantime "I hear from you, your wishes will of course direct me, and I shall persist in my idea of a direct move, even until the middle of November, should it be your Lordships opinion that you can hold out so long." If Cornwallis could not, Clinton noted, "I will immediately make an attempt upon Philadelphia by land, giving you notice, if possible, of my intention." Hopefully this would draw a "part of Washington's force from you," and provide "an opportunity of doing something to save your army; of which, however, you can best judge from being upon the spot."[36]

On October 11, 1781, Cornwallis informed Clinton with resolved pessimism, "...nothing but a direct move to York river, which includes a successful naval action, can save me." He then reported the opening of the siege. "On the evening of the 9th their [allies] batteries opened, and have since continued firing without intermission.... We have lost about seventy men, and many of our works are considerably damaged...we cannot hope to make a very long resistance."[37]

By October 15, 1781, Cornwallis' pessimism turned to desperation: "My situation now becomes very critical."

❧ 15 ❧

A Financial Disaster and French Salvation

The Moment is critical, the Opportunity is precious, the Prospects most happily favorable.

In early August the allies concentrated on operational plans for a move south. Complexities staggered imagination. Washington was swamped by details, which all needed review before the plan's implementation. Even defining challenges, before finding solutions, was a monumental task. The organization, logistics, and mechanics for a southern trek dwarfed previous experiences of either the French or Continental Armies. A move to Virginia by land was longer than either army had previously attempted. The first challenge was to determine routes and whether to deploy forces in large or small groups. As groups of planners huddled together, another serious drawback was immediately obvious. Little was known of the terrain. Maps were incomplete, out of date, and often incorrect. There was general agreement that the topography contained undetermined water and land obstacles.

Not surprisingly, planners agreed that the armies could not carry sufficient supplies. Provisions were needed along the way. Without delay, a commissary had to move ahead to marshal provisions. But financial needs eclipsed all others. Any further action depended on money. In desperation, Washington relied entirely on French aid and the management of recently appointed Superintendent of Finance, Robert Morris.

Headquarters staffs in both French and American camps worked tirelessly in a crisis atmosphere to resolve challenges, prepare action plans, write instructions, and issue orders to start armies in motion. For long periods, Washington personally engaged in writing orders, but financial concerns plagued his consciousness. Development and organization of a logistical platform required five ingredients: persuasion, personality, talent, money and a huge amount of luck, but the scarcest was money. While personality and persuasion were not substitutes for an empty purse, at times they were the only alternatives. Washington soon discovered another pressing difficulty – lack of

talent. Most talented officers wanted field commands with rewards of glory
and recognition. Few laurels came from forging a logistical platform, only
tedious and thankless efforts. Continental Army officers avoided dull logistics with their myriad of failures, corruption, and politics.

For the move to Virginia, Washington's conceptual plan was a work in
progress, evolving over time. At first the prospect was overwhelming and he
exhibited little, if any, enthusiasm. Finally, when he realized the extent of
Rochambeau's resistance to a New York assault, Washington shifted to the
inevitable acceptance of a move south.

The final strategic plan had a creative, audacious military vision, but many
potential flaws. A series of critical assumptions conditioned the plan's feasibility. Support and provisions were needed along the entire route, but confirmation was impossible prior to the move. Sufficient transportation, for
small numerous and separated military forces moving over long distances, did
not exist. Time was another factor frustrating success. To arrive late jeopardized the entire operation and cast a shadow on the allied land forces' capacity to avoid defeat or even annihilation by British forces. Another distinct
threat was starvation. Without the French navy to assist in supplies, many
hungry American soldiers would roam the countryside.

Prospects were gloomy. Washington and Rochambeau faced an insidious dilemma – to move or wait. On one thing they agreed; inaction was no
option. To delay until all tactical flaws were corrected eliminated the opportunity to concentrate the largest allied military force of the war. The chance
of another opportunity was remote. The move, despite overwhelming odds
against success, required decisions seldom made in the annals of military history. The prize for success, attractive to both Washington and Rochambeau,
was a lethal blow to the enemy capable of changing the course of a stalemated
war. But failure meant collapse of the American cause. The hours and days
consumed by the decision process were filled with tension and doubt. The
outcome was uncertain and the stakes so very high. The critical influence after
any decision was luck, or as Washington wrote many years later, "Divine
Providence." Once a decision was made, uncertainty and doubt were subor-
dinated to commitment and determination.

Next, Washington concentrated on information diffusion to individuals and organizations that could supply quick, beneficial assistance to the
plan's success. Activity at headquarters continued twenty-four hours a day.
A sea of humanity arrived and left in droves with a sense of urgency. So
many candles burned at night the smoke filled smaller rooms. Staff officers remained on duty until they collapsed exhausted and fell asleep in
chairs, on tables, on the floor. Fortunately, the weather cooperated and
windows were opened to diffuse the smoke and smell of so many men

confined in close quarters. During thunderstorms, windows were closed against the wind blowing through rooms and hallways disturbing papers and extinguishing candles or betty-lamps.

Maps, sketches, diagrams, and documents covered walls and tables. Complex operational plans began to take shape for the multitude of actions required to move forces more than six hundred miles from New York across five states: New Jersey, Pennsylvania, Delaware, Maryland and finally, Virginia. Aides darted between rooms with information for superior officers who wrote and revised plans. Washington's office had a line of aides waiting to enter, carrying documents for approval. But a nagging and striking realization was unavoidable; during this phase success was more and more a matter of finance. It was folly to start a move until financial matters progressed. Every part of the move depended on money. Again, at just the right time, divine providence intervened. On August 12, Thomas McKean, President of Congress, sent Washington exhilarating news:

> France acts a truly friendly part. We shall certainly obtain from her, this year, twenty millions of liveres; four of which will be retained for Doctor Franklin...and the residue...subject to the directions of Congress. I have the strongest reasons to believe that Colonel Laurens is now on the Ocean, and has with him two millions and an half of this money in specie.[1]

President McKean reinforced his optimism to a friend, writing, "it is with infinite pleasure I can Inform you of our very fair prospects on [financial matters] from abroad as well as at home. France has lately given further proof, that she is a faithful Ally," although, he continued, "I cannot be more particular. Spain continues to act interested and mysterious...but in the end close with us. The United Provinces of the Netherlands appear to be very friendly."[2]

While Washington and Rochambeau, elated by the improved financial prospects, completed operational plans for the campaign, rumors abounded in Congress. Congressional delegates transmitted rumors to family, friends, and politicians throughout the states. Delegate James Duane informed New York Governor George Clinton, "That part of Cornwallis's Army which was supposed to be destined for New York & had been some days on shipboard debarked" and were "Occupied in fortifying York" (Yorktown, Virginia). Another piece of information Duane supplied involved an event with catastrophic potential for the Continental Army. British warships had captured the Dutch island of St. Eustacia, which served as a reservoir for military supplies shipped to the Americans. Fortunately, the French navy recovered twenty-four English ships loaded with plunder and destined for Great Britain.

The American war's enormous cost had a telling effect on French politics. Americans never fully appreciated the financial crisis in France. The war's cost was responsible for serious French political reverberations, eventually causing the resignation of French financial minister, Jacques Necker. As political and financial troubles percolated in France, other financial difficulties developed in the United States. In a short but staggering revelation one Virginia delegate wrote, "On my return to Philadelphia...the beginning of May, I found when I reached Wilmington my continental currency [was] of no use, and when I arrived in Philadelphia, [it had] little or no value, the exchange then being about 700 for one."[3]

The state of financial affairs haunted every decision Washington made. He wrote to Robert Morris, Superintendent of Finance, on August 17; both Washington and Rochambeau signed the letter. In addition to needs "at the Head of Elk to carry the troops down the Bay a very considerable Quantity will be wanted in Virginia." A general order without specifics was needed because only estimates were available for "what will be consumed." The situation was even worse. Until they arrived at the Elk, Washington could not "ascertain the number of men [who] will be drawn together or the time they will be employed."[4]

A shocked Robert Morris read Washington's letter in disbelief. How could anyone conduct a campaign with so many imponderables? Washington had requested provisions for a military force of undetermined size, for an unknown period of time, for shipment to unspecified locations, while the allies were on the move from New York to Virginia. But Washington was not finished; he requested him to send up his "light Vessels of every kind to Elk." He requested Morris to have as many boats as possible sent from "Baltimore and the upper parts of the Bay...take measures at a proper time for that purpose." Then came the jolt. "I am confident it will be necessary to give the American Troops destined for southern service one Months pay in specie."[5]

Previously, Morris made periodic trips to headquarters. He held conferences with Washington and senior staff members on a variety of financial matters. One trip, just after Washington's August 17 letter, included a chance meeting with Washington and Richard Peters, Secretary of the Board of War. The discussions covered the "movement south." Washington, stymied by shortages of "money and material," asked Peters, "What can you do for me?" Peters replied, "With money, everything; without it nothing," and glanced inquiringly at Morris who hesitated, then commented, "Let me know." Without hesitation, Washington motioned to several aides and rose, excused himself, and spent "the rest of the morning" calculating, checking and rechecking cost estimates for the campaign, and gave the information to Morris.

Morris studied Washington's calculations intently. By any measure the sums were enormous, exceeding resources available to the Continental Congress. Morris and Peters returned to Congress and began a series of discussions with delegates on the overall deplorable situation of military finances.

At times discourse was heated, but Morris focused on the monetary infusion necessary to maintain an army and provide for the Virginia campaign. Congressional attitudes were far from encouraging. Some delegates viewed Washington's monetary requirements with great skepticism. Others felt expenses inflated by "bloated expenditures" and a military organization in need of streamlining to reduce excessive costs.

Earlier in August Congress had posed a series of questions to Washington, suggesting that the deplorable financial situation resulted from inefficiencies in the Continental Army. Washington, engaged in directing one of the most complicated military campaigns in history, had to contend with a Congress that had little appreciation for the financial demands of operating a military organization.

On August 21, in careful, measured, respectful, but firm terms, Washington replied to Congress, answering their suggestions point for point in disagreement. The reply was one of the most detailed disagreements ever sent to Congress by the commander-in-chief. Washington answered "with all that frankness, and sincerity, which have from your own candor" been communicated. "I am only unhappy, that I should be forced to dissent [in every] single instance." Washington's reasons for not reducing army size included "glorious opportunities...lost by us [and] almost ruinous advantages...taken by the enemy, in time of our weakness, for want of a permanent force in the field." He reminded Congress of the "great reduction" in regiment strength "from 116 to 50 since the year 1777." His view on the enemy's situation was much different from Congress. He did "not find" the enemy "so much exhausted, or [their] strength so debilitated, as to warrant any further diminution of our established force." Washington further insisted that, "the States are able, by proper exertions to furnish the number of men required." Their populations, in many instances, "have...increased rather than diminished." He had found "the proportion of Officers is not too great" in comparison with British and French forces. The Continental Army required a "full compliment of officers," because of the high number of new recruits continually circulating in the army. "It is likewise an established fact, that every [change] unless founded in the most obvious principles," resulted in an "uneasiness among the Officers."[6]

A big irritant for Washington was the lack of delegate understanding about monetary requirements for maintaining an army in the field. Many delegates suffered a militia mentality, which expected duty discharged on a volunteer basis. The differences in costs between militias and a professional army were not easy for Congress to appreciate.

While Washington engaged in exchanges with Congress, Morris continued to marshal finances. He faced a menacing inflation caused by French forces that paid in hard cash and competed for provisions with the Continental Army. The ability to pay cash enabled the French to construct an effective supply organization, by employing Americans as procurement agents.[7]

All Continental Army military operations desperately needed financial support and Morris was deluged with requests. The first thing he did was to prioritize his effort. His top priority concerned the Allied move – providing magazines along the route. Continental Army and French forces planned different routes, which complicated establishing locations. After much discussion and communication he identified routes, designated magazine locations, then selected, appointed and deployed individuals to implement actions. The magazines contained flour, salted meat, and rum. Even the acquisition of wooden barrels, already in short supply, "caused prices to soar."[8]

In the middle of exhausting efforts to establish logistics support bases, came shocking news from France, the resignation of Minister of Finance, Jacques Necker. The story was that "Necker made misleading claims that ordinary revenues of the French government exceeded expenses and covered interest payments on new war loans for the 1781 campaign."[9] In reality, he knew "the French war effort was financially" near bankruptcy. In desperation he began "secret negotiations with the British to end the war on [terms] acceptable to...the French court."[10] Suddenly, the Necker affair cast an ominous shadow on the future allied operations.

Back at headquarters, a frantic Washington sent streams of requests to Morris. On August 22, as the allies moved south, Morris bluntly acquainted the commander-in-chief with reality. "Money Matters [are] in as bad a Situation as possible." Aware of Washington's disappointment, he added, "but I can assure you...I will make every Exertion possible to place you in the best situation our Means will allow."[11]

As discouraging as the situation was, Morris did not despair. With untiring effort, he worked to establish a process for provisioning the line of march closest to allied forces. The same day he sent the reality check to Washington, Morris notified the "Governors of New Jersey and Delaware" that supplies were needed which Congress had "demanded from your state:"

> It becomes my duty again to press for a compliance with those demands....
> We are on the eve of the most active operations, and should they be in any
> way retarded by the want of necessary supplies...unhappy consequences may
> follow. Those who may be justly chargeable with neglect will have to an-
> swer for it to their country.[12]

Morris challenged the governors by placing their patriotism and dedication to the American cause on the line. He wanted specific answers:

> I beg to know most speedily...what supplies are collected and at what
> places...also the times and places at which the remainder is to be ex-
> pected.... I must assure you that nothing but the urgency of our affairs

would render me this [candid]. I...assure you that while...affairs continue
so urgent I must continue to be demanding.[13]

Morris described financial needs requested during the stay at Washington's
headquarters:

> I had constant applications for money from almost everybody...I had
> conferences with the quartermaster-general, paymaster-general, clothier-
> general, commissary-general of issues, director-general of the hospitals,
> and with many other persons.... I could only recommend the strictest
> economy in their expenditures.[14]

Morris was tenacious addressing the complicated issues surrounding
procurement and revenue generation. At the time, few appreciated his
efforts. Some considered him too free with military finances, not demanding more efficiency. Probably no American other than Washington exercised more influence on the Virginia campaign than Robert Morris. As
wretched as the money supply was, Morris distributed it with amazing
tactical advantage, usually just in time to avoid a catastrophe. He attempted to lower the expectations of those requesting funds, while brow-
beating potential revenue sources. No individual associated with the
Continental Army and Congress was lonelier or less appreciated than the
Superintendent of Finance. At times, Morris was accused of inefficiency,
incompetence, and corruption. Glory, honor, and gratitude were not rewards for Morris or his position. Yet he was key to the success of the
Virginia campaign. Dedicated, committed, determined, and grim, Morris
was the financial wizard of the allied move south.

Morris was appointed on May 14, 1781, but did not start until June 27.
Initially he expected that supply demands would not peak until later in the
year.[15] With the allied plan to move south, his only recourse for financial
support was "Rochambeau who controlled the Kings war chest." They met
and candidly discussed all financial aspects of the campaign, including a full
review of Washington's calculations. Discussions continued for several hours,
but with a sense of relief, Morris realized Rochambeau was committed to a
move south. As they met at a table off to the side, senior French staff officers studied Washington's calculations, while Morris and Rochambeau continued discussions. The atmosphere was cordial and discussions informative.
Each man used the opportunity to get better acquainted with the other. Morris was optimistic; he glanced occasionally at the staff officers nodding in
agreement, as they checked the figures justifying Washington's requests. Finally there was nothing more to discuss and the meeting concluded with
Rochambeau willingly loaning the Americans "twenty thousand dollars in
coin" to begin the campaign.[16]

When he became a member of the Continental Congress, Robert Morris was a wealthy merchant, "married into an aristocratic family."[17] At the time, Congress had no effective financial policy, yet all their actions involved matters around finance. Morris became the initiator of financial policy and his influence in the country was second only to Washington.[18] Effectively, Morris was the commander-in-chief of financial matters and fiscal policy.[19]

On August 27, Washington wrote to Morris before receiving Morris's rather discouraging letter of the same day. Washington explained the needs for transportation, especially "so far as procuring Vessels" and asked Morris to use his "influence with the Gentlemen of Baltimore to permit any Vessels...to assist us in transportation." Then again to the subject of money:

> I must entreat you, if possible to procure one months pay in specie for the detachment which I have under my command; part of those troops have not been paid any thing for a long time past, and have upon several occasions shewn marks of great discontent...but I make no doubt that...a little hard money would put them in proper temper.[20]

Meanwhile Washington continued to refine his communications network. Communication exchanges had to become more expeditious and secure. Occasionally intercepted letters had unintended benefits. One example was the British capture of "Washington's, Rochambeau's and de Barras letters" following the "Wethersfield Conference," which expressed plans to "abandon the southern move in favor of an attack on New York."[21] Without question it was a stroke of luck, because this intelligence convinced Clinton that New York City was the object of allied intentions and froze him there until September 1, several weeks after the allies departed for Virginia.[22]

On August 27, a busy day in letter writing, Washington notified Governors Thomas Nelson of Virginia, and Thomas Sim Lee of Maryland, of a change in plans for the next campaign, which now included a trek to Virginia. Maryland was a transitional state for allied forces and crucial as a source for supplies and provisions. Another important consideration was Maryland's ability to supply water transportation for use in the Chesapeake Bay. Washington informed Governor Lee that he was now marching a large "Detachment from the American Army," and the entire French forces "to Virginia." Reserved, but implied, desperation is reflected in Washington's appeal. "The Moment is critical, the Opportunity is precious, the Prospects most happily favorable. I hope that no "lack of effort on our part may prove the Means of our Disappointments."[23] Governor Sim Lee received a personal request from Washington detailing the critical role Maryland played in the success of the next campaign and how the state's participation was needed in a campaign to determine the war's outcome. For the first time, Lee recognized the sense of urgency and the type of support required to support the allied effort.

Next, Washington prepared Governor Nelson of Virginia, by using a different emphasis. First he congratulated Nelson, a personal friend, for appointment "to the Seat of Government," and expressed anticipation of "the pleasure and advantage of your future official Correspondence and assistance," Washington wrote. "I cannot entertain a doubt of receiving every possible aid and assistance from the State of Virginia." Demands on Virginia exceeded those on other states. Virginia's fate was to sustain allied forces, experience a marauding enemy and the ravages of a military conflict for an indeterminate time with an uncertain outcome.[24] The governors of Maryland and Virginia were now fully informed of the expectations and ordeal heading their way.

✤ 16 ✤

A New Beginning

⊶ *Matters having now come to a crisis.* ⊷

At Washington's Headquarters in Dobbs Ferry, New York, August 10, 1781, was hot and sultry in the morning with a heavy afternoon thunder-shower. Later, when the storm passed, a cool breeze relieved the hot stuffy rooms where earlier the smell of humanity penetrated the air. Noise echoed in the hallways, upstairs and down. Groans, laughter, and voices sometimes revealed heated discussions. Great energy and motion was evident in people rushing from one place to another in endless processions. The day was filled with an unusual flood of correspondence. A continual stream of riders arrived and departed exchanging information, intelligence, and orders from the commander-in-chief. While a busy day for headquarters, nothing eventful occurred. The next day was different. Admiral de Barras, at French Headquarters, notified Washington that dispatches from the "Comte de Grasse" had arrived.[1]

The atmosphere changed immediately with a charged sense of antici-pation. Washington tried to calm the expectations of his junior officers, but even he exuded a twinge of excitement as he waited for a careful trans-lation of information. Nothing was left to nuances of language.

Finally, on August 15, 1781, Washington forwarded information to Lafayette which transformed rumors and expectations into reality. "The Concorde Frigate arrived at Newport" with information "from Count de Grasse," Washington wrote. De Grasse was to depart from "St. Domingo the 3d. of this month with a Fleet of between 25 and 29 [ships] of the line and a considerable Body of land forces." He was headed directly to "the Chesapeak" and "will either be there by the time this reaches you," or if not, wrote Washington, Lafayette was to maintain a constant lookout for the French arrival. Regardless of the enemy's strength, Washington stressed that everything must be done to prevent a British retreat into North Carolina.[2] In conclusion, Washington added:

You shall hear further from me as soon as I have [completed] plans and formed dispositions for sending a reinforcement from [here]. You will be particularly careful to conceal the expected arrival of the Count, because if the enemy is [unaware] they will stay on board their transports in the Bay, which will be the luckiest Circumstances in the World. You will take measures for opening communication with Count de Grasse the moment he arrives.[3]

Washington had stubbornly held the conviction that a successful assault against New York City would end the war. The capture of General Clinton and surrender of British forces with any ships of the Royal navy trapped in New York harbor would inflict a devastating military and political loss. The political ramifications in London were incalculable. Washington argued with reason and experience that allied forces had adequate logistical support around New York and only a powerful French fleet was needed to seal off the city.

From the start, Rochambeau favored a southern operation, but agreed that allied naval superiority was a vital ingredient in any action. Rochambeau never openly opposed Washington's passion for New York, but a lack of enthusiasm was present in all his discussions. Washington sensed the reluctance and realized an unenthusiastic Rochambeau was as damaging to the opportunity as someone openly opposed.

Washington's experience with the climate of southern states, especially this time of the year, shaped his views. He saw danger in Rochambeau's failure to fully appreciate the challenges in an allied move of such distance in the heat of a southern summer. The move faced treacherous road conditions with uncertainty of both provisions and transportation along the entire route.

Washington considered it an absurd idea to move men and artillery such distances under prevailing conditions. The remote wildness encouraged desertions. Disease suffered from poor food, water, insects, and stifling weather was another factor, far more severe than Rochambeau's experiences in Europe. Even if the move succeeded, the French fleet's arrival was not guaranteed. Once in Virginia, after a harrowing trek, the allies still had to achieve a victory over an experienced and determined foe. In Washington's judgment, enormous complications existed, but doing nothing was no option.

Washington and Rochambeau wrestled to complete details for the next move. Progress was slowed by countless conflicting priorities. Unexpectedly, in the middle of all the planning turmoil, fortune influenced events. The enemy received reinforcements from different locations and intelligence indicated more coming from Cornwallis. Enemy reinforcements arrived by the boatload. The steady stream of British reinforcements strengthened Rochambeau's resistance to an assault on New York City. He rebutted Washington's arguments against the move south, not by strenuous objections, but in attempts to weaken them. Rochambeau's major persuasion was money. In earlier correspondence with Admiral de Grasse, lack of money was a central subject. If the Admiral brought money, Rochambeau was certain he could reduce Washington's objections against a southern move.

On or about August 14, 1781, the decision was made to abandon an assault against New York in favor of the Virginia campaign. Washington's thoughts at the time are reflected in a diary entry. "Matters having now come to a crisis," he wrote, there was a need for "a decisive plan" to take advantage of "the shortness of Count de Grasse's promised stay." But "the apparent disinclination" of French Naval Officers "to force the harbour of New York," and "the feeble compliance of the States" in filling manpower requisitions, forced Washington "to give up all idea of attacking New York."[4]

In a letter to Lafayette dated August 15, 1781, Washington sent orders for the first phase of a complex unity of effort. Success depended on speedy, secure, and accurate intelligence. He ordered Colonel Samuel Miles that, "Dispatches for the Marquis de La Fayette are of the greatest importance," and to establish a reliable "Chain of Expresses" to "be depended upon [for delivery] in the shortest conceivable time." Miles was ordered to send this "Letter immediately by a trusty, active Express, with Orders to ride Night and Day." The courier must "deliver the Letter to the Marquis" as quickly as possible. "You will...acknowledge" receipt of the dispatch and inform Washington of the "conveyance by which you have expedited the Dispatch."[5] Effective tactical operations depended on a communication network where exchanges traveled over extreme distances with speed and security previously not achieved.

On August 17, 1781, Washington issued his first order to Rochambeau, exercising unity of command for the Virginia Campaign.[6] "I am of [the] opinion...French Army under your command had better [move] by the following Route" to Trenton, New Jersey, from "Sunday August 19" to "Thursday August 29, 1781."[7] Washington supplied detailed maps for the ten-day trip.

French artillery wagons departed from Philipsburg, New York, on August 18. The next day, at "five in the morning," units of "the French Army left the camp." The Americans departed on the 19th, "but by another route."[8] A French officer described the mood. We "are in perfect ignorance whether we are going against New York or...to Virginia to attack Cornwallis." The troops marched at noon, but the weather was terrible. "A severe rain" made a mess of the roads "and wet us all through." Wagons broke down, even overturned, causing so much of a slow-down "that at eight o'clock in the evening we had made only four miles." Cumbersome French artillery moved at a snail's pace and took six days to go forty miles, "because of the terrible weather and incredible roads."[9]

Later, Washington noted, "much trouble was taken and finesse used to misguide and bewilder Sir Henry Clinton in regard to the real object." When questioned why his troops were not informed of the destination, Washington replied that great pains were "taken to deceive our own army; for I had always conceived, when the imposition did not completely take place at home, it could never sufficiently succeed abroad."[10]

On August 19, 1781, Washington informed Major General William Heath, "Sir: You are to take Command of the Troops remaining in this Department.... The security of West Point and the Posts in the Highlands [are] the first Object of your Attention." In order to discharge this responsibility, "you will make such decisions as the Circumstances shall from Time to Time require."[11]

On August 20, 1781, after months of discussions, uncertainty, and planning, the trek of allied forces was underway. Washington, in command of two thousand "picked American troops," headed south reaching Kings Ferry and crossing the Hudson River rapidly on the 20th and 21st.[12] Pleased with the crossing, Washington wrote to Rochambeau, "I hope your army will be [able] to cross with the same facility when they arrive."

The French Army reached Kings Ferry, New York, on August 22. The next two days were spent crossing the river "in ferry boats collected in great numbers, [but] heavy guns, and much camp equipage...were not all over until the 26th."[13] Washington watched intently, as both armies crossed.[14]

One unexpected result was how little friction occurred between the two armies. A surprised American officer wrote, "The French army and we are in most perfect harmony" and "it extends from the Commander in Chief down to the lowest sentinel." Even Luzerne, the French minister from Philadelphia, "noted the absence of friction," after visiting the two armies.[15]

A French officer described the Americans as ragged Continentals and added, "These brave fellows made one's heart ache. It is almost unbelievable! At times they were almost without clothes. Some had only trousers and a little coat, or jacket of linen." Most had no socks. The officer was "horrified at their emaciated condition and amazed at their unwavering fortitude."[16]

Communications were the core of all action and demanded hourly attention. Washington assigned a body of aides whose only responsibility was to write orders, notify officers and inform politicians of the cascading events. One of the greatest difficulties was finding recipients. Some, close to the commander-in-chief, enjoyed speedy exchanges, but others like Generals Greene and Lafayette, suffered the curse of distance.

In early August, Washington ordered Lafayette, in anticipation of Admiral De Grasse's arrival in "the Chesapeak," to keep "General Wayne with the troops destined for South Carolina...until you hear from me again, and inform Genl. Greene of the cause of their delay." Effectively, his orders redirected Lafayette's efforts. The difficulty was timing. A day lost in orders reaching Lafayette delayed his ability to carry them out.[17]

A piece of encouraging intelligence was the level of enemy forces now in New York City. They made no attempt to send reinforcements to Cornwallis. British forces in the immediate city area totaled "more than 12,000" compared to Washington and Rochambeau's combined force of "9,000."[18] But still missing was critical intelligence about the progress and position of Admiral de Grasse.

On August 21, Washington sent additional intelligence to Lafayette. "Troops destined for the Southern Quarter are now in Motion" and "Our March will be continued with all dispatch that our Circumstances will admit."[19]

As the allies solved challenges, more immediately surfaced. Transportation needs exceeded expectations. Washington, in desperation, prodded Lafayette, "as speedily as possible" to send an account "of the Number of Wagons and Horses which may be collected in Virginia for the use of the Detachment with me, and for the French Army."[20] Washington cautioned Lafayette, "it will be of great importance [for] the Success of our present" effort that the enemy "should not have it in their Power to...Retreat." My "earnest Wish [is] the Land and Naval Force which" are with you "may so combine" to keep the British Army from escaping. How he was to do this, "I shall not at this Distance attempt to dictate. I am confident "your military Genius and Judgment, will lead you to" take the most effective action.[21]

By August 27, the grand allied trek was underway, but with a twist. Enemy observers closely followed the allies and reported every detail. In New York, General Clinton was still convinced the city was the main objective, and moves in New Jersey only reinforced his conviction. He felt the allied advance "on Sandy Hook" was made "to cover the entrance" of New York harbor where French vessels would attempt "an attack on New York."[22] To support Clinton's belief, the allies went into camp on August 29 and "built four baking ovens," indicating a permanency for the camp.[23] The dummy camp faced Staten Island and "fires were kept going for several nights...to...keep the English thinking...we planned to besiege New York."[24] The feint at New York was primarily Washington's idea. French officers "all guessed wrong. Not one...thought...the British general would sit still."[25] The ruse worked and the British remained fixed in New York City. Then, in a sudden move, French forces headed to the Delaware River. By now the allies possessed good maps prepared by Washington's mapmaker and engineer, Simeon De Witt. In August 1781, Washington, after seeing the deplorable state of map intelligence available in the planning sessions, "directed De Witt to survey and prepare maps for the march south to Virginia," an assignment, which he carried out "brilliantly...in a matter of weeks."[26]

Along the route, French soldiers observed the countryside. How strange it seemed, compared to home. One officer described the differences. The "dwellings resemble farm houses; they have no gardens, no fences, no fruit-walls, only some apple...peach...and...scattered cherry trees."[27] To French eyes, the entire country was strange but inviting. A frightening feature was climate and weather – the intense heat and bugs, often accompanied by violent thunderstorms with downpours so heavy it was sometimes impossible to see more than a few feet. Nothing remained dry after these awful deluges.

By the time Clinton learned they "had marched south...to engage Cornwallis," the allies had "crossed the Delaware." On August 31, Washington and Rochambeau, ahead of the two armies, arrived "at Philadelphia."[28] French officers, seeing the capital city for the first time, described it as "a very extensive city...regularly built; the houses are of brick and pretty high...there are sidewalks for persons on foot." The "public buildings... are worthy of a great city," especially "the house where congress meets."[29]

The Continental Army marched into Philadelphia "on the afternoon of September 2...the weather...warm and sultry. There had been no rain for days." The "weary foot-soldiers raised great clouds of dust which was a pity, as the ladies [watched] from the windows of every house." The army stretched "for two miles."[30] On September 4, the French marched into Philadelphia "dressed as elegantly as ever." It was indeed an "imposing spectacle of a French army in the fine style of military array, consisting of six thousand men."[31]

Washington's official announcement of the move south lifted morale, but presented a potential financial disaster for Virginia, already suffering shortages, inflation, and all the ravages of war. They needed "Men, Arms, Ammunition Horse Accoutrements...to An Alarming Degree," Lafayette wrote.[32] How would additional forces be maintained? Perhaps, Lafayette thought, Washington was unaware of the precarious conditions throughout the state. In replying to Washington's letter on the move, he expressed reservations. "There is such Confusion in affairs in this part of the World." There were immense difficulties in "a proper formation of Magazines." But, as usual, the main problem was financial. "Had we anything like Monney [we could] go on Very well." There was "No Cloathing of any Sort – no Heavy Artillery" and a lack of small arms, but a "Great deal of Ammunition." Washington's personal appeals could help alleviate some of these shortages. "I Hope You will Come Your self to Virginia, and if the french Army Moves this way," Lafayette wrote. "[I will see you] at the Head of the Combined Armies." He advised Washington to bring qualified "Heads of departments," for there was no one "equal to the task of a Campaign [on] so large a scale." Lafayette's reservations, while accurate, hardly encouraged an allied army to move south. But Washington faced these problems in most areas.[33]

Lafayette was an intelligence reservoir and provided detailed assessments of conditions and the latest information on enemy activities, including the abandonment of Portsmouth. They "are not yet Fortifying York, [and] do not Appear Very Much Alarmed," he wrote. "[I am keeping] the intelligence Concerning Count de Grasse a...Secret." Accumulating provisions "My dear General," with no working system, "will render our Subsistence difficult." His immediate need was for "Intelligent Commisaries [and] Hard Monney." Since Lafayette had taken command of the army nothing was "Sent from the treasury" and the state's "Monney is Good for nothing."[34] The next day, Lafayette reported the first intelligence that Cornwallis was fortifying York.

Desperation and frustration plagued allied forces during the trek. Sometimes news in the next message changed the entire day's action. The most worrying prospect, as time passed, was the continued lack of intelligence from Admiral de Grasse.

An anxious Washington considered the situation. The small separated units marching long distances presented a new threshold of danger. Defeat of any unit was a potential disaster for the entire allied force. The main defense against enemy surprise attacks depended on reliable intelligence and the prudence of individual unit commanders. Washington, always conscious of the vital need for intelligence, constantly reminded separated forces that their salvation depended on expeditious and accurate communication. Communications, he insisted, was the soul of moving armies and he ordered commanders to create a new, super express intended to maintain open and constant contact between commands.

While Washington was engaged in the massive movement of men and materials, he was unaware of an event which occurred in Virginia. Good fortune intervened again to change the war's course. With favorable winds, Admiral De Grasse arrived in Virginia on August 30, 1781, and immediately started the "disembarkation of his troops." The Admiral's trip was successful, fortuitous, and hopefully a good omen when he captured "every English vessel sighted, bringing needed provisions and preventing knowledge of fleet's movement reaching the enemy."[35]

For a short time, while their troops disembarked, the French expected a British attack. "It was a pleasant surprise for our troops on landing that Cornwallis did not move in the least to hinder them, since...a single cannon could have caused much damage in the narrow and...winding river," wrote a French officer.[36]

On shore three men wearing Continental Army officer uniforms witnessed the French arrival with anticipation and excitement. They had waited for weeks, never certain when or if De Grasse would arrive. Before the French fleet completed deployment, the three officers in a small boat headed for the admiral's flagship. Two assistants accompanied "Brigadier General Duportail, Chief of Engineers," a French national "in the American Army." He carried a letter of introduction signed by Washington and Rochambeau. Duportail and De Grasse became instant friends, and without hesitation, began planning tactical arrangements in aid of the campaign.[37]

Admiral De Grasse wrote to Lafayette. "I have just arrived, sir." He had received his letter with "your position and our enemy's." He agreed with Washington's proposed plans and stated that the next day, "three small frigates [will sail] into the James River...to prevent General Cornwallis's army from [escaping] to Carolina." They would disembark "3,250 effectives...some hussars, artillery, etc." In addition, De Grasse planned to send "three or four vessels up the York River to force General Cornwallis to decide whether to hold the right or left side of the river." He agreed that "destruction of Cornwallis's army is a critical matter," and "if necessary," he could "land 1,800 select troops from the ships garrisons," and "form companies of sailors, who would...be of some assistance and make an effective attack."[38] De Grasse's letter reached Lafayette two days later, but a day after the admiral arrived rumors flowed with a frenzy. Lafayette was skeptical of the rumors. He alerted Anthony Wayne "that a large fleet from the Southward" had arrived in the bay. "I have every Reason to Believe [it is the] Count de Grasse with 25 Ships of the Line," but "the account is not [confirmed]." The suspense kept Lafayette awake at night.[39]

September 1, 1781, would be etched in Lafayette's memory. In the middle of a meeting with subordinates, militia representatives, and state officers, including Governor Nelson, official news of De Grasse arrived. At first the room filled with conspicuous silence. Was it true? The express rider presented the admiral's letter, endorsed by "Brigadier General Duportail, Chief of Engineers." After an initial shocked silence, a charged atmosphere erupted. Both Lafayette and Governor Nelson exploded in an outburst of jubilation. The letter's tone, along with De Grasse's plans, lifted Lafayette's spirit to the heavens.

De Grasse's sudden arrival triggered a flood of communications announcing the good fortune. Orders and instructions streamed from Lafayette's headquarters to exploit what seemed unlimited opportunities. Coordination with French forces was a priority. Lafayette immediately informed Washington, "From the Bottom of My Heart I Congratulate you upon the Arrival of the French fleet." Confirmation was assured after "the Admiral's Dispatches Came to Hand." Governor Nelson "was with me when the letters Came." He left the room immediately, jumped on a horse, and rode "off to His Council." The governor's efforts were solidly behind their situation. "We may depend upon a Quantity of Cattle, but flour [must be sent] from Maryland and Pennsylvania." The governor "Sent people to collect Horses...and Vegetables." There was a desperate need for both.[40]

Nelson issued orders and proclamations to make Virginia's war effort more forceful. He increased pressure for an effective logistical platform throughout the entire state. As encouragement, Nelson invoked martial law with enforcement policies that treated violators as traitors. By September 2, Nelson was back in the capital initiating more actions. He sent a message to Admiral de Grasse congratulating him on the safe arrival with assurances the "commissary general" was ordered to contact French forces "and adopt every measure...to supply them whatever they may want." He issued further orders to gather supplies for other forces in Virginia, including Lafayette. A failure to comply "will be attended with the most fatal consequences," he wrote. "County Lieutenants" were ordered to "procure all the Wagons they possibly can," stressing the need for "an immediate supply."

But reactions to Nelson's orders were slow. Lafayette informed the governor on September 4, "The French troops" have landed and were "without provisions, [especially] flour. I have not seen, nor cannot find a commissary." He implored him to "forward in vessels all the flour within your reach."[41]

Lafayette was desperate; two days later he informed Nelson, "I am sorry to inform you that the French army [is] at this moment without provisions." The little flour received "is just exhausted." There appeared "no prospect of a supply." He knew that cattle were "within a few miles of camp, but we" have received none. "The Commissary has promised to do everything, but nothing is done."[42]

There was more dismal news. The army had to halt for "want of horses and wagons." Lafayette explained, "The persons" empowered "to borrow horses find the people" were "unwilling to lend them," and "our wants do not lessen." In a reply to Lafayette, William Davies, commissioner of Virginia's war office, explained supply difficulties in harsh terms. Before a "few continentals" arrived, many people "were disposed...to assist the British openly...they not only refused the payment of taxes," but rebelled against "the execution of laws," Davies wrote. But now since the "Continentals arrived...All opposition has subsided." He assured him, "I am exerting the whole of my influence to procure supplies for the army."[43]

A few days later, Nelson issued a proclamation banning the "exportation" of provisions, including "all Beef, Pork, Bacon, Wheat, Indian Corn, Pease, or other grain or flour or Meal" from the state. He enforced the proclamation "under pain of incurring the penalties inflicted by the Act of Assembly."[44] Nelson issued the Proclamation, blocking provisions from going out of state or overseas, on September 5. In addition to orders sent to county lieutenants and state commissary officials, Nelson required assistance from county committees of safety. "A large Body of Troops" was "expected in a few Days. [You] will have all the Flour you can procure…sent in Vessels…with all possible dispatch," he ordered.[45]

On September 2, Washington, still unaware of De Grasse's arrival, replied to Lafayette's letter of August 21. Almost point for point Washington addressed the concerns. "Nothing, My Dear Marquis could have afforded me grater satisfaction than the information communicated in your two Letters." With all the forces now available, "I flatter myself we shall not experience any considerable difficulties from the want of Men. Heavy Cannon, Ordinance Stores & Ammunition" were underway. Washington, still fearful of inadequate logistical support, was "extremely anxious respecting the Supplies of the Army…not only Provisions of Bread & Meat…but also Forage & Means of transportation." He had informed "the Governors of Maryland & Virginia on that subject [in] the strongest terms," and sent repeated calls for supplies to "the States of Jersey, Delaware & Maryland." As requested, commissary specialists were on the way "to introduce some kind of System & Method in our Supplies." Lack of intelligence was still a dangerous drawback. Washington implored, "dear Marquis, I am distressed beyond expression, to know what is become of the Count de Grasse." His latest intelligence indicated an "English Fleet" heading for the Chesapeake. If they should occupy "that quarter," they would "frustrate all our flattering prospects." Washington was concerned "for the Count de Barras, who was to have sailed from Rhode Island on the 23d" of August, but "I have heard nothing." The entire operation depended on stopping "the retreat of Lord Cornwallis…by the arrival of either of the French Fleets." He knew "you will do all in your power to prevent his escape by land," and stressed "how critically important the present Moment is. I am determined…to persist, with unremitting ardor…unless some inevitable and insuperable obstacles…If you get any thing New from any quarter, send it…on the Spur of Speed, for I am [filled with] impatience and anxiety."[46]

In a dramatic turn of events, on the same day Washington wrote to Lafayette, De Grasse sent word to Washington announcing the glorious news – the French Fleet has arrived. To reinforce De Grasse's message, Duportail wrote to the commander-in-chief while still on board the admiral's flagship. "Dear General: I arrived here this morning at five o'clock after a long and tedious journey," but the uplifting experience "to see at last a French fleet of 27 [vessels] and meet Admiral De Grasse, makes me forget all the hardships." De Grasse must leave in six weeks, Duportail reported. He intended to go ashore the next day and join the Marquis. He would make the best use "of the short stay of Count de grasse." Still troubling was intelligence that Admiral De Barras had not arrived.

Several days later, in a personal letter to Washington, De Grasse emphasized a spirit of cooperation. He had "not hesitated to open my heart" to General Duportail's requests "with all my resources and orders." The admiral explained how the fleet was deployed "to guard the James river" and prevent Lord Cornwallis's retreat "on the Carolina side." Also, a "few ships" were blockading "the mouth of the York river." The rest of the French navy was "at Cape Henry ready to engage the enemy's maritime forces, should they [try to relieve] Lord Cornwallis." De Grasse planned no further action until Washington arrived. "I am persuaded that my army, who are inflamed only with the desire to give proof of their courage, will surpass themselves under the eyes of Generals worthy to appreciate them," De Grasse wrote. "I shall devote my entire attention to the means of facilitating all the attacks you will judge proper to make on your arrival against the army of Lord Cornwallis."[47]

During the long wait for news of the fleets, Washington and Rochhambeau found little reason for optimism. In public, they projected confidence and determination. Privately, the chances for success seemed slim.

Admiral De Grasse, with a sense of urgency, dashed off the arrival news in a fast "cutter to…Brigadier General Mordecai Gist at Baltimore." Within an hour of receiving the news on September 4, Gist had an express courier on the road with explicit orders "to ride night and day." The next day, the courier reached Washington at Chester. Stunned, the commander-in-chief sat in silence. The dozen or so staff nearby waited for some reaction. They understood that this was news of great significance. Finally, Washington exploded. In a rare emotional outburst, he stood straight up at a full stance in his stirrups. A French officer with Rochambeau described the unforgettable spectacle as they approached Chester by boat. They "saw in the distance" on the docks "General Washington shaking his hat and a white handkerchief, and showing signs of great joy." Before the boat was securely moored, Rochambeau jumped on land. "Washington, usually cool and composed, fell into his arms," shouting the news, "M. de Grasse had arrived in the Chesapeke Bay with 28 ships of the line and 3000 troops, whom had already landed." At first Rochambeau was as stunned by the news as Washington, but then the two commanders "embraced warmly." The waiting was over.[48]

Washington enjoyed his brief respite from the awful possibility of uncertain naval assistance, although not for long. Now he faced new complexities. The French fleet's arrival brought significant improvement in strategic allied potential. But an immediate challenge was quickly constructing an effective operational plan to harness that potential.[49]

When the news reached Philadelphia, shouts of joy echoed through the city with "some merry fellows" pronouncing "funeral orations for Cornwallis." The French Minister's house was surrounded by cheering well-wishers. "Long

Live Louis the Sixteenth." The arrival unleashed high public expectations. Some even declared victory and suggested the war was over.[50] But Washington and Rochambeau still faced executing a complex military campaign with enormous difficulties.

Back in the Chesapeake, De Grasse agreed "to do the impossible" and send "ships to the aid of Washington's and Rochambeau's armies at the Head of the Elk."[51] Washington had assembled enough transportation to begin a journey down the bay, but lacked means to move all the troops. He notified De Grasse "that a Van of the two Armies about two thousand men will be embarked in about two Days," down the bay to join allied forces already "blocking up Ld Cornwallis." The remainder of our troops will follow as soon as additional transportation is available."[52]

The previous two weeks had showered the allies with favorable events. Washington expressed a new optimism in General Orders for September 6: "It is with the highest pleasure and satisfaction the Commander in Chief announces to the Army the arrivals of the Count de Grasse in the Chesapeake with a formidable Naval and Land force." He called "upon all the Gallant Officers, the brave and faithful soldiers he has the honor to command to exert their utmost abilities in the cause of their Country." Then, he elated the troops. "The Commanding Officers of Corps" will send requests "for a Months pay [for] their respective Commands, excluding any infamous characters" who have deserted.[53]

The Superintendent of Finance had responded to Washington's previous request for troop pay. A few weeks later, Robert Morris thanked French Minister Luzerne for the assistance of Rochambeau who "generously made me a very considerable advance of money," and he was able "to give the detachment of our army...one month's pay."[54]

Good fortune continued. Lieutenant Colonel John Laurens arrived from a special mission to France, carrying "2,500,000 livres," a sum sufficiently large to quiet "any further discontent among the troops...concerning pay."[55]

Despite the good news, troubling issues remained. On September 7, Washington wrote to Duportail, "Nothing gives me more uneasiness [than] the two things you mention – not hearing from Count du Barras who sailed" for the Chesapeake on August 24, "and the resolution for the departure of the fleet at a certain time." The "greatest advantage" must be taken, he wrote, of the situation. Some of the army "will I hope be embarked tomorrow." The remainder "will move by land to Baltimore." Washington intended to march ahead "with all possible expedition."[56]

The glorious news of the French Navy's arrival injected a sense of joy and relief throughout the states. It was a boon to the propaganda war. Patriots who doubted French intentions were now energized. A positive public

Lt. Colonel John Laurens, Aide de Camp to General Washington at Yorktown, Virginia, who participated in the British surrender negotiations.

perception of the French allies was a big influence on support as the troops marched south. De Grasse's arrival smothered Tory attempts to drive a wedge between the allies. The Tories had long circulated stories that the French did not intend "to assist the allies in an affective manner, [only] to weaken the English and…Americans by [prolonging a war] that would prove disastrous to both." Tories maintained the French planned to regain losses suffered during the Seven Years' War. British propaganda tried to convince Patriot sympathizers that the French "intended to detach several states to form the nucleus of a Burbon state in America." Rochambeau had sensed latent hostility in the country and worked hard to overcome the effects. Some suspicions grew out the previous failures "of the land and sea forces to coordinate action." Many in the population still harbored bitter memories from the Seven Years' War.

Admiral De Grasse's arrival calmed vestiges of past animosities. Because of Rochambeau's marvelous public relations success, while stationed in Newport, Rhode Island, French troops received cooperation, cheers, and gratitude all along their southern route. Well-disciplined and visually appealing in attractive military attire, they drew enormous crowds.[57]

For Washington, challenges and priorities changed daily – even hourly. With each passing day, the enemy was time. Washington wrote that speed would determine, "success, or disgrace of our expedition."[58]

When Washington wrote to Duportail on September 7, he was unaware that good fortune, already soaring, had achieved higher levels. As predicted, a British fleet arrived with intentions to relieve Lord Cornwallis. Admiral De Grasse discovered "about thirty British ships…heading for the French fleet."[59]

In New York, when the British received intelligence that Admiral De Barras "had sailed for the Chesapeake," they immediately pursued him with a fleet commanded by Admiral Graves. De Barras avoided contact and when Graves arrived off the Chesapeake, he was shocked to find the presence of a superior force under De Grasse.[60] As soon as the British came in view, "de Grasse gave the order to…go out and meet the enemy." The fleets exchanged "the first shots" at 4:20 in the afternoon. By 6:30 all firing ceased. British forces suffered extensive casualties with 336 killed and wounded; the French 200. Damage to British ships was extensive, but French ships experienced no serious harm. A British officer described the encounter. "Graves was outfought, decoyed…from the Capes and out-manoeuvered." While Graves and De Grasse were engaged, Admiral "de Barras' squadron carrying the siege artillery" reached the York River.

Earlier when the French Army reached the "Head of Elk," they found the usual delays caused by an insufficient supply of boats. They sent "as many troops as possible to join the Marquis de Lafayette by sea." The remaining French forces decided not to wait but to march overland to Baltimore.

The trip down the Bay was "300 miles in boats virtually stripped of provisions." French forces traveling by boat endured weather "so terrible and winds so adverse...the journey took them 18 days" of incredible hardships. Those traveling over land fared much better, although when they reached Baltimore on September 12, after a march of sixty-seven miles, there were still no boats. On September 17, they marched to Annapolis, Maryland, forty-two miles south and arrived on the 19th. At last, success, for they found an adequate supply of water transportation and sailed on September 21, arriving at Jamestown, Virginia, on September 25, after "a sea voyage of 250 miles."[61]

On September 8, Washington and Rochambeau went ahead of the main allied vanguard to join De Grasse. Washington traveled a few hours ahead of Rochambeau. He arrived at Mount Vernon sometime before September 10 for the first time "since May 1775." He wrote to Lafayette, "We are...on our way to you. The Count de Rochambeau has just arrived [and] after a resting tomorrow," he expected to arrive "at Fredericksburg on the night of the 12th" and to see Lafayette at his camp on September 14.[62] "Doing sixty miles a day," Washington and Rochambeau reached Williamsburg late on the fourteenth.[63]

Williamsburg was a city consisting "of only a single street, but very broad and very handsome," a French officer wrote.[64] Washington established his headquarters in Williamsburg on September 15, and immediately informed Admiral De Grasse. Washington was elated to find the run of good fortune holding when he received details of the French victory at the Capes. He was especially relieved that De Grasse had sent ships to transport "troops waiting at the head of the Chesapeake," and thanked the admiral:

> I am at a loss to express the Pleasure...I have in congratulating your Excellency on your Return to your former station in the Bay – And the happy Circumstance of forming a Junction with the Squadron of the Count De Barras. I take particular satisfaction in felicitating your Excellency on the Glory of having driven the British Fleet from the Coast...these happy Events, and the decided superiority of your fleet. Gives us the happiest Presages of the most compleat Success in our combined Operations in this Bay.[65]

Even Washington, usually cautious of exaggerations, exuded unusual optimism. With time still a relentless enemy, the commander-in-chief was attentive to the one individual with influence, Admiral de Grasse. "It is very much the Wish of the Count De Rochambeau, as well as myself, to have the Honor of an interview with your Excellency." But, as Washington noted, he was "dependent on your Goodness for the means of Conveyance."[66]

Washington's arrival spurred Governor Nelson into even more urgency. A torrent of activity flooded his office from the first morning light and often, with a mass of candles, after midnight. When the entire state was surveyed, Virginia clearly possessed sufficient provisions and manpower to supply allied requirements. An angry Nelson was frustrated in attempts to muster manpower and collect provisions. Again the governor raised the tempo of demands. On September 14, he informed David Jamison, Lieutenant Governor, that "His Excellency Genl Washington arrived here about two Hours ago." He reminded him "to urge...the greatest...activity and industry [from] every Officer within your reach, whose business it is to provide forage or provisions for the Army." The immediate needs were "Beef, Flour, Corn, and means of Transportation."[67]

Nelson also urged Colonel James Hendricks of the Virginia Militia that, "we cannot depend on procuring sufficient Supplies" in the local areas, "but must...draw from Parts more remote." He noted a desperate "Want of Waggons," and Hendricks must impress, "as many as you can."[68]

Demands escalated beyond food, horses, and wagons. Arrival of the allied forces exploded needs. Collect "Spades, Axes, Hatchets, & hilling hoes," for entrenching tools, Nelson ordered.[69] Nelson worked relentlessly to improve the supply situation, but flour came in slowly and he wrote, "I am still full of Anxiety on this."[70] The key was enforcement; he needed to make an example. As punishment for a group of citizens who had "been guilty of Conduct [against] this Government & the Interest of the United States," Nelson authorized the apprehension of "their Persons & papers, & to have them conveyed to the Town of Richmond under proper Guard."[71]

Soon provisions arrived more regularly but with grudging compliance and still too slow. Increased supplies were offset when new militia arrived in the field. Additional forces needed more supplies, which occasionally placed allied forces in competition. Nelson excoriated one Virginia county Colonel: "I have Information that 29 Boxes of Arms were seized...by you [and given] to the People of your County [against] express Orders to bring then on to Camp." He considered "nothing...more criminal or meriting severe Notice."[72] In the middle of September, Nelson wrote to Captain John Pierce, Virginia Commissary General, "The Millers and Country people must be obliged to lend their aid to the support of the army." If they refused, he told Pierce, "you are hereby empowered to impress any grain...wagons, carts, Horses or negroes...the Commissioners in the different Counties are [not doing their duty, and] if you find this so...appoint other persons." When cattle "are not sufficient to supply the Army...seize...any that [are available] for the purpose."[73] Still resistance plagued Nelson, but slowly supplies reached an adequate level. The issues Nelson addressed determined the campaign's outcome. Washington backed up Nelson's efforts and scolded the Virginia Board of War. "Upon

viewing the troops of the Virginia Line...I find they are almost totally des-
titute of Cloathing...upwards of one third of them are...at present unfit for
service."[74]

On September 18, Washington and Rochambeau boarded the *Ville de
Paris*, Admiral de Grasse's flagship. The occasion was treated with all
the pomp and ceremony of a royal French military event. Of great historical significance, it was the first meeting of three senior commanders
who would shape the future of international affairs. Intense, candid discussions dominated the meeting, but in a respectful, friendly atmosphere.
During the four-day meeting, subjects shifted from broad strategy to
minute details of tactical operations.

Military actions on this scale required careful personal considerations. An
unprecedented unity of effort was required for success, and harmony between
the commanders was essential. Washington observed De Grasse and
Rochambeau together – their mutual respect and ease of association. As for
the French, they measured Washington's opinions, judgments, and responses
to many military questions. Formal at first, the atmosphere evolved into one
of comradeship. The commanders and their staffs spent four days in close
association with formal and informal gatherings. Hour after hour, the different staffs became better acquainted. Harmony between senior commanders
did not always overcome friction in the lower levels of command. To
everyone's relief, the mingling of staffs, at first cordial, developed friendships.
Three personal benefits emerged from the meetings, trust, respect, and confidence. By the meeting's conclusion, Washington was satisfied sufficient harmony existed between allies to overcome inevitable tensions and challenges
inherent in future operations. This meeting, more than any other, provided
the basic operational unity of effort for the Yorktown campaign. With details
for the next move against Cornwallis settled, try as he did, Washington could
not influence De Grasse to remain longer than November 1.[75]

Upon returning to headquarters, Washington found that fortune had turned
again, this time against the allies. Intelligence arrived "containing disturbing news." Immediately it was forwarded to Rochambeau and De Grasse. A
letter from Congress dated September 15 disclosed information from New
York. A British fleet commanded by Admiral Digby was momentarily expected to arrive from England. The fleet carried army reinforcements and a
sizable addition of naval power. From English accounts, "Digby's Fleet is said
to consist of ten Ships of the line," although they "they may be less." More
disturbing intelligence indicated, "Between thirty & forty large Transports lay
at New York...ready to sail, and more were getting ready."[76]

Washington cautioned Rochambeau that the intelligence was not verified.
Besides, New York was a long distance from the Chesapeake Bay and rein-

forcements for Cornwallis required days, even weeks to arrive. His caution proved well founded. On September 18, James Madison, Virginia delegate in Congress informed a friend, "the arrival of Digby is far from certain, and circulating reports have reduced his force to six ships of the line."[77] As late as September 21, Washington received a report: "We have not yet heard that Admiral Digby is arrived."[78]

Meanwhile General Cornwallis attempted an offensive operation in response to his increasingly obvious state of siege. On the evening of September 22, the British sent fire ships down river towards the French fleet. The objective was destruction of as much French shipping as possible and hope any British relief vessels lurking offshore might sneak by in the confusion. It was a desperate, but not risky, attempt by Cornwallis.

A French officer described the event. "In the dark of the night it was a beautiful and at the same time terrifying sight [as we observed] 5 burning ships in full sail floating down the stream past our eyes." Fortunately no harm occurred, except a harrowing experience for one ship that cut its anchor lines to avoid a collision. For awhile the ship drifted, threatened by a narrow passage. Finally an American pilot came on board, but only one officer, "a swede" spoke English. The "value of knowing several languages" helped guide the ship to safety.[79]

The next day, a shaken Admiral De Grasse replied to Washington's intelligence of an additional English fleet. De Grasse's concern centered on the sudden arrival of a British fleet from New York, trapping French vessels inside the Chesapeake Bay.[80] The Admiral felt headed "into an affair that can turn out to be my own disadvantage and into the humiliation of the nation.[81] De Grass assembled his officers for a council of war. After several hours of discussions he "began formulating a new plan of operation."[82]

De Grasse notified Washington, "I see that our position is changed by the arrival of Admiral Digby." He intended "to hoist sail" and engage any British attack from "a less disadvantageous position." Unfortunately, "the course of the battle may drive us to leeward and put it beyond our power to return." The Admiral's immediate concern was the safety of the fleet, independent of other considerations. A short time later, after the original panic subsided, De Grasse evaluated his planned action on the overall campaign. He was aware that fleet redeployment presented serious consequences to the allied forces on land. If in the tradition of past naval actions, De Grasse acted solely to protect the navy, regardless of consequences, allied success at Yorktown was jeopardized. After review, he wrote a more concessionary letter to Washington. "I impatiently await your answer and that of the Count de Rochambeau, for whom this letter is also intended." Please forward a copy, "and let me have your reflections on the future."[83]

The alliance and the Yorktown Campaign reached another test of confidence. What De Grasse planned, if executed, almost assured Cornwallis' escape from the tightening allied encirclement. Great personal diplomacy by Rochambeau and Washington changed the Admiral's mind.[84] On September 25, Washington responded in the strongest manner, but with patience and respect. "I cannot conceal from your Excellency the painful anxiety under which I have labored since the receipt of [your letter]. The naval movements which Your Excellency states…make it incumbent upon me to represent the consequences that [would] arise, and to urge perseverance in the plan already agreed upon." Washington was convinced that the plan against Lord Cornwallis and Yorktown, "under the protection of your Ships, is as certain as any military operation can be rendered…it is in fact reducible to calculation…the surrender of the british Garrison will be so important [and] go a great way towards terminating the war." The departure of his fleet "would frustrate these brilliant prospects," and be a disgrace to all the efforts and "expectations of the allies…after the most expensive preparations and uncommon exertions."

The removal of De Grasse's fleet meant many problems, all-leading to a potential allied debacle. One especially dangerous consequence was "disbanding…the whole Army for want of provisions." Virginia was "so much exhausted," Washington wrote, "by the ravages of the enemy, and the subsistence of our own army that our supplies can only be drawn from a distance, and under cover of a fleet," one that is "Mistress of the Chesapeake." Washington hoped after considering "the consequences which must follow your departure, [you] will determine the measure [with] the dearest interests of the common cause [would] dictate." More recent intelligence indicated "the strength of…Admiral Digby may not only be exaggerated, but" an attempt to mislead. Convinced departure of the French fleet doomed the allied campaign; in desperation, Washington sent Lafayette to personally deliver the letter and explain "any particularities of our situation, which could not well be comprised in a letter."[85]

An anxious Lafayette watched De Grasse read the letter. The letter was in English, but a carefully translated copy was included. Finally, without comment, the Admiral gave a barely discernable nod of approval. After a few moments pacing back and forth in deep thought, De Grasse informed Lafayette of his decision. He called another "council of war to consider the situation." Lafayette waited, suffering in suspense. Finally with the council completed, Lafayette received a letter for Washington. "I have the honor to inform Your Excellency" that "a general council of my officers" confirmed that while his plans "for getting underway [were] brilliant and glorious, [they] did not appear to fulfill the aims we had in view." Therefore, it was decided, "the major part of the fleet should proceed to anchor in the York River…Four or five vessels should be stationed in the James to pass up and down the river, and you should aid us [by] erecting a battery."[86]

Washington's appeal, Rochambeau's encouragement ,and De Grasse's reason, passed another test for allied unity of command. Washington responded on September 27 with gracious applause. "The resolution that your Excellency has taken…proves that a great Mind knows how to make personal Sacrifices to secure an important general Good."[87]

Back in New York, the British officially reported the arrival of Rear Admiral Digby on September 21.[88] President McKean sent more intelligence on September 27. "Admiral Digby had but three Ships…under his Command from England." In addition, the enemy had four "large Ships…are so damaged," they were unable to go to sea.[89]

At least temporarily, another critical threat to the Yorktown campaign diminished. On September 28, Washington informed the president of Congress, that the whole Army had marched "At daybreak. Our armies broke camp at Williamsburg," and moved to "the advance upon York." Additional good news was the arrival of increasing numbers of Virginia militia. By noon the army reached their assigned position and "bivouacked in the line of battle."[90]

On September 28, a French officer reported, "We arrived about six o'clock…before the town of York and immediately began its investment."[91] On October 1, Washington wrote, "American Troops moved forward and took their Ground in front of the Enemys Works." The enemy was now fully encircled "except on the River" where he expected De Grasse would shortly "compleat the Blockade."[92]

Cornwallis had sealed his fate with a decision to move into Virginia and fortify Yorktown for his final military adventure in North America. In contrast, the French Army's move from Newport, Rhode Island, to Yorktown, Virginia, was "The March of History." The French moved a total distance of seven hundred fifty-six miles, while the Americans covered more than five hundred miles.[93] Both armies endured extreme hardships.

One modern historian considered the French Navy's action at the Battle of the Capes "the most significant event of Modern times." The effects were "infinitely more important than those of Waterloo." When Graves's disabled fleet "sailed away…the surrender of the army at Yorktown was a matter of time."[94]

After overcoming seemingly insurmountable odds, with exceptional valor, audacious actions, and a remarkable exercise of command and control, the final phase of the Yorktown campaign, the siege, began.

African-American Continental Army private,
Lt. Colonel Gaskins' Virginia Battalion at Yorktown, Virginia, 1781.

❖ 17 ❖

An Analysis

*Each period existed for itself, not as part of
a grand scheme, and could be only
understood on its own terms.*

French financial support, Rochambeau's vision, and Washington's power of leadership charisma drove the "March of History."

A striking aspect of the American War of Independence was the thin line between success and failure. For eight years the outcome staggered precariously on a precipice of fractal events, many beyond anyone's control. People were engaged in a conflict with no idea of the outcome. Even more perplexing was the uncertainty of what success or failure would bring.

A few different responses by the British or Americans might have changed the outcome, but upon reflection some significant events occurred on a timeline beyond any human control. The challenge was to make the fewest mistakes, while taking advantage of fortuitous opportunities to influence a fragile outcome.

The march south was a microcosm of the entire war. People made decisions and undertook actions, aware that chances for success were remote. Glory, fame, or public accolades are not awarded to individuals who demonstrate enterprise in moving armies or solving logistic problems. The allied victory at Yorktown, Virginia, in 1781 was no exception. While a victory with great military and political significance, the actual siege was carried out in a routine 18th century manner. The people who supplied and deployed the allied armies exhibited the real brilliance of Yorktown – brilliance unsurpassed in the annals of American military history. In case of failure the purveyors of these audacious actions were destined for the scrap heap of history, dismissed as incompetent and stupid. But the amazing deployment shifted acclaim to the next and last event, the Yorktown victory. Many individuals participated in both the deployment and final Yorktown victory.

There are several beginnings to this story, the "March of History," but the one chosen began in Boston Harbor on a cold January morning in 1779, when the Marquis de Lafayette embarked on an epic return to Paris, France. His Paris accomplishments fueled the final phase on the road to American independence. Lafayette's persuasion was instrumental in Louis XVI, King of France's unprecedented decisions to increase American assistance. The king's appointment of George Washington as commander-in-chief of French forces in North America was unparalleled for the times. As a part of the increased assistance French General Rochambeau arrived in Newport, Rhode Island, with more than 5000 troops to an unenthusiastic welcome from the town residents or George Washington. Rochambeau's response to his American allies is a superb demonstration of patience, diplomacy, and determination.

But Washington had to pass another test before addressing opportunities provided by the French arrival. The test was a challenge to the Continental Army's survival, an abominable infection of mutinies in January 1781. The mutinies were on a scale unprecedented in Washington's or the army's experience. The method of solution affected the army's future and was watched intently throughout the army and with concerned interest by the French allies. After thirty agonizing days, as the army held together in a precarious existence, the mutinies of January were concluded with a military solution.

Although the January mutinies ended, and Washington had survived an immediate threat to the army's existence, he next faced a long-range challenge, one with geopolitical consequences. Before cooperating with the French allies, there was an embarrassing question: what could Washington and the Americans offer the alliance? In the south two Continental Army commands were destroyed during 1780, leaving patriot influence or control problematic. If Washington approached the alliance without a southern military component, it was admission of British control in the southern states, a situation that offered a reasonable chance for the French to question a continued alliance.

In an act of desperation, late in 1780, Washington sent Major General Nathanael Greene south to reconstruct a third Continental Army and reclaim military influence for the patriot cause. Greene's southern mission was one of Washington's finest command decisions; it began the war's most complex series of military moves. Early in 1781, Washington made another command decision. He sent Major General Lafayette with a force of 1200 for the expressed purpose of reinforcing Greene. Lafayette's deployment was a pilot study of all the challenges that a much larger allied army faced during the "March of History" later in 1781. The difficulties confronting Lafayette in Virginia highlighted many systemic problems, both military and political, that were addressed before the Virginia campaign was possible. A move south by the larger allied army in August 1781 without Lafayette's probe would have probably ended in disaster.

Shortly after Lafayette's arrival in Virginia the entire war situation changed. Benedict Arnold ceased to be a viable target, leaving Lafayette without a mission in the state. The alternative plan was a march to join Greene, something with little attraction for the Marquis. Lafayette's persuasive powers and British reinforcements arriving in Virginia helped establish a need for his detachment to remain. But then began the real work. The state had no existing means to support an army in the field or to counter British offensive operations. Governor Jefferson suspected northern intentions of abandoning the south in favor of northern interests. Jefferson floundered in addressing administrative necessities to conduct war. But after prodding by Lafayette, the governor began to address Virginia's deplorable supply conditions. Then came General Cornwallis' fateful decision to leave the Carolinas and march north to Virginia. General Greene responded with a brilliant strategic move, doing the unexpected. He did not pursue Cornwallis, but headed south to reestablish patriot influence in the Carolinas and Georgia.

At the time, British land forces were widely deployed to protect important cities and seaports. As long as the British maintained superior naval forces, they could sail from location to location and defend against serious assaults by enemy land forces.

If the allies assembled superior naval forces and concentrated forces against any one significant British location, they might achieve a major victory. The trend of allied tactics drifted toward a concentration of forces, but the question was where? Tension continued between two objectives: Washington's stubborn refusal to consider any serious objective except New York City and another objective, gaining support especially from Rochambeau, to strike the British in Virginia. Two events eroded Washington's resistance – Cornwallis's move to Virginia and Admiral de Grasse's move to the Chesapeake.

Lafayette continued to wrestle with the challenges of his separate command and the sudden change of enemy strategy by General Cornwallis' march north. The deplorable support situation in Virginia exposed Lafayette to destruction from a stealthy foe with expertise in surprise attacks and entrapments. His major defense was to keep on the move and gather accurate intelligence on the enemy's deployment. At the same time he worked to improve communications with headquarters in the north and General Greene to the south. But salvation for Virginia's desperate circumstances had to come from within the state. Lafayette flooded Governor Jefferson with appeals. But Jefferson lacked political will to solve administrative and military deficiencies. Lafayette pressured for necessary changes. He threatened, exaggerated, and generally made Jefferson's life miserable, until slow grudging changes began to take place.

Back at headquarters Washington got his way. In tepid agreement, New York City was selected as the first priority for the next campaign, but support disappeared quickly.

In contrast to allied unity, the British senior command was rife with contentiousness and abrasive egos that promoted clashing tactics and strategies. A major influence affecting this devastating British planning was the absence of an effective communications network.

At the time, the British operated as three separate commands even though General Clinton was commander-in-chief of British forces in North America. Clinton commanded his own forces in the New York area; General Cornwallis acted as a *de facto* separate command in the south, and Admiral Arbuthnot commanded the Royal Navy as an independent military force. Each of the three commanders developed strategies and tactics which often differed from operations in other British commands. But Cornwallis' move into Virginia was the fateful decision that resulted in the war's last phase.

Nathanael Greene's reconstruction and deployment of a third Continental Army was a spectacular achievement under desperate conditions. Greene's aggressive harassment of Cornwallis' forces and later, British coastal ports in the Carolinas, had a decided influence on the eventual success at Yorktown. With a masterful strategic move, Greene did not pursue Cornwallis into Virginia, a move that reclaimed the Carolinas and Georgia for the patriot cause. While Greene influenced progress in the Carolinas and Georgia, Lafayette continued to send a steady flow of intelligence to northern headquarters describing the changing situation in Virginia – intelligence which demanded a military response, but where? At the time any attempted military response was an effort in futility without financial or administrative support. Belatedly, Congress appointed Robert Morris to be Superintendent of Finance and financial support began trickling into military affairs.

Stubbornly Washington held his passion to attack New York City and requested General Rochambeau to head south to join forces. On June 9, 1781, French forces left Newport, Rhode Island, and began the fateful "March of History."

Political pressures from Congress and the patriot public mounted for Washington to take action. Americans were still unconvinced of the benefits of a French association. On July 2, the allies probed the northern tip of Manhattan Island. Nothing of military advantage was accomplished, but it kept the British convinced the allies' interest was New York City. On July 6, the full French and American armies joined for the first time, giving soldiers from each army an opportunity to observe the other. The juncture was a public relations bonanza with many public officials and civilians witnessing the festivities.

Earlier, Admiral De Grasse wrote to inform Rochambeau of his anticipated arrival in North American waters not earlier than July 15. The letter arrived on June 9 during the junction celebrations. Immediately Rochambeau informed Washington and replied to De Grasse stressing financial and manpower needs. Rochambeau acquainted the admiral with the need for an expedited reply and supplied subtle persuasion directing attention to the Chesapeake Bay as an area of opportunity.

Political pressure increased for Washington to conduct a southern campaign toward Virginia. By July 14 he acknowledged the futility of an assault against New York City, but was not quite ready to concede. Washington ordered another allied probe in the city suburbs at Kings Bridge. After skirmishing, the allies withdrew, but the probe strengthened British convictions that it was the beginning of a major assault on New York.

In August came the lightening strike. Admiral De Grasse sent word of his expected arrival in the Chesapeake area with additional manpower and a significant financial war chest. The news cast the final vote in favor of Washington and Rochambeau's Virginia campaign.

From early 1781, Virginia's transformation to a support platform for allied armies continued as a work in progress. The first steps advanced grudgingly, hardly discernable, but progress occurred just the same. Advances came from the personal sacrifices of a few determined and dedicated men: Greene, von Steuben, Lafayette, and eventually Governor Thomas Nelson. The British helped, not overtly, but with an inability to harness their arguably superior military assets and exercise a unity of command to destroy allied hopes. For more than eight months in 1781 Virginia teetered precariously close to becoming the caldron for allied defeat.

Virginia's transformation to an allied support platform was a slow tedious process filled with agony, tension, and outright hostility. At the time, many Virginians considered forsaking the patriot cause to return to the king's protection. The British dominated Virginia's landscape with increased intrusions, attacking patriot enclaves with relentless brutality. Lafayette and von Steuben found the Virginia military situation in chaos. A change in governors from Thomas Jefferson to Thomas Nelson advanced the process of building support.

As Lafayette improved communications in Virginia, enemy efforts weakened. The contentious relationship between British commanders Clinton and Cornwallis assured continuation of separate commands and strategies. Cornwallis made the fateful decision to abandon the Carolinas and move into Virginia without input from Clinton. This was interpreted as defiance by Clinton, who was appalled by an act he considered an insubordinate and serious blunder.

Meanwhile the allies struggled in a financial morass. But the appointment of Robert Morris as superintendent of finance added the essential ingredient to advance a fiscal approach to supplying army needs. With direct French monetary assistance, and relentless pressure on Congress and various state legislatures, Morris extracted adequate monetary resources to support the next campaign.

Deployment of French forces from Newport, Rhode Island to Yorktown in 1781 was "The March of History." While various French brigades traveled different distances, they moved more than seven hundred miles. At least one brigade moved seven hundred fifty-six miles.[1]

General Rochambeau's First Brigade departed from camp near Providence, Rhode Island ,on June 10, 1781, marching south to Phillipsburg, New York, where they arrived on July 6 – a march of two hundred twenty-six miles in twenty-six days. The First Brigade was headquartered at Phillipsburg until August 19 when they continued the march south. They arrived at the Head of the Elk River in Maryland on September 7, a march of 219 miles in nineteen days. On September 9 and 10, part of the French Army headed overland to Annapolis and the rest embarked for the Chesapeake Bay. They reached Annapolis on September 18 and sailed down the Chesapeake on September 21, landing at College Landing, Virginia, on September 25. The next day they marched seven miles to Williamsburg and set up headquarters; they were now only twelve miles from Yorktown. The distance traveled from Newport to Yorktown was seven hundred twenty-four miles. Except for an interlude at Phillipsburg, the French Army was on the move for fifty-six days.[2]

This move of allied forces to Yorktown, Virginia, was unprecedented, unique in its time, and unparalleled since. Their unity of command was unlike any experienced by allies before or after. The possibilities and conditions for failure were unlimited. Modem commanders undertaking such a move under the conditions prevailing in Virginia during the eighteenth century, could expect nothing less than charges of incompetence and dereliction of duty. But such an anachronistic judgment is invalid. Carl von Clausewitz, noted military strategist who served on the Prussian General Staff during the Napoleonic period, cautioned against historical comparisons between time periods. "Each period existed for itself, not as part of a grand scheme, and could be only understood on its own terms."[3]

The Virginia campaign to Yorktown had complexities and challenges far beyond the experience of its planners and participants. The success was a great accomplishment that still baffles military historians today. No single episode of the American War of Independence influenced the outcome more than the Virginia campaign.

Sometimes the outcome is explained as allied good luck – and bad luck for the British. Another facetious explanation suggests stealth; the allies jumped on horses and marched with well-conceived plans to Yorktown and completely surprised British General Cornwallis. The reasons for success are complicated and deserve continued research.

Any analysis of critical contributions to the brilliance of Yorktown has one common ingredient – people. Ordinary and extraordinary people performed daily, tedious, unglamorous tasks vital for success. They performed with valor, dedication, and determination above and beyond reasonable expectations. Always shadowed by failure, defeat, and death, many remain unheralded, perhaps yet to be discovered, but their accomplishments can never be forgotten.

Seven Critical Contributions

Many events contributed to the successful Yorktown campaign. Seven are selected as the most dominating. Failure of any could have doomed the entire campaign.
1. Personal relationships
    a. George Washington with General Rochambeau.
    b. British Generals Clinton, Cornwallis and British Admiral Arbuthnot.
2. Interaction of American subordinate officers.
    a. Major General the Marquis de Lafayette
    b. Major General Baron von Steuben
    c. Major General Nathanael Greene
    d. Virginia Governor Thomas Nelson
3. King Louis XVI's appointment of General George Washington as commander-in-chief of French Force in North America.
4. Inordinate allied good luck (Providence)
5. A superb performance from French and American soldiers who suffered extreme hardships with resolute courage and determination.
6. Infusion of French financial support into the campaign at propitious times.
7. An unprecedented exercise of a command and control process, allied style.

1. PERSONAL RELATIONSHIPS
Washington and Rochambeau's personal relationship dominated the Virginia campaign to Yorktown. At first, uncertain of French intentions, Washington was cautious. Did the French have territorial ambitions with their army at Newport, Rhode Island? Washington had no sense of the man, Rochambeau; he needed to find out more. He did not understand

French culture nor speak the language. The French General did not speak English, but moved to gain Washington's acceptance and confidence, always with respect, dignity, and patience. At any time in the year, after the French arrived, an ego-clashing episode might have dashed the alliance. But on the other hand, Washington appreciated that without French assistance the American cause was in peril. Slowly, the relationship evolved into a bulwark of strength and mutual support. The Washington and Rochambeau relationship was an essential catalyst for the successful exercise of allied command and control.

In contrast, relationships among enemy commanders were striking. Contentious relationships between senior British commanders dominated tactics during the allied move south. Friction between British Generals Clinton and Cornwallis, and Clinton's differences with Admiral Arbuthnot, were roadblocks to an effective military strategy. If senior British commanders had personal relationships to support an effective unity of effort, the war's outcome might have been different.

2. INTERACTION OF AMERICAN SUBORDINATE OFFICERS

Officers serving under Washington and Rochambeau exhibited diversity in training, nationality, and experience. Many native-born American officers lacked professional military training and learned from "on the job training." But the Continental Army did have French, German, Polish, and British officers, some with extensive military experience and training in Europe.

Major General the Marquis de Lafayette — Lafayette's contributions to the American cause are real, legendary, and underestimated. The thought of a nineteen-year-old foreigner, commissioned a major general of the Continental Army in 1777, was not, at first, widely appreciated. But eventually zeal, bravery, and learning quickly from experience overcame immaturity and lack of military experience. At times vanity and pride overshadowed good judgment, but during the Virginia campaign Lafayette demonstrated intelligence, loyalty, astute military sense, and a deft ability at public relations. No commission of major general better served the Continental Army than Lafayette's.

In January 1779, on a return trip to France, Lafayette initiated a series of actions that changed the war's course. His determined effort in the royal court was a crucial influence. Patiently for more than a year, he trumpeted the American cause. Lafayette pleaded, persuaded, and explained the benefits for France of increasing aid to the Americans. Finally, ministers, royal representatives, and the King agreed to send General Rochambeau with a French military force, money, and the amazing appointment of George Washington as commander-in-chief of all French forces in North America. These actions provided the foundation for a

Virginia campaign to Yorktown. Following his return to America in 1780, Lafayette was ordered south where his Virginia activities prepared support for the arrival of large allied forces.

Major General Baron Von Steuben — During the Virginia campaign, no Continental army officer suffered more politics of personal destruction than Baron Von Steuben. His gruff Prussian drillmaster manner offended Virginian's sensitivities, when he attacked widespread incompetence of military and political administrations. Many problems the baron identified needed solutions before Virginia transformation to a support platform for allied forces. Without the Baron's critical appraisals, which forced changes, a large allied army arriving under existing conditions easily would have failed. Fortunately for the Baron, Lafayette arrived and calmed bruised Virginia egos that demanded the Baron's resignation. Lafayette's public relations blitz persuaded needed changes, many already identified by the Baron.

Major General Nathanael Greene — Major General Nathanael Greene's contributions to the eventual victory at Yorktown are significant. His harassment of Cornwallis in the Carolinas reduced the size of forces available to the British general for his move north into Virginia.

Nathanael Greene lacked professional military training, and in the early days of the war his inexperience was apparent. But as the war progressed, he learned quickly. Loyal, determined, and dedicated, Washington recognized him as a most likely replacement if personal disaster befell the commander-in-chief. Greene maintained an excellent rapport with Lafayette, Baron von Steuben, Washington, and other fellow officers. His southern command was as lonely and unappreciated as any during the war.

Virginia Governor Thomas Nelson — Thomas Nelson replaced Thomas Jefferson as governor of Virginia in 1781. He was a personal friend of Washington with extensive military experience in Virginia state forces. Nelson was an aggressive governor and employed "almost dictatorial powers" to change Virginia into a military support base. He worked tirelessly with Lafayette to improve the quality and administration of state forces. Nelson commanded Virginia state forces during the Yorktown siege.

3. KING LOUIS XVI'S APPOINTMENT OF GENERAL GEORGE WASHINGTON

Two decisions by the French king, one to send a French auxiliary force under the command of General Rochambeau and the other to appoint George Washington as commander-in-chief of all French army and naval forces in North America, created an unprecedented unity of command. These two decisions created a chain of command which evolved into the most dominating organizational structure of the American War of Independence.

4. INORDINATE AMOUNT OF ALLIED GOOD LUCK

The entire period of the American War of Independence was laced with substantial amounts of good luck for the Patriot cause. Not that the American cause lacked its share of potentially devastating events, which easily could have influenced the war's outcome in a different direction. For eight years the American War floundered on a thin line between victory and defeat with unknown consequences for either outcome. Uncertainty was the rule of the day, moving quickly in one direction and then the other. But always, when the cause drifted against the Americans toward a precipice of defeat, people and events rose to reroute the course toward victory. But the struggle was agonizing, brutal, and bloody. The Virginia Campaign of 1781 was the last major episode that moved the cause to victory, but while in progress, the outcome teetered more toward collapse than success.

Later, Washington referred to many events of the Virginia campaign as acts of "Devine Providence." Admiral de Grasse arriving in the Chesapeake at an auspicious moment was nothing less than an act of providence. His arrival with a large fleet, land forces, and financial support was critical to the eventual victory. De Grasse's subsequent and successful action against the British off the Capes sealed Cornwallis' fate at Yorktown.

5. UNHERALDED EFFORTS BY FRENCH AND AMERICAN SOLDIERS

Efforts by allied soldiers during the move to Virginia can never be fully appreciated. Contributions by most private soldiers will remain lost in history. But Washington wrote perhaps the best tribute to the private soldier in a letter to Major General Nathanael Greene in 1783:

> ...for it will not be believed that such a force as Great Britain has employed for eight years in this Country could be baffled in their plan of Sujigating it by numbers infinitely less, composed of Men sometimes half starved; always in Rags, without pay, and experiencing, at times, every species of distress which human nature is capable of undergoing.[4]

6. FRENCH FINANCIAL SUPPORT

A successful outcome to the American War of Independence was impossible without French financial and materiel contributions. French monetary gifts and loans fueled the Virginia campaign to Yorktown. A Yorktown victory required sizable amounts of cash supplied by French sources. Most Americans never fully appreciated the amount of French capital infused into the war effort.

Money was often squandered by a corrupt or incompetent American financial administration. With Robert Morris' appointment as Superintendent of Finance, financial management improved, but the task was massive. Incompetence plagued finances and they remained in a precarious state for the balance of the war. The French always seemed to appear at the most appropriate times and with adequate funds that avoided a collapse of the war effort.

7, THE EXERCISE OF COMMAND AND CONTROL, ALLIED STYLE

No precise definition of military command and control exists. In any definition there always is an exception. "It is a process easier described than defined." A "general agreement is that people are its most important ingredient." Advances in technology "impact modern military control practice," but people are the driving force in a "successful exercise of command and control." People, in a military context, "are the total human resources brought to bear against an enemy."[5]

Unity of Command Described

In the final analysis, it was the dedication to the cause of independence and the faith in Washington's command, supported by Rochambeau and De Grasse that brought a beleaguered Continental Army to victory.

Appendix A

Details of Command and Control

It is often difficult to describe a word conceptually through several centuries. While definitions may travel a little easier through time, concepts and semantics do not, especially in a military context. Not recognizing these dangers can be a source of anachronistic contamination. The following definitions and descriptions are submitted in a form to minimize anachronisms, but explain a modern process of command and control in a military context of the 18th century.

A Clear Chain of Command: Successful exercise of military command and control is based on a well-defined and clearly understood chain of command, beginning with a supreme authority and traveling down the chain to the lowest ranking soldier. Congress was responsible for the higher direction of the war, especially political and economic considerations.[1] They communicated their direction to the army, whose primary concern was tactical military exercise to achieve the objectives of Congress's *higher* considerations. The initial reality of Congressional relationships with the army was confusion, misunderstanding, ambiguity, chaos, contradiction and suspicion.

Command:[2]
[To] direct with authority.[3]

In today's military jargon, command is the primary means of relaying a vision to the organization. The focus is not on individual soldiers, but on issues affecting everybody. The objective of command is to provide a direction for producing results. It is a coordinated effort of many units where soldiers think, act, and achieve to accomplish a mission. Command is flexible and its effectiveness is measured by battlefield success.

The Continental Congress had no experience or precedent to guide its efforts for achieving the higher or political direction of the war. Before it could command, Congress had to establish a balance of authority and responsibility with the army. The Continental Army lacked effective command and control until Congress created an organizational framework for operational command.

Command and Control together.[4]

Segments: of military command and control include systems, method and process. Additional important concerns are the design of effective strategies and tactics. Before the genesis of command and control, Continental Army style, occurred at the Valley Forge encampment of 1778, the segments were missing. The six months breather gave Congress and its army an opportunity to engage, communicate, debate, and reform. The Genesis evolved into a allied command and control process that was exercised during the Virginia campaign in 1781.

System: An organized set of doctrines, ideas, or principles usually intended to explain the arrangement. System suggests a fully developed or formulated method often emphasizing orderliness.

Method: Denotes the means or procedure required to achieve an end. It implies orderly effective arrangement and available skills or techniques.

Process: a series of actions or operations that lead towards a particular result. In a military context, the command and control process is the operation, performance, function or action-taking place.

Communications:[5] Communications technology is a major distinction between the practice of modern military command and control and the 18th century. Sophisticated technology provides instantaneous contact for a modern military hierarchy. Speed of 18th century communications exchanges rarely exceeded a fast horse. Battles contain chaos and confusion caused by changing military situations and consequences are disastrous without clear and well-understood orders. A critical influence on the outcome of a battle is the accurate and speedy conversion of a commander's intentions into cohesive action. Military communications were mainly in two forms, written or verbal.[6] Verbal communications, the quickest to prepare, suffered from potential distortion. Written communications required more preparation time but were more precise.

Control:[7]
To exercise authority over [regulate].

Control is a process that sets limits and provides structure, serving primarily as a compensating and correcting device for command. High quality command uses control as an exception. A low quality of command overuses control, creating tension and confusion. Initially, a low quality of command existed between the Continental Army and its supreme authority – Congress did not ignore its army, but its attempts to control often lacked a realistic understanding.

Hierarchy and Mission:[8] Hierarchy is an organization's authority defined in a graded order or rank. While Congress established a theoretical hierarchy, the reality differed. On June 15, 1775, the Continental Congress unanimously elected "George Washington, esq., to command all the continental forces, raised or to be raised, for the defense of American liberty..." One year later, on July 4, 1776, the Declaration of Independence focused the Continental Army's "mission" from defense of American liberty (redress of grievances), to pursuit of independence

Infrastructure: Selected consolidated groups described as critical for the organization to achieve and perpetuate its mission, distinguished from structure by selectivity and implied experience and quality required from the groups. The difficulty for the Continental Army was that while it was an organization based on the Congressional "Resolves" of June 1775, it had no sufficiently developed infrastructure to support the mission to which it was assigned. This study describes the development of the infrastructure that supported the Continental Army's exercise of command and control during the Yorktown campaign.

The Americans created a "national" political (Continental Congress) and military (Continental Army) structure where none existed. Those responsible for creation were, with few exceptions, inexperienced and by European standards lacked professional expertise in required technical skills.

American military practice in the 18th century, prior to the American War for Independence, was rooted in British tradition. Military proficiency was judged successful if it imitated a European approach. Departure from these methods was deemed inferior. Americans were not viewed as accomplished in the military arts, especially by British officers. British military tradition emphasized social and economic considerations for high-ranking officers. Most military commissions were purchased; the means to acquire commissions suggested a privileged social class.

Military Tactics: Includes the method for employing forces in combat, the science and art of disposing and maneuvering forces in combat, i.e., the art or skill of employing available means to accomplish an end.

Tactics teaches the use of the armed forces in the engagement.

Strategy is distinguished from tactics by describing the former as the plan and the latter as the practice or application.

Modern Military Command and Control:[9] Successful exercise of military command and control includes a well-defined and understood chain of command in theory and practice, reliable communication and a sound plan of action with an effective method of execution.[10]

Organization: It is difficult to explain in the context of a modern process of command and control and still retain a comparative relationship with the 18th century. Organization is not a word whose military context retains a similarity over the centuries. In this, the military organization is described as the consolidated groups, resolved by the Continental Congress in 1775, to be the Continental Army and includes any revisions. There are two additional terms that influence the context of organization. They are: structure and infrastructure.

People: Organization, hierarchy and mission are command and control ingredients that depend on people: not just any people: often individuals with indeterminate qualities. Intangible personal relationships develop under life and death challenges. Teamwork is vital.

The heart of the command and control process is people, and the development of personal relationships that include trust and competency. From a soldier's point of view, it helps to have confidence in anyone commanding and controlling his life. In addition to military authority confirmed by rank, attributes associated with a successful commander include good judgment, a willingness to delegate, decisiveness, and most importantly, the "power of leadership charisma." Orders, given with confidence, inspire effort.[11] The Continental Army's short existence made it difficult to find individuals with the intangible "power of leadership charisma."[12]

Strategy: Includes the science and art of employing political, economic, psychological, and military forces of a nation to adopted policies in peace or war. Military strategy is: the science and art of military command exercised to meet the enemy, in combat, under advantageous conditions. The Continental Congress was responsible for originating the higher direction or strategy of the war. Strategy teaches the use of engagements for the object of war.

Structure: The arrangement or interrelation of the total consolidated groups in the military organization described as the Continental Army. It includes something made up of interdependent parts [the organization] and its relationship with others.

Training: Effective exercise of command and control places a high priority on personnel selection and training. When trained personnel are either nonexistent or lost, severe consequences in operational performance result. The Continental Army began the war with few professionally trained officers and fewer individuals experienced in technical skilled positions vital to conduct the business of war. As the war progressed the British lost many of their experienced soldiers; by comparison the Americans became better trained with both French assistance and battlefield exposure.

Lack of training in the methodology of European warfare standards was a factor contributing to British low respect for the Americans. Any possibility that a military organization constructed by the rebels could seriously compete with the British military was not considered a rational possibility.[13] Senior

American officers coming from such a varied background of class, politics, and economic pursuits were a departure from European tradition and when European volunteers first arrived to serve in the Continental Army there were military culture clashes.[14]

One American methodological deficiency was in the execution of linear tactics, including the use of the bayonet – a challenge for the untrained Americans. At times deficiency in execution resulted in an entire regiment's disintegration. The Continental Army's overall performance level was no better than its least trained unit in a specific battle. The least trained units provided the enemy with an opportunity, quickly identified and exploited.

18th Century Unity of Command is impossible to define in the context of modern command and control, but a description can be formulated in an 18th century context with modern parallels.

In a modern context, unity of command exercised during the Vietnam War provides parallels with the allied unity of command exercised during the Yorktown campaign. Unity of command ensures control over the total military effort and encourages improvements in the operational capabilities of indigenous forces and promotes cooperation that is flexible to adjust to changes during the course of the war.[15]

From a modern perspective the allied unity of command during the Yorktown Campaign could be described as a unity of effort rather than a unity of command. From an 18th century perspective, it was a unity of command with an unprecedented basis. King Louis XVI of France appointed Washington commander-in-chief of French forces in North America and effectively paid for the service when he sent both troops, and the navy to be placed at Washington's disposal.

The distinction and differences between unity of effort and command in the 18th century becomes apparent when contrasting British and Allied approaches during the Yorktown Campaign. The British did not develop an effective unity of effort between their naval and land forces, essentially maintaining a separate command status, which performed to the individual commanders agenda. While crude and basic, the allied effort required more than cooperation. Had Louis XVI intended only cooperation it is doubtful he would have issued instructions and sent financial support to Washington. The relationship forged between the allies was more than cooperation in an 18th century context.

Appendix B

Rochambeau's Instructions

THE INSTRUCTIONS:

Article I: Rochambeau to always be under command of Washington.

Article II: All plans, campaigns or private expeditions to be decided upon by GW., keeping in view the harmony which his majesty hopes to see between the two commanders and the Generals and soldiers of the two nations.

Article III: The French troops should, as was done in Germany in 1757 yield precedent to and the right to the American troops. Rochambeau to give this information to the General officers and the troops under his command in order to avoid any difficulty that might disturb the good understanding which the King hopes to see between the two armies under the command of George Washington.

Article IV: American officers with equal rank and the same date of commission shall have the command, and in all *cases the American troops shall take the right.* In all military acts and capitulations the American general and troops shall be named first and will sign first, as has always been the custom, and in accordance with the principles above laid down with regard to auxiliary troops (probably explains Rochambeau's actions deferring to Washington at Yorktown).

Article V: It is his Majesty's expectations and very positive order to Count De Rochambeau that he will see to the exact and literal execution of the above four articles.

Article VI: The French troops will retain full jurisdiction and rights of trial over every individual belonging to it. The decision of the King over a question of this nature, which arose at Brest concerning Spanish troops, is to serve as a precedent in this matter, according to the laws of nations.

Article VII: The King provides for the needs of his troops and expects Congress and General Washington have been informed of the number of troops and their needs. The Marquis de Lafayette having been charged to give them notice and also at the moment of arrival orders issued for furnishing the necessary provisions needed, also horses for french artillery, and that these supplies will be on hand where ever the French troops land.

The King sends with Lafayette a commissary of war for these troops and it should be used for provisions, hospitals and anything else needed by the French troops. This article is of highest importance to the King and he trusts that Congress and General George Washington will feel its indispensable necessity.

Article VIII: The King commands to Rochambeau the need of maintaining the most severe and exact discipline in all respects among the French troops under his command. Above all it is up Rochambeau to promote by all possible means the greatest harmony and good understanding between the French troops and the American troops and all inhabitants who are subjects or allies of the Congress of the United States of North America.

Although it is entirely up to General George Washington to dispose of the auxiliary troops (French) sent to North America, but if the French troops are detached for any expedition with an American Corps, the two French and American general officers might be independent of each other, whatever their rank, and act in concert without either giving or receiving orders.

In an a further instructions to Rochambeau, the Articles were paraphrased in two directives:

I: The King ordered, as far as circumstances will permit, that his troops stay together, and at the proper time to represent to General GW under whose orders the French troops are to serve that it is the king's intention that the French troops not be dispersed, but they should act as a body under French generals except in the case of temporary detachments which would rejoin the principal corps in a few days.

II: The King intends that French troops keep their own guards and should perform all duties involving their security in camps, cantonments or quarters, which they occupy.

Reproduced from *Rochambeau. A Commemoration by the Congress of the United States of America of the Services of the French Auxiliary Forces in the War of Independence.* Prepared by authority of Congress under direction of the Joint Committee on the Library by Deb. Randolph Keim, Government Printing Office, Washington, DC, 1907, 296-298.

Appendix C

The March of History

The First Brigade of Rochambeau's army began the "March of History" on June 10, 1781, at Newport, Rhode Island, and arrived at Yorktown, Virginia, on September 28, 1781, after covering a distance of 724 miles.

Departure: June 10, Newport, Rhode Island Arrival: July 6, at Phillipsburg, New York	226 miles
Departure: August 19, Phillipsburg, New York Arrival: Head of Elk, Maryland, on September 7	219 miles
Departure: September 10, Head of Elk Arrival: Annapolis, Maryland, on September 18	92 miles
Departure: September 21, Annapolis, Maryland Arrival: Yorktown, Virginia, on September 28, 1781	187 miles
TOTAL	724 miles

The above information was extracted from an unpublished *Journal of the Siege of Yorktown* as recorded by Gaspard De Gallatin and translated by the French department of the College of William and Mary. Mr. Fess presented it on March 3, 1931, and then printed in Senate Document No. 322, 71st Congress, 3rd Session, 1931.

In the marvelous account of the march detailed in *Rochambeau, A Commemoration by the Congress of the United States of America* by Deb. Randolph Keim, printed by the Government Printing Office in Washington, 1907, pages 429-430, is the following:

The entire distance marched from Providence, Rhode Island to Yorktown by the Army of Rochambeau was 536 miles, with water transportation, Newport to Providence 30 miles, and Annapolis to Jamestown, 178 miles — 208miles; and march Williamsburg to Yorktown, 12 miles, or a total of 756 miles, Newport to Yorktown.

Endnotes

Chapter 1

1. Paul H. Smith, ed., *Letters of Delegates to Congress* (Washington: 1982), Vol. 9, 782.
2. Paul H. Smith, ed., *Letters of Delegates to Congress* (Washington: 1983), Vol. 10, 134 fn 1 (Marine Committee to Eastern Navy Board).
3. *Ibid.*, 358.
4. Stanley J. Idzerda, ed., *Lafayette in the Age of the American Revolution*, Vol. II (Ithaca: Cornell University Press, 1979), 221; Andreas Latzko, *Lafayette A Life,* trans. by E. W. Dickes (Garden City: Doubleday, Doran & Company, Inc., 1937), 75.
5. Paul H. Smith, ed., *Letters of Delegates to Congress*, Vol. 11 (Washington: Library of Congress, 1985), 120.
6. *Ibid.*, 134.
7. Idzerda, Vol. II, 225.
8. Stanley J. Idzerda, Vol. I, 14 fn 21.
9. *Ibid.*, Latzko, 35-39.
10. Latzko, 77.
11. Idzerda, Vol. II, Chronological Outline, xxxviii-xxxiv.
12. *Ibid.*, 226, 514.
13. *Ibid.*, 226.
14. *Ibid.*, 230.
15. *Ibid.*, 230-231.
16. *Ibid.*, 226.
17. Latzko, 78.
18. Idzerda, Vol. II, 289 fn 2.
19. D. Randolph Keim, *Rochambeau, A Commemoration by the United States of America of the Services of the French Auxiliary Forces in the War of Independence* (Washington, 1907), 264.
20. Idzerda, Vol. II, Genealogical Chart; Latzko, 83.
21. Latzko, 83.
22. Keim, 268-269.
23. *Ibid.*, 267.
24. L. Edward Purcell, *Who was Who in the American Revolution* (New York: Facts on File, 1993), 411-412.
25. Jean-Edmond Weelen *Rochmbeau Father and Son, The Journal of the Vicomte de Rochambeau*, trans, Lawrence Lee (New York: Henry Holt and Company, 1936), 7.
26. Purcell, 411-412.
27. Weelen, viii.
28. *Ibid.*, x.
29. Idzerda, Vol. II, 373; Latzko, 83.
30. Idzerda, Vol. II, 373 fn 1.
31. *Ibid.*, 377.
32. *Ibid.*, 379.
33. Latzko, 88.
34. Stanley J. Idzerda, ed., *Lafayette in the Age of the American Revolution*, Vol. III (Ithaca: Cornell University Press, 1979), 3.
35. Latzko, 88.
36. *Ibid.*, 88-89.
37. Idzerda, Vol. III, 6.
38. *Ibid.*, 10 fn 3.
39. *Ibid.*, 10 fn 4.
40. Keim, 263-269; Idzerda, Vol. III, xxxiv.
41. Latzko, 89.
42. *Ibid.*, 90.

Chapter 2

1. Keim, 276-277.
2. Weelen, 82.
3. Keim, 284-285, 307; Richard K. Showman, ed., *The Papers of Nathanael Greene*, Vol. VI (Chapel Hill: 1991), xiii, Introduction. French fleet anchored at Newport, RI on July 10, 1780; Howard C. Rice, Jr., and Anne S.K. Brown, Editors and translators, *The American Campaigns of Rochambeau's Army 1780, 1781, 1782,1783* (Princeton & Providence, Jointly published: Princeton University Press &Brown University Press, 1972), Vol. I, 17, 17 fn 6.
4. Rice and Brown, Vol. I, 18-19, fn 10.
5. *Ibid.*, 17.
6. Keim, 290-291.
7. Ibid., 299, 300-301; Rice and Brown, Vol. I, 18.
8. Keim, 302, 306.
9. Rice and Brown, Vol. I, 18.
10. *Ibid.*, 20.
11. *Ibid.*, 21.
12. Keim, 276-280.
13. *Ibid.*, 311-313.
14 Latzko, 91.
15. Keim, 294-295.
16. *Ibid.*, 313.
17. James A. Huston, *Logistics of Liberty* (Newark: University of Delaware Press, 1991), 259-260.
18. Keim, 311, 313.
19. *Ibid.*, 323.
20. *Ibid.*, 325.
21. *Ibid.*, 326.
22. *Ibid.*

23. *Ibid.*
24. *Ibid.*, 327.
25. *Ibid.*, 328.
26. Idzerda, Vol. III, xxxvi (Chronological Outline). Meetings took place from July 24-August 3, 1780.
27. *Ibid.*, 104. A British force under the command of Admiral Graves was cruising off New York and Rochambeau was not risking his force without French naval protection.
28. *Ibid.*, 131-136.
29. *Ibid.*
30. *Ibid.*,139-141.
31. *Ibid.*, 139-156.
32. *Ibid.*, 137-139, 139 fn 2-3.
33. *Ibid.*, 144-148.
34. *Ibid.*, 147. This passage, as well as any, illustrates the difficulties of comparing 18th century semantics in a modern context. In the modern vernacular this passage appears effeminate, hardly an expected discourse between two military men. Yet this was often the style and form in 18th century correspondence. The style is more noticeable in French communications printed in English.
35. *Ibid.*, 155.
36. Latzko, 92.
37. W.T.T. Pakenham, Captain, RN, *Naval Command and Control* (London: Brassey's Defense Publishers, 1989), 127-128.
38. Keim, 294-295.
39. William C. Stinchcombe, *The American Revolution and the French Alliance,* (Syracuse: 1969), 48-55.
40. Richard L. Blanco, ed., *The American Revolution 1775-1783, An Encyclopedia* (New York: Garland Publishing, 1993), 1499-1501.
41. Stinchcombe, 78.
42. Keim, 295.
43. John C. Fitzpatrick, ed., *The Writings of George Washington* (Washington: United States Printing Office, 1937), Vol. 20, 2.
44. *Ibid.*
45. Blanco, Vol. II, 942. General Benjamin Lincoln had been forced to surrender the southern Continental Army at Charleston, SC on May 12, 1780.
46. Fitzpatrick, Vol. 20, 58.
47. Rice and Brown, Vol. I, 19.
48. *Ibid.*, 20.
49. Latzko, 92
50. Fitzpatrick, Vol. 20, 58.
51. Latzko, 93.
52. Keim, 344.
53. Latzko, 94.
54. Showman, Vol. VI, xv-xvi.
55. *Ibid.*, 385-387.
56. Rice and Brown, Vol. I, 20, 20 fn 13.
57. Weelen, 214-216.

Chapter 3

1. Herman O. Benninghoff, II, *Valley Forge: A Genesis for Command and Control, Continental Army Style* (Gettysburg: Thomas Publications, 2001). Hereafter referred to as *Genesis.*
2. Mark M. Boatner, *Encyclopedia of the American Revolution* (Mechanicsburg: 1994), 758; The Mutiny of Thomas Hickey.
3. *Ibid.*, 758-759.
4. *Ibid.*, 758; Van Doren, *Mutiny in January* (New York: The Viking Press, 1943), 20.
5. Fitzpatrick, Vol. 21, 56 fn 94.
6. Smith, Vol. 16, 549 fn 1.
7. Fitzpatrick, Vol. 21, 55-58.
8. Van Doren, 53-54.
9. *Ibid.*, 55.
10. *Ibid.*, 56.
11. Smith, Vol. 16, 549 fn 1.
12. Fitzpatrick, Vol. 21, 173.
13. *Ibid.*, 61-63.
14. *Ibid.*, 64-66.
15. Van Doren, 74.
16. Boatner, Names given.
17. Van Doren, 128-129; William Reed, *Life and Correspondence of Joseph Reed* (Philadelphia: Lindsay and Blakiston, 1847). Vol. II, 319-333.
18. Boatner, 764-765.
19. Van Doren, 200.
20. Fitzpatrick, Vol. 21, 74.
21. Van Doren, 133-134.
22. Boatner, 759-760.
23. Van Doren, 206.
24. Fitzpatrick, Vol. 21, 119-122.
25. *Ibid.*, 123-124.
26. *Ibid.*, 124.
27. *Ibid.*, 128.
28. Van Doren, 220.
29. *Ibid.*, 221.
30. Fitzpatrick, Vol. 21,137-138.
31. *Ibid.*
32. *Ibid.*, 147-148.
33. Van Doren, 222-223.
34. Fitzpatrick, Vol. 21, 151.
35. Van Doren, 238.

Chapter 4

1. Theodore Thayer, *Nathanael Greene, Strategist of the American Revolution,* (New York: Twayne Publishers, 1960), 25.
2. *Ibid.*
3. *Ibid.*, 42.
4. *Ibid.*, 50.
5. *Ibid.*, 65.
6. Maureen Harrison & Steve Gilbert, eds., *George Washington in His Own Words* (New York: 1997), 253.

7. *Ibid.*, 258.
8. *Ibid.*
9. Fitzpatrick, Vol. 20, 181-182.
10. *Ibid.*, 215-216.
11. *Ibid.*, 238-239.
12. *Ibid.*, 247-248.
13. John McCauley Palmer, *General von Steuben* (New Haven, CT: Yale University Press, 1937), 237.
14. Showman, Vol. VI, 508.
15. See *Genesis* for reference to Washington's 13 Armies.
16. H. R. McIlwayne, ed., *Official Letters of the Governors of the State of Virginia, Letters of Thomas Jefferson* (Richmond: 1928), Vol. II, 261.
17. Palmer, 247.
18. *Ibid.*
19. Smith, Vol. 16, 616, John Sullivan to Meshech Weare.
20. Palmer, 248-249.
21. *Ibid.*, 250.
22. *Ibid.*
23. McIlwayne, Vol. II, 333-334.
24. Palmer, 253.
25. Smith, Vol. 16. 608-609. James Madison to Edmund Pendleton.

Chapter 5
1. Fitzpatrick, Vol. 21, 253-256.
2. *Ibid.*, 257.
3. *Ibid.*, 270-271.
4. *Ibid.*, 305.
5. Showman, Vol. VII, 337-341, 339 fn 1, 339-340 fn 12.
6. *Ibid.*, 362-363. The Facilitator heads south.
7. Purcell, 276-277.
8. *Genesis*. Lafayette's ascendancy to a trusted member of Washington's inner circle is described.
9. Fitzpatrick, Vol. 21, 322-323.
10. McIlwayne, Vol. II, 63-377.
11. Idzerda, Vol. III, 369.
12. *Ibid.*, 370-371, 371 fn 2.
13. Showman, Vol. VII, 385-386.
14. Palmer, 257.
15. *Ibid.*
16. *Ibid.*, 257 fn.
17. Keim, 276-277.
18. Fitzpatrick, Vol. 21, 358-359.
19. Idzerda, Vol. III, 371-372.
20. *Ibid.*, 381-382.
21. *Ibid.*, 382-383.
22. *Ibid.*, 384-385.
23. *Ibid.*, 386-387.
24. *Ibid.*, 387-389.
25. *Ibid.*, 390.
26. *Ibid.*, 390-391 fn 1.

27. *Ibid.*, 391.
28. Fitzpatrick, Vol. 21, 331.
29. Idzerda, Vol. III, 392-393, 393 fn 1.
30. *Ibid.*, 395.
31. *Ibid.*, 396-397.
32. *Ibid.*, 397-398, 398 fn 3.
33. *Ibid.*, 410-413.
34. *Ibid.*, 413-416.
35. *Ibid.*, 417.
36. *Ibid.*, 419 fn1.
37. *Ibid.*, 419-421.
38. *Ibid.*, 423-424.
39. Fitzpatrick, Vol. 21, 387-388.
40. *Ibid.*, 396-399.
41. *Ibid.*, 399-400, March 31, 1781.
42. *Ibid.*, 402-403.
43. Idzerda, Vol. IV, 1.
44. *Ibid.*, 3-5.
45. *Ibid.*, 5-6.
46. *Ibid.*, 6-7.
47. *Ibid.*
48. *Ibid.*, 8-9.
49. *Ibid.*
50. *Ibid.*, 9

Chapter 6
1. McIlwaine, Vol. II, 382 –532. These pages provide an insight into the governorship of Thomas Jefferson between March 2, 1781, and the balance of his term to June 3, 1781. His letters reveal a governor struggling with a military challenge for which he had neither training nor experience. His approach to solving military problems came from a political perspective. While he communicated frequently to the field, his requests for action and information were frequently delayed or remained unanswered. He showed little interest or aptitude for enforcement and less on placing Virginia on the war footing necessary to provide the support necessary to effectively resist the enemy.
2. *Ibid.*, 427.
3. *Ibid.*, 467.
4. *Ibid.*
5. *Ibid.*
6. *Ibid.*
7. Idzerda, Vol. IV, 16-17.
8. *Ibid.*, 23-24.
9. *Ibid.*, 24-26.
10. *Ibid.*
11. *Ibid.*, 35-41.
12. *Ibid.*, 41 fn11, Battle during Seven Years War in 1759.
13. *Ibid.*, 43-45.
14. *Ibid.*, 47-48.
15. *Ibid.*, 51.
16. *Ibid.*, 52.

17. *Ibid.*, 54-56.
18. *Ibid.*, 56-58.
19. *Ibid.*, 56-60.
20. *Ibid.*, 60-61.
21. *Ibid.*, 60 fn 1.
22. *Ibid.*, 62-63.
23. McIlwaine, Vol. II, p 498.
24. Idzerda, Vol. IV, 68-69.
25. *Ibid.*, 74-75.
26. Dennis M. Conrad, ed., *The Papers of General Nathanael Greene* (Chapel Hill: 1994), Vol. VIII, 185-186.
27. Idzerda, Vol., IV, 82-84.

Chapter 7

1. Keim, 355.
2. Wheelen, 215-216.
3. *Ibid.*
4. *Ibid.*, 100.
5. *Ibid.*, 100-101.
6. Weelen, 101.
8. *Ibid.*
9. Fitzpatrick, Vol. 22, 63-66.
10. *Ibid.*, 68-69.
11. John B.B. Trussell, Jr., *Birthplace of an Army: A Study of Valley Forge* (Harrisburg: 1979), 31, 80; Fitzpatrick, Vol. 22, 70-72.
12. Fitzpatrick, Vol. 22, 70-72.
13. James Ferguson, *The Power of the Purse* (Chapel Hill: 1961), 32.
14. Keim, 379.
15. Fitzpatrick, Vol. 22, 80.
16. Weelen, 102.
17. Fitzpatrick, Vol. 22, 86-87; Destouche had taken command of the French navy at Newport when Admiral; Ternay had died in March, 1781; later Admiral de Barras was sent from France to take command over Destouches; Purcell, 136-137.
18. Keim, 378-380.
19. Fitzpatrick, Vol. 22, 107.
20. xenophogroup (internet), *Yorktown Campaign Decision,* 4.
21. Keim, 380-386; Fitzpatrick, Vol. 22, 105-107.
22. Keim, 386.
23. *Ibid.*, 387.
24. *Ibid.*
25. *Ibid.*
26. *Ibid.*
27. Fitzpatrick, Vol. 22, fn 95, 132-133.
28. Henry P. Johnston, *The York town Campaign* (New York: Harper Brothers, 1881), 72.
29. Fitzpatrick, Vol. 22, 129.
30. *Ibid.*, 135-137.
31. Smith, Vol. 17, 402-403, 403 fn 5.
32. *Ibid.*, 403 fn 4.
33. *Ibid.*, 183-185, 185 fn 6.
34. *Ibid.*, 219.

35. *Ibid.*, 224-225.
36. *Ibid.*, 273-274.
37. Idzerda, Vol. IV, 134 fn 2. He became Minister of the Marine in October 1780.
38. *Ibid.*, 134 fn 3. Somewhat reluctantly, Rochambeau changed his mind on the feasibility of attacking New York during a conference with Washington in May, 1781, and agreed to a joint French-American expedition against the city; but his correspondence with De Grasse almost assured it would be the Chesapeake Bay rather than New York harbor.
39. *Ibid.*, 132-134, 134 fn 6; De Castries son was the Comte de Charlus who joined Lafayette in March 1781.
40. Fitzpatrick, Vol. 22, 209-210.

Chapter 8

1. Idzerda, Vol. IV, 89-91.
2. William B. Wilcox, ed., *The American Rebellion* (New Haven: 1954), 508-510; Earl Cornwallis, *An Answer to Sir Henry Clinton Narrative* (Philadelphia: Campbell, 1866), reprint, Number III, 9-13.
3. Wilcox, 511-512; Cornwallis, Number III, 20-21.
4. Idzerda, Vol. IV, 91.
5. *Ibid.*, 92-93.
6. *Ibid.*
7. *Ibid.*, 93 fn 3.
8. *Ibid.*, 93-95.
9. *Ibid.*, 95 fn 1.
10. *Ibid.*, 93-95.
11. *Ibid.*, 96-98.
12. *Ibid.*, 98 fn 4.
13. McIlwaine, Vol. II, 515-516.
14. *Ibid.*
15. Idzerda, Vol. IV, 102-103.
16. *Ibid.*, 106-108.
17. McIlwaine, Vol. II, 518.
18. Idzerda, Vol. IV, 120-121.
19. *Ibid.*, 121 fn 3.
20. *Ibid.*, 123-124.
21. *Ibid.*, 121.
22. *Ibid.*, 121-125.
23. *Ibid.*, 136-137.
24. *Ibid.*
25. McIlwaine, Vol. II, 522-523.
26. Idzerda, Vol. IV, 143-146.
27. *Ibid.*, 148-149.
28. *Ibid.*, 150-151.
29. *Ibid.*, 151-153.
30. *Ibid.*, 156-157, 157 fn 1.
31. *Ibid.*, 109 fn 3.
32. Fitzpatrick, Vol. 22, 140, 140 fn 9.
33. *Ibid.*, 139-140, 143-144, 144 fn 14.

Chapter 9

1. Cornwallis, Introduction i-ii.
2. Wilcox, 183, 183 fn 20.
3. *Ibid.*, 184.
4. *Ibid.*, 185.
5. Wickwire, 133.
6. *Ibid.*, 129.
7. Wilcox, 449.
8. *Ibid.*, 450.
9. *Ibid.*, 204.
10. *Ibid.*, 451.
11. *Ibid.*, 205 fn 16, 454-455.
12. *Ibid.*, 205, 467-468.
13. Wickwire, 132.
14. Wilcox, 176.
15. *Ibid.*, 180.
16. Wickwire, 184.
17. Wilcox, 20; Wickwire, 151. Clinton did send 1900 men into the Carolinas in November, 1780, Clinton's figures of Cornwallis's strength is suspect [Details given], in addition to the British troops, Cornwallis commanded 2 German infantry regiments (Huyne & Ditfurth). He had six Provincial regiments.
18. Wickwire, 158.
19. Wilcox, 230.
20. Wickwire, 192-193.
21. *Ibid.*, 195.
22. *Ibid.*, 196-198. Wickwire's description of Hanger's character is colorful; Boatner, 318.
23. Wickwire, 195-199.
24. Lieut. Col. Banastre Tarleton, *A History of the Campaigns of 1780 and 1781 in the Southern Provinces of North America* (North Stratford, NH: Ayer Publishers, 1999), 159.
25. *Ibid.*, 160. Author's note: this is a significant impact on command and control and may indicate the real advantage and contribution of the American Partisans.
26. Wilcox, 220.
27. *Ibid.*, 469, 471, correspondence: October 29, 1780.
28. Wickwire, 223.
29. Wilcox, 230.
30. Wickwire, 231.
31. *Ibid.*, 230.
32. *Ibid.*
33. *Ibid.*, 251.
34. *Ibid.*, 252.
35. *Ibid.*, 257.
36. *Ibid.*, 259.
37. Cornwallis, Part 1, Number I, 1-4.
38. Wickwire, 274-275. Very important distinction from a command and control concept. The mere existence of a British force in the south was pointless: to be worthwhile it had to do something to speed the reestablishment of royal government. The Americans on the other hand merely had to exist to cast doubt on British authority and as long as they existed they were winning.
39. *Ibid.*, 276-278.
40. *Ibid.*, 279.
41. Wickwire, 279-283; Tarleton, 227-228.
42. Tarleton, 229-230.
43. Wickwire, 885, 284-285.
44. *Ibid.*, 289.
45. Cornwallis, Number II, 5-8.
46. Wickwire, 290, 291, 448 fn 49.
47. *Ibid.*, 289.
48. *Ibid.*, 311, 451 3n.
49. Wilcox, 508-510; Earl Cornwallis, Number III, 9-13.
50. Wilcox, 512. Clinton received this letter on May 22, 1781. Cornwallis also notified Lord Germain on the same day (April 23, 1781); Cornwallis, Number III, 20-21.
51. Wilcox, 512-513. Phillips received Cornwallis's April 24, 1781 letter on May 6; Wickwire, 325.
52. Wilcox, 284.
53. *Ibid.*, 293.
54. Wilcox, *Portrait of A General,* 386-387; a route and operation of Cornwallis in the South.
55. Wickwire, 314-321, 325, 327.
56. *Ibid.*, 314-321, 327.
57. *Ibid.*, 328.
58. *Ibid.*, 325-326, 327 map of Cornwallis from Halifax to Yorktown.
59. Cornwallis, 85-87.

Chapter 10

1. Showman, Vol. VI, 488-489.
2. *Ibid.*, 533.
3. *Ibid.*, 542.
4. *Ibid.*, 543.
5. *Ibid.*, 544.
6. *Ibid.*, 546 fn 9.
7. Fitzpatrick, Vol. 20, 469-470.
8. Showman, Vol. I, 82-83.
9. Fitzpatrick, Vol. 22, 146-147. In his reference to before "Campden," Washington is referring to Greene's encounter at Guilford Court House on March 15, 1781.
10. *Ibid.*, 154-158.
11. *Ibid.*, 159.
12. Erna Riach, *Supplying Washington's Army* (Washington: Center of Military History, 1981), 59, 90.
13. *Ibid.*, 58-59.
14. Fitzpatrick, Vol., 22, 163-165.
15. *Ibid.*, 170-171.
16. *Ibid.*, 174-175.
17. *Ibid.*, 177-178.
18. *Ibid.*, 182-183.

19. *Ibid.*, 189-190.
20. *Ibid.*, 191-192, 191 n 69.
21. Keim, 391.
22. Wheelen, 105 fn 3.
23. *Ibid.*, 106.
24. Keim, 387.
25. Fitzpatrick, Vol., 22, 206 fn 91.
26. *Ibid.*, 207.
27. *Ibid.*, 204-209, 206 n 91, 208 n 93. Series of letters in exchange of information between GW, Rochambeau and associated individuals regarding de Grasse appearance on the coast and his eventual effort in the Chesapeake.
28. Keim, 392.
29. Showman, Vol. VIII, 273.
30. Fitzpatrick, Vol. 22, 215-218.
31. *Ibid.*, 229-230.
32. *Ibid.*, 234-235.
33. Boatner, 853-854.
34. Enrique Fernandez Y Fernandez, *Spain's Contribution to the Independence of the United States* (Philadelphia: Spanish Embassy,1985), 16; Fitzpatrick, The *Writings of George Washington,* Vol., 22, 242.
35. Count William De Deux-Ponts, *My Campaigns in America, 1780-81* (Boston: J. K. Wiggin and Wm. Parsons Lunt, 1868), Appendix, 163.
36. Keim, 395.
37. Fitzpatrick, Vol. 22, 258-259.
38. *Ibid.*
39. Keim, 395.
40. Rice and Brown, Vol. I, 30.
41. Keim, 395; Rice and Brown, Vol. 1, 30.
42. Rice and Brown, Vol. 1, 30.
43. Fitzpatrick, Vol., 22, 267-268.
44. Purcell, 303.
45. Fitzpatrick, Vol., 22, 268-269.
46. *Ibid.*, 285-286.
47. *Ibid.*, 286-288.
48. *Ibid.*, 293-295, 296-306.
49. *Ibid.*, 306-308.

Chapter 11

1. Fitzpatrick, Vol. 22, 324-325.
2. *Ibid.*, 327.
3. David B. Mattern, *Benjamin Lincoln and the American Revolution* (Columbia: University of South Carolina Press, 1995), 116.
4. Fitzpatrick, Vol. 22, 324-325.
5. *Ibid.*, 328.
6. Keim, 400.
7. Rice and Brown, Vol. I, 32-33.
8. Fitzpatrick, Vol. 22, 332-333.
9. Stephen Bonsal, *When the French were Here* (Garden City: Doubleday, Doran and Company, 1945), 97.
10. *Ibid.*, 98.
11. *Ibid.*, 99-100.
12. *Ibid.*, 101.
13. Rice and Brown, Vol. I, 33.
14. Stinchcombe, 146.
15. Rice and Brown, Vol. I, 33-34 fn 36.
16. Fitzpatrick, Vol. 22, 204-209 with special attention to 206 fn 91 & 208 fn 93. Series of communication exchanges between Washington, Rochambeau and associated individuals regarding de Grasse appearance on the coast and his eventual effort in the Chesapeake are in both; Keim, 387.
17. *The Naval Campaigns of Count De Grasse, During the American Revolution 1781-1783*, Karl Gustaf Tornquist, (trans) Amandus Johnson (Philadelphia: Swedish Colonial Society, 1942), 53.
18. Keim, 387.
19. *Ibid.*, 401.
20. Fitzpatrick, Vol. 22, 367-369.
21. Keim, 388.
22. Fitzpatrick, Vol. 22, 382 fn 19; Purcell, 288-289.
23. Fitzpatrick, Vol. 22, 382-384. Authors note: This is an important letter because it highlights both the political and military aspects of command and control as well as GW's approach to declining dictatorial powers. Richard Henry Lee was not an ardent supporter of Washington at the time of the Valley Forge encampment. Washington makes every effort to get his understanding and support in this letter.
24. Keim, 405.
25. *Ibid.*, 406-410.
26. *Ibid.*, 410.
27. Fitzpatrick, Vol. 22, 400-402.
28. *Correspondence of General Washington and Comte De Grasse 1781, Aug 17–Nov 4*, Ed. by The Institut Francais de Washington (Washington: 1930), 4.
29. Fitzpatrick, Vol. 22, 495-496.
30. Fitzpatrick, Vol. 23, 8.
31. De Grasse had a large margin of discretion as to where to head, New York or the Chesapeake; Sparks "Washington" Vol. 8, appendix indicated that De Grasse had concluded from the tenor of letters from Washington, Rochambeau and Luzerne to head for Virginia.

Chapter 12

1. Idzerda, Vol. IV, 147-148.
2. *Ibid.*, 150-151.
3. *Ibid.*, 157.
4. *Ibid.*, 158.
5. Benninghoff Collection, 91B44 and Catalogue in MASTER FILE 91B44.
6. Idzerda, Vol. IV, 166-167.

7. *Ibid.*, 168-169.
8. McIlwaine, Vol. II, Preface, iii.
9. Fitzpatrick, Vol. 9, 93.
10. Fitzpatrick, Vol. 22, 413-416, 415, 415 fn 70.
11. *Ibid.*, 472.
12. Idzerda, Vol. IV, 271-272, 272 fn 3.
13. Fitzpatrick, Vol. 9, 421.
14. Showman, Vol. VI, Biography, 483 484 fn 1.
15. Benninghoff Collection 91B90.
16. McIlwaine, Vol. III, 2.
17. *Ibid.*, 5-6.
18. *Ibid.*, 11-12.
19. *Ibid.*, 13-14.
20. *Ibid.*
21. *Ibid.*, 17.

Chapter 13

1. Dennis M. Conrad ed., *The Papers of General Nathanael Greene* (Chapel Hill, 1995), Vol. VIII, 406.
2. Smith, Vol. 17, 282-283.
3. *Ibid.*, 336-338.
4. Purcell, 264.
5. Idzerda, Vol. IV, 194-196.
6. *Ibid.*, 197-201. A reference to a previous letter to Greene sent on June 18. This reference was to von Steuben and his failure to protect the stores against Simcoe's raid at Point of Forks, Virginia (see Steuben to Lafayette, June 5, 1781). Lafayette was considerably more critical of Steuben in private letters to Greene and Washington than he was in public correspondence to others (June 18, 20, 1781).
7. Fitzpatrick, Vol. 22, 352-355.
8. *Ibid.*
9. *Ibid.*, 367-369.
10. Conrad, 415-416.
11. Rhys Isaac, *The Transformation of Virginia, 1740-1790* (New York: W.W. Norton & Company, 1982), 275-277.
12. Idzerda, Vol. IV, 206.
13. Photo and explanation of findings in Benninghoff Collection.
14. Idzerda, Vol. IV, 217 n1, n2, n3.
15. *Ibid.*, 228-231.
16. McIlwaine, Vol. III, 17.
17. Idzerda, Vol. IV, 231-235.
18. Harold A. Larrabee, *Decision At Chesapeake* (New York: Clarkson N. Potter, 1964), 125.
19. Idzerda, Vol. IV, 235-236.
20. General Robert Lawson, Brigadier General, Virginia militia.
21. Idzerda, Vol. IV, 235-236.
22. *Ibid.*, 236-239, 238, fn 1& 3.
23. *Ibid.*, 240-241.
24. *Ibid.*, 242-245.
25. *Ibid.*, 244 fn 3.

26. Fitzpatrick, Vol. 22, 367-369; Idzerda, Vol. IV, 247-248.
27. *Ibid.*
28. *Ibid.*
29. Idzerda, Vol. IV, 286.
30. McIlwaine, Vol. III, 10-11.
31. *Ibid.*, 16.
32. Fitzpatrick, Vol. 22, 432-434; Idzerda, Vol. IV, 288-290.
33. Idzerda, Vol. IV, 293.
34. *Ibid.*, 294 fn 1.
35. *Ibid.*, 303.
36. *Ibid.*, 307.
37. *Ibid.*
38. *Ibid.*
39. *Ibid.*, 321-322.
40. *Ibid.*, 329-331.

Chapter 14

1. Purcell, 112-113; Wickwire, 312; Cornwallis, 162.
2. Wickwire, 326.
3. *Ibid.*, 310.
4. *Ibid.*
5. *Ibid.*, 325.
6. *Ibid.*, 325-326.
7. *Ibid.*, 328.
8. *Ibid.*, 325-326, 327. Map of Cornwallis move from Halifax to Yorktown.
9. *Ibid.*, 326.
10. *Ibid.*
11. Cornwallis, 85-87.
12. Wickwire, 328-335.
13. *The Continental Journal and Weekly Advertiser*, Thursday, May 17, 1781, Boston, 2.
14. Wickwire, 335-336. Good map on page 327.
15. *Ibid.*, 336.
16. *Ibid.*, 338-338.
17. *Ibid.*, 339-340; Cornwallis, 112-118.
18. Wickwire, 337.
19. Cornwallis, 118-126; Wickwire, 339-340.
20. Wickwire, 345-346.
21. Wickwire, 347; Cornwallis, 126-158. A series of letters.
22. Wickwire, 349.
23. Cornwallis, 170-174.
24. *Ibid.*, 179, 181-182.
25. Wickwire, 353; Cornwallis, 182.
26. Wickwire, 355.
27. *Ibid.*, 357.
28. *Ibid.*, 359.
29. *Ibid.*, 360.
30. Boatner, 58.
31. Wickwire, 360.
32. Bonsal, 134-137.
33. Wickwire, 361-362.
34. Cornwallis, 193.
35. *Ibid.*, 201-202; Tarleton, 423-424.

36. Cornwallis, 202-203; Tarleton, 424-425.
37. Cornwallis, 204; Tarleton, 425.

Chapter 15

1. Smith, Vol. 17, 502-503.
2. *Ibid.*, 505.
3. *Ibid.*, 535-536.
4. Fitzpatrick, Vol. 23, 11-12.
5. *Ibid.*
6. *Ibid.*, 28-32.
7. Erna Rish, Supplying Washington's Army (Washington: Center of Military History, United States Army, 1980), 246. Risch indicates 450 miles New York to Yorktown.
8. *Ibid.*
9. Smith, Vol. 17, 547 fn 3.
10. *Ibid.*
11. Francis Wharton, ed., *Diplomatic Correspondence of the American Revolution,* (Washington: 1889), Vol. IV, 650; Fitzpatrick, Vol. 23, 12 fn 23.
12. Wharton, Vol. IV, 651.
13. *Ibid.*
14. Wharton, Vol. IV, 651 fn August 21.
15. James A. Huston, *Logistics of Liberty* (Newark: University of Delaware Press, 1991), 263.
16. Keim, 413-414; Wharton, Vol. IV, 700 (Morris to Rochambeau).
17. E. James Ferguson, *The Power of the Purse* (Chapel Hill: 1961), 117.
18. *Ibid.*, 119.
19. *Ibid.*, 121.
20. Fitzpatrick, Vol. 23, 52.
21. L.G. Shreve, *Tench Tilghman, The Life and Times of Washington's Aide-de-Camp* (Centerville MD: Tidewater Publishers, 1982), 148.
22. *Ibid.*
23. Fitzpatrick, Vol. 23, 57-58.
24. *Ibid.*, 55-56.

Chapter 16

1. Idzerda, Vol. IV, 331 fn 3.
2. Fitzpatrick, Vol.. 22, 501-502.
3. *Ibid.*
4. Rice and Brown, Vol. I, 39-40 fn 54.
5. Fitzpatrick, Vol. 22, 503.
6. Unity of Command in the modern vernacular has no comparison with the concept in the 18th century.
7. Fitzpatrick, Vol., 23, 6-7.
8. Rice and Brown, Vol. I, 40, 254.
9. Count William De Deux-Ponts, *My Campaigns in America,* trans, Samuel Abbot Greene (Boston: J.K. Wiggin & Wm. Parsons Lunt, 1868) 121-122; Rice and Brown, Vol. I, 40.

10. Colonel H. L. Landers, *The Virginia Campaign and The Blockade and Siege of Yorktown 1781*(Washington: F.A. Historical Section, Army War College, 1931); http://army.mil/cmh-pg/books/RevWar/Yorktown/AWC-Ytn-14.htm, Part XIV, (Washington's Intentions and Plans), 2 .
11. Fitzpatrick, Vol. 23, 20.
12. Keim, 416; Henry P. Johnston, *The Yorktown Campaign and Surrender of Cornwallis* (New York: Harper Brothers, 1881), 88 fn 2.
13. Keim, 416-417; *The Journal of Claude Blanchard*, Thomas Balch, ed., trans, William Duane (New York: Arno Press, 1969), reprint, 129: Johnston, 88 fn 2.
14. *The Journal of Claude Blanchard*, 129.
15. Stinchcombe, 146.
16. Bonsal, 121.
17. Fitzpatrick, Vol. 22, 502.
18. *Ibid.*, 411.
19. Fitzpatrick, Vol. 23, 33-34.
20. *Ibid.*
21. *Ibid.*
22. Keim, 419-420.
23. Weelen, 109.
24. Rice and Brown, Vol. I, 42-43.
25. Bonsal, 122.
26. Purcell, 138 (De Witt, Simeon), 153 (Erskine, Robert); Bonsal, 123; Fitzpatrick, Vol. 23, 68-69.
27. *The Journal of Claude Blanchard*, 134.
28. Keim, 419-420.
29. *The Journal of Claude Blanchard*, 137.
30. Bonsal, 126.
31. *Ibid.*, 129.
32. Idzerda, Vol. IV, 324-325.
33. *Ibid.*, 338-339.
34. *Ibid.*, 350-351.
35. *Correspondence of General Washington and Comte De Grasse 1781, Aug 17–Nov 4*, Edited by The Institut Francais de Washington (Washington: 1930), 4.
36. Karl Gustaf Tornquist, *Naval Campaigns of Count De Grasse*, trans. by Amandus Johnson (Philadelphia: Swedish Colonial Society, 1942), 57.
37. *Correspondence of General Washington and Comte De Grasse 1781*, 4-5.
38. Idzerda, Vol. IV, 373-376.
39. *Ibid.*, 378.
40. *Ibid.*, 380-383.
41. *Ibid.*, 387.
42. *Ibid.*, 388-389.
43. *Ibid.*, 389-390.
44. McIlwaine, Vol. III, 29-35.
45. *Ibid.*, 42.
46. *Correspondence of General Washington and Comte De Grasse 1781*, 5-7; Fitzpatrick, Vol. 23, 77.

47. *Correspondence of General Washington and Comte De Grasse 1781*, 8-11.
48. Rice and Brown, Vol. I, 50 fn 85.
49. *Correspondence of General Washington and Comte De Grasse 1781*, 14.
50. *Ibid.*, 17.
51. *Ibid.*, 18.
52. *Ibid.*, 21-22.
53. Fitzpatrick, Vol. 23, 93-94.
54. Wharton, Vol. IV, 718 (Morris to Luzerne).
55. Keim, 419.
56. *Correspondence of General Washington and Comte De Grasse 1781*, 22.
57. Kathryn Sullivan, *Maryland and France 1774-1779* (Philadelphia: University of Pennsylvania, 1936), Dissertation, 113-117.
58. Fitzpatrick, Vol. 23, 101 (Letter to Major General Benjamin Lincoln).
59. *Correspondence of General Washington and Comte De Grasse 1781*, 23-24.
60. Keim, 427.
61. Rice and Brown, Vol. I, 52-55.
62. Idzerda, Vol. IV, 397.
63. Weelen, 112.
64. *The Journal of Claude Blanchard*, 141.
65. *Correspondence of General Washington and Comte De Grasse 1781*, 30-31.
66. *Ibid.*, 31.
67. McIlwaine, Vol. III, 51.
68. *Ibid.*
69. *Ibid.*, 53.
70. *Ibid.*
71. *Ibid.*, 55-56.
72. *Ibid.*, 60-61.
73. *Ibid.*, 63-64.
74. Fitzpatrick, Vol. 23, 121.
75. *Correspondence of General Washington and Comte De Grasse 1781*, 35.
76. Smith, Vol. 18, 45-46.
77. *Ibid.*, 57.
78. *Ibid.*, 68-69.
79. Tornquist, 65, 65 fn 132, 66.
80. *Correspondence of General Washington and Comte De Grasse 1781*, 44.
81. Weelen, 112.
82. *Correspondence of General Washington and Comte De Grasse 1781*, 44.
83. *Ibid.*, 46.
84. Weelen, 112.
85. *Correspondence of General Washington and Comte De Grasse 1781*, 48-51.
86. *Ibid.*, 51.
87. *Ibid.*, 54.
88. French Ensor Chadwick, ed., *The Graves Papers* (New York: De Vinne Press, 1916), Vol. VII, 97.
89. Smith, Vol.18, 84.
90. Fitzpatrick, Vol. 23, 158-159; Keim, 438.
91. Rice and Brown, Vol. I, 57.
92. Fitzpatrick, Vol. 23,158-159.
93. Keim, 429.
94. *Correspondence of General Washington and Comte De Grasse 1781*, 23-24.

Chapter 17

1. Keim, 429.
2. *Journal of the Siege of York-town*, recorded in the hand of Gaspard De Gallatin, transl. by the French Department of the College of William and Mary, United States Government Printing Office, 1931, 44-48.
3. Carl von Clausewitz, *On War* (Princeton: 1984), 23.
4. *Genesis*, 160.
5. For a more expanded explanation of command and control see *Genesis*, 1-8.

Appendix A

1. Clausewitz, 7.
2. FM 22-103 *Leadership and Command at Senior Levels, Headquarters, Department of the Army*, 41.
3. *Ibid*, 41-42.
4. Capt. W.T.T. Packenham, R.N., *Naval Command and Control* (London: 1989), vii-viii.
5. Paddy Griffith, *Battle Tactics of the American Civil War, Command and Control* (Wilks: 1996), 53.
6. Some communications took place over short distances by sight, i.e. waving flags or lights, but these were exceptions.
7. FM 22-103 *Leadership and Command at Senior Levels, Headquarters, Department of the Army*, 41-47.
8. Raphael P. Thian, *Legislative History of the General Staff of the Army of the United States From 1775-1901* (Washington: 1901), 3.
9. Clausewitz, 71.
10. *Ibid*, 128.
11. Packenham, 127-128.
12. The Continental Army needed an individual(s) with the power of leadership charisma. If one could not be found, he would have to be invented. Washington, as Commander-in-Chief, was found and invented.
13. Mark V. Kwansy, *Washington's Partisan War, 1775-1783* (Kent: 1996), 3.
14. Clausewitz, 145.
15. Major General George S. Eckhardt, *Command and Control 1950-1969,* Department of the Army (Washington, D.C.: 1974), 85-86.

Bibliography

PAPERS, CORRESPONDENCE AND MEMOIRS

Butterfield, L. H., and Wendell D. Garrett, (Editors), *The Adams Family Correspondence*, The Belknap Press of Harvard University Press, Cambridge, MA, 1973.

Fitzpatrick, John E., *The Writings of George Washington*, George Washington Bicentennial Edition, United States Printing Office, Washington, DC.

Heath's Memoirs of the American War. Books for Libraries Press, Freeport, New York, NY, 1970.

Idzerda, Stanley J.(Editor), *Lafayette in the Age of the American Revolution, Selected Letters & Papers, 1776-1790,* Cornell University Press, Ithaca, NY, 1977.

Johnson, Herbert A. (Editor), *The Papers of John Marshall*. Volume 1, University of North Carolina Press, Chapel Hill, N.C. 1974.

Journals of the Continental Congress, 1774-1789. Government Printing Office, Washington, DC, 1907-1908.

Reese, George H. (Editor) *The Cornwallis Papers*. The University Press of Virginia, Charlottesville, VA, 1978.

Smith, Paul H., (editor), *Letters of Delegates to Congress, 1774-1789,* Library of Congress, Washington, DC, 1981-1982.

Showman, Richard K. and Margaret Cobb (Editors), *The Papers of General Nathanael Greene, January 1777-October, 1778,* University of North Carolina Press, Chapel Hill, NC, 1980.

Sparks, Jared, *Correspondence of the American Revolution, Letters of Eminent Men to George Washington, From the Time of His Taking Command of the Army to the End of His Presidency.* Volume 2, Books for Libraries Press, New York, NY, 1970.

Syrett, Harold C. and Jacob E. Cooke, (Editors), *The Papers of Alexander Hamilton, 1768-1777,* Columbia University Press, New York, NY, 1961.

Taylor, Robert J. and Gregg L. Lint, (Editors), *The Papers of John Adams,* Belknap Press of Harvard University Press, Cambridge, MA, 1983.

Von Zemensky, Edith (Editor), *The Papers of General Friedrich Wilhelm von Steuben 1777-1794*. Microfilm Edition, Guide and Index, Kraus International Publications, Millwood, NY, 1984.

MANUAL SOURCES

A Plan of Discipline, Composed for the Use of the Militia of the County of Norfolk. Originally printed by Shuckburgh, London, England, 1759, Reprint by Museum Restoration Service, Ottawa, Canada, 1969.

FM 22-103 Leadership and Command at Senior Levels. Headquarters, Department of the Army, Washington, DC, 1987.

FM 100-5 Operations. Headquarters, Department of the Army, Washington, DC. 1993.

Pickering, Timothy, Jr., *An Easy Plan of Discipline for a Militia.* Samuel and Ebenezer Hall, Salem, MA. 1775.

ARTICLES

Griffith, Paddy, "Battle Tactics of the American Civil War" *Command and Control,* The Crowood Press, Ltd., Ramsbury Wilks, England. 1996.

Kramer, Lloyd S., "America's Lafayette and Lafayette's America: A European and American Revolution", *William & Mary Quarterly.* XXVIII (1981), 228-241.

Zabecki, David T., "Kazimierz Pulaski in the Birth of American Cavalry." *Military History.* Leesburg, VA, March, 1997

PRIMARY SOURCES, PRINTED SOURCES
Archives of Maryland, 45:329-31.

Baurmeister, Adjutant General Major, *Revolution in America, Confidential Letters and Journals 1776-1784 of Adjutant General Major Baurmeister of the Hessian Forces.* Bernhard A. Uhlendorf (Translator). Rutgers University Press, New Brunswick, N.J. 1957.

Boyer, Melville J., (Editor) *The Book of Jacob Weiss, Deputy Quartermaster of the Revolution.* Lehigh County Historical Society, Allentown, PA, 1956.

Brown, A. Lloyd and Howard H. Peckham, (Editors) *Revolutionary War Journals of Henry Dearborn, 1775-1783.* Heritage Books, Bowie, MD, 1994.

Burgoyne, Bruce E. (Editor), *Diaries of Two Anspach Jaegers.* Heritage Books, Bowie, MD, 1997.

Burgoyne, Bruce E. (Translator), *Eighteenth Century America, A Hessian Report on the People, the Land, the War. As Noted in the Diary of Chaplain Philip Waldeck (1776-1780).* Heritage Books, Inc. Bowie, MD, 1995.

Chinard, G. (Editor), *The Treaties of 1778 and Allied Documents.* John Hopkins Press, Baltimore, MD, 1928.

Cornwallis, Earl, *Answer to Sir Henry Clinton's Narrative of the Campaign in 1781 in North America.* John Campbell, Philadelphia (Reprint), 1866.

Cornwallis, Earl, *Letter, to Sir Henry Clinton, July 17, 1780*, Charleston, South Carolina. Original Letter in Benninghoff Collection.

Dann, John C. (Editor), *The Revolution Remembered, Eyewitness Accounts of the War for Independence.* The University of Chicago Press, Chicago, IL, 1980.

Davies, William, *Letter, to The County Lieutenant of War Office,* Berkley, Virginia, June 22, 1781. Original Letter in Benninghoff Collection.

Deux-Ponts, Count William De, *My Campaigns in America, 1780-1781.* Samuel Abbot Green (Translator), J. K. Wiggin and Wm. Parson Lunt, Boston, MA, 1868.

Douglas, Robert B., (Editor & Translator), *The Chevalier de Pontgibaud, A French Volunteer of the War of Independence.* Kennikat Press, Inc., Port Washington, NY, 1898, reissued 1968.

Drake, Francis S., *Life and Correspondence of Henry Knox, Major-General in the American Revolutionary Army.* Samuel G. Drake, Boston, MA, 1873.

Ewald, Johann, Captain, *Diary of American Revolution.* Yale University Press, New Haven, CT, 1979.

Field, Edward, *Diary of Colonel Israel Angell, 1778-1781, Commanding the Second Rhode Island Continental Regiment.* Preston & Rounds Company, Providence, RI, 1899.

Greenman, Jeremiah, *Diary of a Common Soldier in the American Revolution, 1775-1783.* Northern Illinois University Press, Dekalb, IL, 1978..

Gruber, Ira D. (Editor), *John Peebles' American War, 1776-1782.* Sutton Publishing, Ltd., Phoenix Mill, England, 1998.

Harrison, Maureen & Steve Gilbert, (Editors), *George Washington In His Own Words.* Barnes & Noble Books, New York, NY, 1997.

MacKenzie, Frederick, *Diary of Frederick MacKenzie, Giving a Daily Narrative of his Military Service as an Officer of the Regiment of Royal Welch Fusiliers During the Years 1775-1781 in Massachusetts, Rhode Island and New York.* 2 Volumes, Harvard University Press, Cambridge, MA. 1930.

Martin, Joseph Plumb, *Private Yankee Doodle.* George F. Sheer (editor). Eastern Acorn Press, New York, N. Y. 1988.

Muster and Pay Rolls of the War of the Revolution, 1775-1783 (Collections of The New York Historical Society). Genealogical Publishing Company, Inc., Baltimore, MD. 1996.

Robertson, Archibald, *Archibald Robertson, Lieutenant-General, Royal Engineers, His Diaries and Sketches in America, 1762-1780.* Facsimile Copy, 1930.

Turner, Joseph B. Rev. (Editor), *The Journal and Order Book of Captain Robert Kirkwood.* Kennikat Press, Port Washington, NY, 1970.

Ward, John, *A Memoir of Lieut.-Colonel Samuel Ward, First Rhode Island Regiment, Army of the American Revolution.* John Ward, New York, NY, 1875.

Wilcox, William B. (Editor), *The American Rebellion, Sir Henry Clinton's Narrative of His Campaigns, 1775-1782.* Yale University Press, New Haven, CT.

SECONDARY SOURCES

Alden, John R., *The South in the Revolution 1763-1789.* Louisiana State University Press, Baton Rouge, LA, 1976.

Allen, E. M. *LaFayette's Second Expedition to Virginia*. Maryland Historical Society, Baltimore, MD, 1891.

Baldwin, Alice M., *The New England Clergy and the American Revolution*. Frederick Ungar Publishing Company, New York, NY, 1965.

Bass, Robert D., *The Green Dragoon, The Lives of Banastre Tarleton and Mary Robinson*. Henry Holt and Company, New York, NY, 1957.

Bennett, Charles E. & Donald R. Lennon., *A Quest for Glory, Major General Robert Howe and the American Revolution*. University of North Carolina Press, Chapel Hill, NC, 1991.

Benninghoff, Herman O. II, *Valley Forge: A Genesis of Command and Control, Continental Army Style*. Thomas Publications, Gettysburg, PA, 2001.

Berg, Fred A., *Encyclopedia of the Continental Army Units*. Stackpole Books, Harrisburg, PA,1972.

Berger, Carl, *Broadsides & Bayonets*. Presidio Press, San Rafael, CA, 1976.

Billias, George A., (Editor), *George Washington's Generals and Opponents*. Da Capo Press, New York, NY, 1994.

Billias, George A., *General John Glover and His Marblehead Mariners*. Henry Holt and Company, New York, NY, 1960.

Black, Jeannette D. & William G. Roelker, *A Rhode Island Chaplin in the Revolution*. Kennikat Press, Port Washington, NY, 1949.

Blair, Bruce G., *Strategic Command and Control*. The Brookings Institution, Washington, DC, 1985.

Blanco, Richard L. (Editor), *The American Revolution 1775-1783, An Encyclopedia*. Garland Publishing, Inc. New York, NY, 2 Volumes,1993.

Blumenthal, Walter H., *Women Camp Followers of the American Revolution*. Arno Press, New York, NY, 1974.

Boatner, Mark M., III, *Encyclopedia of the American Revolution*. Stackpole Books, Mechanicsburg, PA, 1994.

Bodinier, Gilbert, Capitaine, *Dictionnaire des officiers de l'armee royale qui ont combattu aux Etats-Unis pendant la guerre d'Independance 1776-1783 suivi d'un Supplement a Les Francais sous les treize etoiles du commandant Andre Lasseray*. Chateau de Vincennes, France, 1983.

Bolles, Albert S., *The Financial History of the United States from 1774-1789*. Augustus M. Kelly, New York, NY, 1976.

Bolton, Charles K., *The Private Soldier under Washington*. Corner House Publishers, Williamstown, MA, 1976.

Boyes, Jon L., Dr.Vice-Adm, USN (Ret.) & Stephen J. Andriole, *Principles of Command & Control*. AFCEA International Press, Washington, DC, 1987.

Bonsal, Stephen, *When The French Were Here*. Doubleday, Doran and Company, Inc., Garden City, NY, 1945.

Boyle, Joseph L., *From Redcoat to Rebel: The Thomas Sullivan Journal.* Heritage Books, Inc. Baltimore, MD, 1997.

Brown, Richard D., *Knowledge is Power, The Diffusion of Information in Early America, 1700-1865.* Oxford University Press, New York, NY, 1989.

Builder, Carl H. and Richard N. Bankes, *Command Concepts, A Theory Derived from the Practice of Command and Control.* National Defense Research Institute, RAND, 1999.

Callahan, North, *Henry Knox, General Washington's General.* A. S. Barnes and Company, South Brunswick, NJ, 1958.

Camus, Raoul F., *Military Music of the American Revolution.* University of North Carolina Press, Chapel, NC, 1976.

Carp, Wayne E., *To Starve an Army at Pleasure, Continental Army Administration and American Political Culture.* University of North Carolina Press, Chapel Hill, NC, 1984.

Caughey, John W., *Bernardo de Galvez in Louisiana, 1776-1783.* University of California Press, Berkley, CA, 1943.

Chadwick, French Ensor, editor. *The Graves Papers and Other Documents Relating to the Naval Operations of the Yorktown Campaign July to October 1781.* Naval History Society, New York, NY, 1916.

Clinton, Henry, K. B., *Narrative of the Campaign in 1781 (Reprint).* John Campbell, Philadelphia, PA, 1865.

Commager, Henry S., *Documents of American History.* Appleton-Century-Crofts, Inc. New York, NY, 1958.

Commager, Henry S. and Richard B. Morris, *The Spirit of "Seventy-six."* Harper and Row Publishing, Philadelphia, PA, 1967.

Cress, Lawrence D., *Citizens in Arms, The Army and Militia in American Society.* University of North Carolina Press, Chapel Hill, NC, 1982.

Curtis, Edward E., *The Organization of the British Army in the American Revolution.* Corner House History Publishers, Ganservoort, NY, 1998.

De Jomini, Antoine Henri, Baron, *The Art of War, Precis di l'Art de Guerre.* Stackpole Books, Mechanicsburg, PA, 1995.

Diamant, Lincoln, *Bernard Romans, Forgotten Patriot of the American Revolution.* Harbor Hill Books, Harrison, NY, 1985.

Doyle, Joseph B. *Frederick William von Steuben and the American Revolution.* H. C. Cook Co. Steubenville, OH, 1913.

Eckardt, George S., Major General. *Vietnam Studies, Command and Control, 1950-1969.* Department of the Army, Washington, DC, 1974.

Eckenrode, H.J., *The Story of the Campaign and Siege of Yorktown.* Government Printing Office, Washington, DC, 1931.

Egleston, Thomas, *The Life of John Patterson, Major General in the Revolutionary Army.* G. P. Putnam Sons, New York, NY, 1898.

Everest, Allan S., *Moses Hazen and the Canadian Refugees in the American Revolution.* Syracuse University Press, Syracuse, NY, 1976.

Ferguson, E. James, *The Power of the Purse.* University of North Carolina Press, Chapel Hill, NC, 1961.

Flexner, James T., *The Young Hamilton.* Little Brown & Company, Boston, MA, 1978.

Flexner, James T., *Washington, the Indispensable Man.* Little, Brown & Company, New York, NY, 1969.

Frey, Sylvia R., *The British Soldier in America, A Social History of Military Life in the Revolutionary Period.* University of Texas Press, Austin, TX, 1981.

Graham, James, *The Life of Daniel Morgan.* Derby & Jackson, New York, 1858.

Grant, Alfred, *Our American Brethren, A History of Letters in the British Press During the American Revolution, 1775-1781.* McFarland & Company, Inc., Jefferson, N.C. 1995.

Griffith, Paddy, *Battle Tactics of the American Civil War, Command and Control.* Crowood Press, Ltd., Ramsbury, Wilks, England, 1996.

Griffith, Samuel B. (Translator), *Sun Tzu, The Art of War.* Oxford University Press, New York, NY, 1996.

Gruber, Ira D., *The Howe Brothers and the American Revolution.* University of North Carolina Press, Chapel Hill, NC, 1972.

Haiman, Miecislaus, *Kosciuszko in the American Revolution.* Library of Polish Studies, Jersey City, NJ, 1975.

Handel, Michael I., *Masters of War: Sun Tzu, Clausewitz and Jomini.* Frank Cass & Co., Ltd. London, England and Portland, OR, 1992.

Harrison, Maureen and Steve Gilbert, (Editors), *George Washington in His Own Words.* Barnes and Nobel Books, New York, NY,1997.

Heitman, Francis B. *Historical Register and Dictionary of the United States Army from Its Organization, September 29, 1789 to March, 1903.* Government Printing Office, Washington, DC, 1903.

Higginbotham, Don, *Daniel Morgan.* University of North Carolina Press, Chapel Hill, NC, 1961.

Higginbotham, Don, *The War of American Independence, Military Attitudes, Policies, and Practice, 1763-1789.* Northeastern University Press, Boston, MA, 1983.

Hillard, E. B., Rev., *The Last Men of the Revolution.* Barre Publishers, Barre, MA, 1968.

Holliday, Carl, *The Wit and Humor of Colonial Days.* Corner House Publishers, Williamstown, MA, 1975.

Houlding, J.A., *French Arms Drill of the 18th Century.* Museum Restoration Service, Alexandria Bay, NY, 1988.

Huston, James A., *Logistics of Liberty, American Services of Supply in the Revolutionary War and After.* University of Delaware Press, Newark, 1991.

Jackson, Harvey H., *Lachland McIntosh and the Politics of Revolutionary Georgia.* University of Georgia Press, Athens, GA, 1979.

Jenkins, E. H., *A History of the French Navy from Its Beginnings to the Present Day.* Naval Institute Press, Annapolis, MD, 1973.

Johnson, Cecil, *British West Florida, 1763-1783.* Archons, Hamden, England, 1971.

Johnston, Henry P., *The Yorktown Campaign and the Surrender of Cornwallis.* Harper and Brothers, New York, NY, 1881.

Katcher, Philip R. N., *Encyclopedia of British, Provincial, and German Army Units 1775-1783.* Stackpole Books, Harrisburg, PA, 1973.

Kapp, Freidrich, *Life of Major General Frederich William von Steuben.* Mason, NY, 1859.

Keim, D. Randolph, *Rochambeau, A Commemoration by the Congress of the United States.* The Government Printing Office, Washington, DC, 1907.

Ketman, Marvin, (Editor), *George Washington's Expense Account.* Simon & Shuster, New York, NY, 1970..

Kite, Elizabeth S., *Brigadier-General Louis Lebegue Duportail, 1777-1783.* John Hopkins Press, Baltimore, MD, 1983.

Kurtz, Stephen G. and James H. Hutson, *Essays on the American Revolution.* University of North Carolina Press, Chapel Hill, NC, 1973.

Kwasny, Mark V., *Washington's Partisan War, 1775-1783.* Kent State University Press, Kent, OH, 1996.

LaFarelle, Lorenzo G., *Bernardo de Galvez, Hero of the American Revolution.* Eakin Press, Austin, TX, 1992.

Landers, H. L. *The Virginia Campaign and the Blockade and Siege of Yorktown, 1781.* Government Printing Office, Washington, DC, 1931.

Langguth, A. J., *Patriots, The Men Who Started the American Revolution.* Simon & Schuster, New York, NY, 1989.

Leach, Douglas E., *Roots of Conflict.* The University of North Carolina Press, Chapel Hill, NC, 1986.

Lossing, Benson J., *The Pictorial Field-Book of the Revolution.* 2 Volumes, Harper & Brothers, New York, NY, 1860 (reprint).

Lowell, Edward J., *The Hessians and Other German Auxiliaries of Great Britain in the Revolutionary War.* Corner House Publishers, Williamstown, MA, 1975.

Lumpkin, Henry, *From Savannah to Yorktown, The American Revolution in the South.* Paragon House, New York, NY, 1981.

Mackesy, Piers, *The War for America, 1775-1783*. University of Nebraska Press, Lincoln, NE, 1993.

Marshall, John, *The Life of George Washington*. Chelsea House, New York, 1983.

Mattern, David B., *Benjamin Lincoln and the American Revolution*. University of South Carolina Press, Columbia, SC, 1995.

May, Robin, *The British Army in North America, 1775-1783*. Reed Consumer Books Ltd., London, England, 1974.

Merlant, Joachim, Captain, *Soldiers and Sailors of France in the American War for Independence*. Mary Bushnell (Translator), Charles Scribners & Sons, New York, NY, 1976.

Meyer, Edith P., *Petticoat Patriots of the American Revolution,* The Vanguard Press, Inc., New York, NY, 1976.

Mitchell, Broadus, *Alexander Hamilton, Youth to Maturity, 1735-1788*. Macmillan Company, New York, NY, 1962.

Montross, Lynn, *The Reluctant Rebels, The Story of the Continental Congress, 1774-1789*. New York, NY, 1950.

Montross, Lynn, *The Story of the Continental Army*. Barnes & Nobel, Inc., New York, NY, 1952.

Moore, Frank, *Dairy of the American Revolution From Newspapers and Original Documents*. Charles Scribner, New York, NY, 1860.

Morrill, Dan L., *Southern Campaigns of the American Revolution*. The Nautical & Aviation Publishing Co. of America, Baltimore, MD, 1993.

Muller, John, *A Treatise of Artillery, 1780*. Museum Restoration Service, Bloomfield, IL,1977.

Muller, John, *A Treatise of Fortifications*. Museum Restoration Service, Ottawa, Canada, 1968.

Museum Restoration Service, *A Plan of Discipline, Composed for Use of the Militia of the County of Norfolk*. Ottawa, Canada, 1969.

Nash, Gary B., *Race and Revolution*. Madison house, Madison, WI, 1990.

Neimeyer, Charles P., *America Goes to War, A Social History of the Continental Army*. New York University Press, New York, NY, 1996.

Nelson, Paul D., *Anthony Wayne*. Indiana University Press, Bloomington, 1985.

Nelson, Paul D., *The Life of William Alexander, Lord Stirling*. University of Alabama Press, Tuscaloosa , AL, 1987.

Pakenham, W.T.T., Captain, R.N., *Naval Command and Control*. Brassey's Defense Publishers, London, England, 1989.

Palmer, John M., *General von Steuben*. Yale University Press, New Haven, CT, 1937.

Pancake, John S., *This Destructive War, The British Campaign in the Carolinas, 1780-1782*. University of Alabama Press, Tuscaloosa, AL, 1992.

Peckham, Howard H., *The Toll of Independence, Engagements and Battle Casualties of the American Revolution.* University of Chicago Press, Chicago, IL, 1974.

Peckham, Howard H., *The War for Independence.* The University of Chicago Press, Chicago, IL, 1979.

Petrie, Charles, Sir, *King Charles III of Spain.* Constable and Company, Ltd, London, England, 1971.

Pinkowski, Edward, *Washington's Officers Slept Here.* Sunshine Press, Philadelphia, PA, 1953.

Purcell, L. Edward, *Who Was Who in the American Revolution.* Facts on File, Inc., New York, NY, 1993.

Quarles, Benjamin, *The Negro in the American Revolution.* W. W. Norton and Company, New York, NY, 1966.

Raines, Edgar F., Jr. and David R. Campbell, *The Army and the Joint Chiefs of Staff: Evolution of Army Ideas on the Command, Control, and Coordination of the Armed Forces, 1942-1985.* Analysis Branch, U.S. Army Center of Military History, Washington, DC, 1985.

Ramsay, David, MD, *The History of the American Revolution.* 2 Volumes, Lester H. Cohen (Editor), Liberty Classics, Indianapolis, IN, 1990 (reprinted from the original of 1789).

Reed, William B., *Life and Correspondence of Joseph Reed.* Lindsay and Blakiston Publishers, Philadelphia, PA, 1847.

Rice, Howard C. Jr. and Anne S. K. Brown (Translator & Editor), *The American Campaigns of Rochambeau's Army, 1780-1783.* 2 Volumes, Princeton and Brown University Press, Princeton, NJ, 1972.

Risch, Erna, *Supplying Washington's Army.* Center of Military History, U.S. Army, Washington, DC,. 1981.

Rogers, Truett, *Bibles and Battle Drums.* Judson Press, Valley Forge, PA, 1976.

Rossie, Jonathan G., *The Politics of Command in the American Revolution.* Syracuse University Press, Syracuse, NY, 1975.

Rossman, Kenneth R., *Thomas Mifflin and the Politics of the American Revolution.* University of North Carolina Press, Chapel Hill, NC, 1952.

Royster, Charles, *A Revolutionary People at War, The Continental Army and American Character, 1775-1783.* W. W. Norton and Company, New York, NY, 1981.

Sellers, Charles C., *Patience Wright, American Artist and Spy in George III's London.* Wesleyan University Press, Middletown, CT, 1976.

Seymour, William, *The Price of Folly.* Bassey's Publishers, London England, 1995.

Shreve, L. G., *Tench Tilghman, The Life and Times of Washington's Aide-de-camp.* Tidewater Publishers, Centreville, MD, 1982.

Shy, John, *A People Numerous & Armed.* Ann Arbor Paperbacks, The University of Michigan Press, Ann Arbor, MI, 1990.

Silverman, Kenneth, *A Cultural History of the American Revolution.* Thomas Y. Crowell Co. New York, NY, 1976.

Smith, Page, *John Adams.* 2 Volumes, Doubleday and Company, Garden City, NY, 1962.

Stewart, Bruce W., *Morristown: A Crucible of the American Revolution.* New Jersey Historical Commission, Trenton, NJ , 1975.

Stinchcombe, William C., *The American Revolution and the French Alliance.* Syracuse University Press, Syracuse, NY, 1969.

Sullivan, Kathryn, *Maryland and France, 1774-1789.* University of Pennsylvania Press, Philadelphia, PA, 1936.

Summer, William G., *The Financier and the Finances of the American Revolution.* Dodd, Mead and Company, New York, NY, 1891.

Swiggett, Howard, *The Extraordinary Mr. Morris.* Doubleday and Company, Inc., Garden City, NY, 1952.

Tarleton, Lieutenant-Colonel, *A History of the Campaigns of 1780 and 1781, in the Southern Provinces of North America (Reprint).* Ayer Company Publishers, Inc., North Stradford, NH, 1999.

Thayer, Theodore, *Nathanael Greene, Strategist of the American Revolution.* Wayne Publishers, New York, NY, 1960.

Thian, Raphael P., *Legislative History of the General Staff of the Army of the United States (Its Organization, Duties, Pay & Allowances) 1775-1901.* Government Printing Office, Washington, DC., 1901.

Tolzman, Don. H. (Editor), *German Allied Troops in the American Revolution.* J. R. Rosegarten's Survey of German Archives and Sources, Heritage Books, Bowie, MD, 1993.

Toth, Charles W. (Editor), *Liberte', Egalite', Fraternite'. The American Revolution and European Response.* Whitson Publishing Company, Troy, NY, 1989.

Townsend, Sara B., *An American Soldier, The Life of John Laurens.* Edwards and Broughton Company, Raleigh, NC, 1959.

Trevelyan, George O., Sir, *The American Revolution.* Part 3, Longman, Green and Company, New York, NY, 1907.

Troiani, Don, *Soldiers in America 1754-1865.* Stackpole Books, Mechanicsburg, PA, 1998.

Trussell, John B. B., Jr., *The Pennsylvania Line, Regimental Organization and Operations, 1776-1783.* Pennsylvania Historical/Museum Commission, Harrisburg, PA, 1977.

Trussell, John B. B., Jr., *Birthplace of an Army: A Study of Valley Forge.* Pennsylvania Historical/Museum Commission, Harrisburg, PA, 1979.

Upton, Richard F., *Revolutionary New Hampshire.* Octagon Books, New York, NY, 1971.

Van Creveld, Martin, *Command in War*. Harvard University Press, Cambridge, MA, 1985.

Van Doren, Carl, *Mutiny in January*. The Viking Press, New York, NY, 1943.

Van Doren, Carl, *Secret History of the American Revolution*. The Viking Press, New York, NY, 1941.

Van Every, Dale, *A Company of Heroes*. William Morrow, New York, 1993.

Von Clausewitz, Carl, *On War*. Edited and translated by Michael Howard & Peter Paret, Princeton University, Princeton, NJ, 1984.

Wallace, David D., *The Life of Henry Laurens*. Russell & Russell Publishers, New York, NY, 1967.

Ward, Christopher, *The War of the Revolution*. Volume 2, Macmillan Company, New York, NY, 1952.

Ward, Christopher, *The Delaware Continentals, 1776-1783*. Delaware Historical Society, Wilmington, DE, 1941.

Whiteley, Emily S., *Washington and His Aides-de-Camp*. The Macmillan Company, New York, NY, 1936.

Wickwire, Franklin B., *British Sub Ministers and Colonial America 1763-1783*. Princeton University Press, Princeton, NJ, 1966.

Wickwire, Franklin and Mary, *Cornwallis: The American Adventure*. Houghton Mifflin Company Boston, MA, 1970.

Willcox, William B., *Portrait of a General, Sir Henry Clinton in the War of Independence*. Alfred A. Knoph, New York, NY, 1962.

Willcox, William B., *The American Rebellion*. Yale University Press, New Haven, CT, 1954

Wood, George C., *Congressional Control of Foreign Relations During the American Revolution, 1774-1789*. H. Ray Haas & Co. Publishers, Allentown, PA, 1919.

Wright, Robert K. Jr., *The Continental Army*. United States Army, Washington, DC, 1986.

Wright, John Womack, Col., *Some Notes on the Continental Army*. New Windsor Cantonment Publication No, 2, National Temple Hill Association, Vails Gate, NY, 1963.

Young, Philip, *Revolutionary Ladies*. Alfred A. Knoph, New York, NY, 1977.